How Private George Peck Put Down the Rebellion

How Private George Peck Put Down the Rebellion

The humorous exploits of
a Union Cavalryman during
the American Civil War

George Peck

LEONAUR

How Private George Peck
Put Down the
Rebellion
The humorous exploits of
a Union Cavalryman during
the American Civil War
by George Peck

First published under the title
How Private George Peck
Put Down the Rebellion
or
The Funny Experiences
of a Raw Recruit

Leonaur is an imprint
of Oakpast Ltd

ISBN: 978-1-84677-880-3 (hardcover)
ISBN: 978-1-84677-879-7 (softcover)

http://www.leonaur.com

Publisher's Notes

In the interests of authenticity, the spellings, grammar and place names
used have been retained from the original editions.

The opinions of the authors represent a view of events in which he
was a participant related from his own perspective,
as such the text is relevant as an historical document.

The views expressed in this book are not necessarily
those of the publisher.

Contents

CHAPTER 1

Why I Became a Raw Recruit

For the last year or more I have been reading the articles in the *Century* magazine, written by generals and things who served on both the Union and Confederate sides, and have been struck by the number of "decisive battles" that were fought, and the great number of generals who fought them and saved the country. It seems that each general on the Union side, who fought a battle, and writes an article for the aforesaid magazine, admits that his battle was the one which did the business. On the Confederate side, the generals who write articles invariably demonstrate that they everlastingly whipped their opponents, and drove them on in disorder.

To read those articles it seems strange that the Union generals who won so many decisive battles, should not have ended the war much sooner than they did, and to read the accounts of battles won by the Confederates, and the demoralization that ensued in the ranks of their opponents, it seems marvellous that the Union army was victorious. Any man who has followed these generals of both sides, in the pages of that magazine, must conclude that the war was a draw game, and that both sides were whipped. Thus far no general has lost a battle on either side, and all of them tacitly admit that the whole thing depended on them, and that other commanders were mere ciphers. This is a kind of history that is going to mix up generations yet unborn in the most hopeless manner.

It has seemed to me as though the people of this country had got so mixed up about the matter that it was the duty of some private soldier to write a description of *the* decisive battle of the war, and as I was the private soldier who fought that battle on the Union side, against fearful odds, *viz.*: against a Confederate soldier who was braver than I was, a better horseback rider, and a better poker player, I feel it my duty to tell about it. I have already mentioned it to a few veterans, and they have advised me to write an article for the *Century*, but I have felt a delicacy about entering the lists, a plain, unvarnished private soldier, against those generals. While I am something of a liar myself, and can do fairly well in my own class, I should feel that in the *Century* I was entered in too fast a class of liars, and the result would be that I should not only lose my entrance fee, but be distanced. So I have decided to contribute this piece of history solely for the benefit of the readers of my own paper, as they will believe me.

It was in 1864 that I joined a cavalry regiment in the department of the Gulf, a raw recruit in a veteran regiment. It may be asked why I waited so long before enlisting, and why I enlisted at all, when the war was so near over. I know that the most of the soldiers enlisted from patriotic motives, and because they wanted to help shed blood, and wind up the war. I did not. I enlisted for the bounty. I thought the war was nearly over, and that the probabilities were that the regiment I had enlisted in would, be ordered home before I could get to it. In fact the recruiting officer told me as much, and he said I would get my bounty, and a few months' pay, and it would be just like finding money. He said at that late day I would never see a rebel, and if I did have to join the regiment, there would be no fighting, and it would just be one continued picnic for two or three months, and there would be no more danger than to go off camping for a duck shoot.

At my time of life, now that I have become gray, and bald, and my eyesight is failing, and I have become a grandfather, I do not want to open the sores of twenty-two years ago. I want a quiet life. So I would not assert that the recruiting officer deliberately lied to me, but I was the worst deceived man that ever enlisted, and if I ever meet that man, on this earth, it will go hard with him. Of course, if he is dead, that settles it, as I shall not follow any man after death, where I am in doubt as to which road he has taken, but if he is alive, and reads these lines, he can hear of something to his advantage by communicating with me. I would probably kill him. As far as the bounty was concerned, I got that all right, but it was only three-hundred dollars.

Within twenty-four hours after I had been credited to the town from which I enlisted, I heard of a town that was paying as high as twelve-hundred dollars for recruits. I have met with many reverses of fortune in the course of a short, but brilliant career, have loaned money and never got it back, have been taken in by designing persons on three card *monte*, and have been beaten trading horses, but I never suffered much more than I did when I found that I had got to go to war for a beggarly three-hundred dollars bounty, when I could have had twelve hundred dollars by being credited to another town. I think that during two years and a half of service nothing tended more to dampen my ardour, make me despondent, and hate myself, than the loss of that nine-hundred dollars bounty. There was not an hour of the day, in all of my service, that I did not think of what might have been. It was a long time before I brought to my aid that passage of scripture, "There is no use crying for spilled bounty," but when I did it helped me some. I thought of the hundreds who didn't get any bounty.

I joined my regiment, and had a cavalry horse issued to me, and was assigned to a company. I went up to the captain of the company, whom I had known as a farmer before the war commenced, and told him I had come to help him put down the rebellion. I never saw a man so changed as he was. I thought he would ask me to bring my things into his tent, and stay with him, but he seemed to have forgotten that he had known me, when he worked on the farm. He was dressed up nicely, and I thought he put on style, and I could only think of him at home, with his overalls tucked in his boots, driving a yoke of oxen to plow a field. He seemed to feel that I had known him under unfavourable circumstances before the war, and acted as though he wanted to shun me.

I had drawn an infantry knapsack, at Madison, before I left for the front, and had it full of things, besides a small trunk. The captain called a soldier and told him to find quarters for me, and I went out of his presence. At my quarters, which consisted of what was called a pup-tent, I found no conveniences, and it soon dawned on me that war was no picnic, as that lying recruiting officers had told me it was. I found that I had got to throw away my trunk and knapsack, and all the articles that I couldn't strap on a saddle, and when I asked for a mattress the men laughed at me. I had always slept on a mattress, or a feather bed, and when I was told that I would have to sleep on the ground, under that little tent, I felt hurt. I had known the colonel when he used to teach school at home, and I went to him and told him what kind of a way they were treating me, but he only laughed. He had two nice cots in his tent, and I told him I thought I ought to have a cot, too. He laughed some more.

Finally I asked him who slept in his extra cot, and intimated that I had rather sleep in his tent than mine, but he sent me away, and said he would see what could be done. I laid on the ground that night, but

I didn't sleep. If I ever get a pension it will be for rheumatism caught by sleeping on the ground. The rheumatism has not got hold of me yet, though twenty-two years have passed, but it may be lurking about my system, for all I know.

I had never rode a horse, before enlisting. The only thing I had ever got straddle of was a stool in a country printing office, and when I was first ordered to saddle up my horse, I could not tell which way the saddle and bridle went, and I got a coloured man to help me, for which I paid him some of the remains of my bounty. I hired him permanently, to take care of my horse, but I soon learned that each soldier had to take care of his own horse. That seemed pretty hard. I had been raised a pet, and had edited a newspaper, which had been one of the most outspoken advocates of crushing the rebellion, and it seemed to me, as much as I had done for the government, in urging enlistments, I was entitled to more consideration then to become my own hostler.

However, I curbed my proud spirit, and after the nigger cook had saddled my horse, I led the animal up to a fence to climb on. From the remarks of the soldiers, and the general laugh all around, it was easy to see that mounting a cavalry horse from off the top of a rail fence was not according to tactics, but it was the only way I could see to get on, in the absence of step-ladders. They let me ride into the ranks, after mounting, and then they laughed. It was hard for me to be obliged to throw away all the articles I had brought with me, so I strapped them on the saddle in front and behind, and only my head stuck out over them. There was one thing, it would be a practicable impossibility to fall off.

The regiment started on a raid. The colonel came along by my company during the afternoon, and I asked him where we were going. He gave me an evasive answer, which hurt my feelings. I asked his pardon, but told him I would like to know where we were going, so as to have my letters sent to me, but he went off laughing, and never told me, while the old soldiers laughed, though I couldn't see what they were laughing at. I did not suppose there was so much difference between officers and privates, and wondered if it was the policy of this government to have a cavalry regiment to start off on a long raid and not let the soldiers know where they were going, and during the afternoon I decided to write home to the paper I formerly edited and give my opinion of such a fool way of running a war.

Suppose anybody at home was sick, they wouldn't know where to write for me to come back. There is nothing that will give a man such

MOUNTING MY ARAB STEED FROM THE TOP OF A RAIL FENCE

an appetite as riding on a galloping horse, and along about the middle of the afternoon I began to get hungry, and asked the orderly sergeant when we were going to get any dinner. He said there was a hotel a short distance ahead, and the colonel had gone forward to order dinner for the regiment. I believed him, because I had known the orderly before the war, when he drove a horse in a brickyard, grinding clay. But he was a liar, too, as I found out afterwards. There was not a hotel within fifty miles, and soldiers did not stop at hotels, anyway. Finally the orderly sergeant came along and announced that dinner was ready, and I looked for the hotel, but the only dinner I saw was some raw pork that soldiers took out of their saddle bags, with hard tack. We stopped in the woods, dismounted, and the boys would cut off a slice of fat pork and spread it on the hard tack and eat it.

I had never supposed the government would subject its soldiers to such fare as that, and I wouldn't eat. I did not dare dismount, as there was no fence near that I could use to climb on to my horse, so I sat in the saddle and let the horse eat some grass, while I thought of home, and pie and cake, and what a condemned fool a man was to leave a comfortable home to go and put down anybody's rebellion. The way I felt then I wouldn't have touched a rebellion if one lay right in the road. What business was it of mine if some people in the South wanted to dissolve partnership and go set up business for themselves? How was I going to prevent them from having a southern confederacy, by riding an old rack of bones of a horse, that would reach his nose around every little while and chew my legs?

If the recruiting officer who inveigled me into the army had come along then, his widow would now be drawing a pension. While I was thinking, dreaming of home, and the horse was eating grass, the fool animal suddenly took it into his head to lay down and roll, and before I could kick any of his ribs in, he was down, and I was rolling off, with one leg under him. The soldiers quit eating and pulled the horse of me, and hoisted me up into the space between my baggage, and then they laughed, lit their pipes and smoked, as happy as could be. I couldn't see how they could be happy, and wondered if they were not sick of war.

Then they mounted, and on we went. My legs and body became chafed, and it seemed as though I couldn't ride another minute, and when the captain came along I told him about it, and asked him if I couldn't be relieved some way. He said the only way was for me to stand on my head and ride, and he winked at a soldier near me, and, do you know, that soldier actually changed ends with himself and stood on his head and hands in the saddle and rode quite a distance, and the captain said that was the way a cavalry soldier rested himself. Gracious, I wouldn't have tried that for the world, and I found out afterwards that the soldier who stood on his head formerly belonged with a circus.

I suppose it was wrong to complain, but the horse they gave me was the meanest horse in the regiment. He would bite and kick the other horses, and they would kick back, and about half the time I was dodging the heels of horses, and a good deal of the time I was wondering if a man would get any pension if he was wounded that way. It would seem pretty tough to go home on a stretcher, as a wounded soldier, and have people find out a horse kicked you.

I never had been a man of blood, and didn't enlist to kill anybody, as I could prove by that recruiting officer, and I didn't want to fight, but from what I could gather from the conversation of the soldiers, fighting and killing people was about all they thought about. They talked about this one and that one who had been killed, and the hundreds of confederates they had all shot or killed with sabres, until my hair just stood right up. It seems that twelve or fifteen men, more or less, had been shot off the horse I was riding, and one fellow who rode next to me said no man who ever rode that old yellow horse had escaped alive.

This was cheering to me, and I would have given my three hundred dollars bounty, and all I could borrow, if I could get out of the army. However, I found out afterwards that the soldier lied. In fact they all lied, and they lied for my benefit. We struck into the woods, and travelled until after dark, with no road, and the march was enlivened by remarks of the soldiers near me to the effect that we would probably never get out of the woods alive. They said we were trying to surround an army of rebels, and cut them off from the main army, and the chances were that when tomorrow's sun rose it would rise on the ghostly corpses of the whole regiment, with jackals and buzzards eating us.

One of the soldiers took something from his pocket, about the size of a testament, pressed it to his heart, and then kissed it, and I felt as though I was about to faint, but by the light of a match which another soldier had scratched on his pants to light his pipe, I saw that what I supposed to be a testament, was a box of sardines the soldier had bought of the sutler. I was just about to die of hunger, exhaustion, and fright at the fearful stories the veterans had been telling, when there was a shout at the head of the regiment, which was taken up all along the line, my horse run under the limb of a tree and raked me out of the saddle, and I hung to the limb, my legs hanging down, and—

Chapter 2

A Desperate Conflict

The careful readers of this history have no doubt been worried about the manner in which the first chapter closed, leaving me hanging to a limb of a tree, like Absalom weeping for her children, my horse having gone out from under me. But I have not been hanging there all this time. The soldiers took me down, and caught my horse, and the regiment dismounted and a council of war was held. I suppose it was a council of war, as I noticed the officers were all in a group under a tree, with a candle, examining a map, and drinking out of a canteen. I had read of councils of war, but I had never seen one, and so I walked over to the crowd of officers and asked the colonel if there was anything particular the matter.

I never saw a crowd of men who seemed so astonished as those officers were, and suddenly I felt myself going away from where they were consulting, with somebody's strong hand on my collar, and an unmistakable cavalry boot, with a man in it, in the vicinity of my pantaloons. I do not know to this day, which officer it was that kicked me, but I went away and sat under a tree in the dark, so hungry that I was near dead, and I wished I *was* dead. I guess the officers wished that I was, too. The soldiers tried to console me by telling me I was too fresh, but I couldn't see why a private soldier, right from home, who knew all about the public sentiment at the north in regard to the way the war was conducted, should not have a voice in the consultations of officers.

I had written many editorials before I left home, criticising the manner in which many generals had handled their commands, and pointed out to my readers how defeat could have been turned into victory, if the generals had done as I would have done in their places. It seemed to me the officers of my regiment were taking a suicidal course in barring me out of their consultations. A soldier had told me that we were lost in the woods, and as I had studied geography when at school, and was well posted about Alabama, it seemed as though a little advice from me would be worth a good deal. But I concluded to let them stay lost forever before I would volunteer any information. It was crawling along towards midnight, of my first day in the army, and I had eaten nothing since morning.

As I sat there under the tree I fell asleep, and was dreaming of home, and warm biscuit, with honey, and a feather bed, when I was rudely awakened by a corporal who told me to mount. I asked him what for, and told him that I didn't want to ride any more that night. What I wanted was to be let alone, to sleep. He said to get on the horse too quick, and I found there was no use arguing with a common corporal, so the boys hoisted me on to the horse, and about nine of us started off through the woods in the moonlight, looking for a main road.

The corporal was kind enough to say that as soon as we found a road we would put out a picket, and send a courier back to the regiment to inform the colonel that we had got out of the woods, and the rest of us would lay down and sleep till morning. I don't think I was ever so anxious to see a road in all my life, because I *did* want to lay down and sleep, and die.

O, if I could have telegraphed home, how I would have warned the youth of the land to beware of the allurements held out by recruiting officers, and to let war alone. In an hour or so we came to a clearing, and presently to a road, and we stopped. The corporal detailed me to go up the road a short distance and stand picket on my horse. That was not what I had expected of the corporal. I used to know him before the war when he worked in a paint shop in a wagon factory, and I had always treated him well, and it seemed as though he ought to favour me by letting somebody else go on picket. I told him that the other boys were more accustomed to such work than I was, and that I would resign in their favour, because what I wanted was rest, but he said I would have to go, and he called me "Camp and Garrison Equipage," because I carried so much luggage on my horse, a name that held to me for months.

I found that there was no use kicking against going on picket duty that night, though I tried to argue with the corporal that it would be just as well to all lay down and sleep till morning, and put out a picket when it got light enough to see. I was willing to work during the day time for the government, but it seemed as though it was rushing things a little to make a man work day and night for thirteen dollars a month. So the corporal went out on the road with me about a quarter of a mile, and placed me in position and gave me my instructions. The instructions were to keep a sharp lookout up and down the road for Confederate cavalry, and if I saw anybody approaching to sing out "halt!" and if the party did not halt to shoot him, and then call for the corporal of the guard, who would come out to see what was the matter. I asked him what I should do if anybody came along and shot me, and he said that would be all right, that the boys would come out and bury me. He said I must keep awake, for if I got to sleep on my post I would be court-martialled and shot, and then he rode away and left me alone, on a horse that kept whinnying, and calling the attention of possible Confederates to my position.

I do not think any reader of these papers will envy me the position I was in at that time. If I remained awake, I was liable to be killed by the enemy, and if I fell asleep on my post I would be shot anyway. And if I was not killed, it was probable I would be a murderer before morning. Hunger was gnawing at my stomach, and the horse was gnawing at my legs, and I was gnawing at a hard tack which I had found in the saddle-bag. Every little while I would hear a noise, and my hair would raise my hat up, and it would seem to me as though the next minute a volley would be fired at me, and I shrunk down between the piles of baggage on my saddle to be protected from bullets.

Suddenly the moon came out from behind a cloud and around a turn in the road a solitary horseman might have been seen coming towards me. I never have seen a horse that looked as high as that horse did. He seemed at least eighteen feet high, and the man on him was certainly twelve feet high. My heart pounded against a tin canteen that I had strung around my shoulder, so I could hear the beating perfectly plain. The man was approaching, and I was trying to think whether I had been instructed to shoot and then call for the corporal of the guard, or call for the corporal and then ask him to halt.

I knew there was a halt in my instructions, and wondered if it would not conciliate the enemy to a certain extent if I would say "Please Halt." The fact was, I didn't want to have any fuss. If I could have backed my horse up into the woods, and let the man go by, it seemed as though it would save precipitating a conflict. It is probable that no military man was ever in so tight a place as I was that minute. The enemy was advancing, and I wondered if, when he got near enough, I could say "halt," in a commanding tone of voice. I knew enough, then, to feel that to ask the stranger to halt in a trembling and husky voice would give the whole thing away, that I was a recruit and a coward. Ye gods, how I suffered! I wondered if I could hit a man with a bullet.

Before the war I was quite a good shot with a shotgun, shooting into flocks of pigeons and ducks, and I thought what a good idea it would be if I could get that approaching rebel into a flock. The idea seemed so ridiculous that I laughed right out loud. It was not a hearty, happy laugh, but it was a laugh all the same, and I was proud that I could laugh in the face of danger, when I might be a corpse any minute. The man on the horse stopped. Whether he heard me laugh it is impossible to say, but he stopped. That relieved me a great deal. As he had stopped it was unnecessary for me to invite him to halt. He was welcome to stay there if he wanted to. I argued that it was not my place to go howling around the Southern Confederacy, ordering people to halt, when they had already halted. If he would let me alone and stay where he was, what sense was there in picking a quarrel with him?

Why should I want to shoot a total stranger, who might have a family at home, somewhere in the South, who would mourn for him. He might be a dead shot, as many Southern gentlemen were, and if I went to advising him about halting, it would, very likely cause his hot Southern blood to boil, and he would say he had just as much right to that road as I had. If it come right down to the justice of the thing, I should have to admit that Alabama was not my state. Wisconsin was my home, and if I was up there, and a man should trespass on my property, it would be reasonable enough for me to ask him to go away from there, and enforce my request by calling a constable and having him put off the premises.

But how did I know but he owned property there, and was a taxpayer. I had it all figured out that I was right in not disturbing that rebel, and I knew that I could argue with my colonel for a week, if necessary, on the law points in the case, and the courtesy that I deemed proper between gentlemen, if any complaint was made for not doing my duty. But, lordy, how I *did* sweat while I was deciding to let him alone if he would let me alone. The war might have been going on now, and that rebel and myself might have been standing there today, looking at each other, if it hadn't been for the action of the fool horse that I rode.

My horse had been evidently asleep for some time, but suddenly he woke up, pricked up his ears, and began to prance, and jump sideways like a race horse that is on the track, and wants to run. The horse reared up and plunged, and kept working up nearer to my Southern friend, and I tried to hold him, and keep him still, but suddenly he got the best of me and started towards the other man and horse, and the other horse started, as though someone had said "go".[1]

I do not suppose any man on this earth, or any other earth, ever tried to stop a fool horse quite as hard as I did that one. I pulled until my arms ached, but he went for all that was out, and the horse ahead of me was buckling in as fast as he could. I could not help wondering what would happen if I should overtake that Southern man. I was gaining on him, when suddenly eight or nine men who were sleeping beside the road, got up and began to shoot at us. They were the friends of the rebel, who believed that the whole Union army was making a charge on them.

We got by the shooters alive, and then, as we passed the rickety old judge's stand, I realized that we were on a race track, and for a moment I forgot that I was a soldier, and only thought of myself as a rider of a race horse, and I gave the horse his head, and kicked him, and yelled like a Comanche Indian, and I had the satisfaction of seeing my horse go by the rebel, and I yelled some more. I got a glimpse of my rebel's, face as I went by him, and he didn't look much more like a fighting man than I did, but he was, for as soon as I had got ahead of him he drew a revolver and began firing at me on the run. I thought that was a mean trick, and spoke to him about it afterwards, but he said he only wanted me to stop so he could get acquainted with me.

Well, I never could find any bullets in any of the clothes strapped on the back of my saddle, but it *did* seem to me as though every bul-

---

1. Before I get any further on this history of the war, it is necessary to explain. The facts proved to be that my regiment had got lost in the woods, and the scouting party, under the corporal, who had been sent out to find a road, had come upon the three-quarter stretch of an old private race track on a deserted southern plantation, instead of a main road, and I had been placed on picket near the last turn before striking the quarter stretch. A small party of Confederates, who had been out on a scout, and got lost, had come on the track further down, near the judges' stand, and they had put a man, on picket up near where I was, supposing they had struck the road, and intending to wait until morning so as to find out where they were. My horse was an old race horse, and as soon as he saw the other horse, he was in for a race and the other horse was willing. This will show the situation as well as though I had a race track engraved, showing the positions of the two armies. The Confederates, except the man on picket, were asleep beside the track near the quarter stretch, and our fellows, except myself, were asleep over by the three-quarter pole.

On went the two night riders

let from his revolver hit very near my vital parts. But a new danger presented itself. We were rapidly approaching the corporal and his men, with whose command I belonged, and they would wake up and think the whole Confederate army was charging them, and if I was not killed by the confounded rebel behind me, I should probably be shot all to pieces by our own men.

As we passed our men they fired a few sleepy shots towards us, and took to the woods. On went the two night riders, and when the rebel had exhausted his revolver he began to urge his horse, and passed me, and I drew my revolver and began to fire at him. As we passed the judge's stand the second time a couple of shots from quite a distance in the woods showed that his rebel friends had taken alarm at the frequent charges of cavalry, and had skipped to the woods and were getting away as fast as possible.

We went around the track once more, and when near the judge's stand I was right behind him, and his horse fell down and my horse stumbled over him, and I guess we were both stunned. Finally I crawled out from under my horse, and the rebel was trying to raise up, when I said, "What in thunder you want to chase a man all around the Southern Confederacy for, on a dark night, trying to shoot him?"

He asked me to help him up, which I did, when he said, "Who commenced this here chasing? If you had kept whar you was, I wouldn't a had no truck with you."

Then I said, "You are my prisoner," and he said, "No, you are my prisoner."

I told him I was no hand to argue, but it seemed to me it was about a standoff, as to which was 'tother's prisoner. I told him that was my first day's service as a soldier, and I was not posted as to the customs of civilized warfare, but I was willing to wait till daylight, leaving matters just as they were, each of us on the defensive, giving up none of our rights, and after daylight we would play a game of seven-up to see which was the prisoner. That seemed fair to him, and he accepted the situation, remarking that he had only been conscripted a few days and didn't know any more about war than a cow.

He said he was a newspaper man from Georgia, and had been taken right from the case in his office before his paper could be got out. I told him I was only a few days out of a country printing office myself, the sheriff having closed out my business on an old paper bill. A bond of sympathy was inaugurated at once between us, and when he limped along the track to the fence, and found that his ankle was hurt by the fall, I brought a bottle of horse liniment out of my saddle-bags, and a rag, and bound some liniment on his ankle. He said he had never seen a Yankee soldier before, and he was glad he had met me. I told him he was the first rebel I had ever met, and I hoped he would be the last, until the war was over.

By this time our horses had gone to nibbling grass, as though there were no such thing as war. We could hear occasional bugle calls off in the woods in two directions, and knew that our respective commands had gone off and got lost again, so we concluded to camp there till morning. After the excitement was over I began to get hungry, and I asked him if he had anything to eat. He said he had some corn bread and bacon, and he could get some sweet potatoes over in a field. So I built a fire there on the track, and he hobbled off after potatoes.

Just about daylight breakfast was served, consisting of coffee, which I carried in a sack, made in a pot he carried, bacon fried in a half of a tin canteen, sweet potatoes roasted in the ashes, and Confederate corn bread, warmed by holding it over the fire on a sharp stick. My friend, the rebel, sat on my saddle, which I had removed from my horse, after he had promised me on his honour to help me to put it on when it was time to mount. He knew how to put on saddles, and I didn't , and as his ankle was lame I gave him the best seat, he being my guest, that is, he was my guest if I beat him in the coming game of seven-up, which we were to play to see if he was my prisoner, or I was his.

It being daylight, I could see him, and study his character, and honestly he was a mighty fine-looking fellow. As we eat our early breakfast I began to think that the recruiting officer was more than half right about war being a picnic. He talked about the newspaper business in the South, and before breakfast was over we had formed a partnership to publish a paper at Montgomery, Ala., after the war should be over. I have eaten a great many first-class meals in my time, have feasted at Delmonico's, and lived at the best hotels in the land, besides partaking pretty fair food camping out, where an appetite was worked up by exercise and sporting, but in all my life I have never had anything taste as good as that combination Union-Confederate breakfast on the Alabama race track, beside the judges stand.

After the last potato peeling, and the last crumb of corn bread had been "sopped" in the bacon gravy and eaten, we whittled some tobacco off a plug, filled our pipes and leaned up against the fence and smoked the most enjoyable smoke that ever was smoked. After smoking in silence a few minutes my rebel friend said, as he blew the smoke from his handsome mouth, "War is not so unpleasant, after all." Then we fell to talking about the manner in which the different generals on each side had conducted things. He went on to show that if Lee had taken his advice, the Yankees would then be on the run for the North, and I showed him, by a few well-chosen remarks that if I could have been close to Grant, and given him some pointers, that the Confederates would be hunting their holes.

We were both convinced that it was a great mistake that we were nothing but private soldiers, but felt that it would not be long before we were called to occupy high places. It seemed to stand to reason that true merit would find its reward. Then he knocked the ashes out of his pipe and said if I had a pack of cards we would go up in the judges stand and play seven-up to see whether I was his prisoner, or he was mine. I wanted to take a prisoner back to the regiment, at I thought it would make me solid with the colonel, and I played a strong game of seven-up, but before we got started to playing he suggested that we call it a stand-off, and agree that neither of us should be a prisoner, but that when we got ready to part each should go hunt up his own command, and tell the biggest lie we could think of as to the fight we had had.

That was right into my hand, and I agreed, and then my friend suggested that we play poker for money. I consented and he put up Confederate money, against my greenbacks, ten to one. We played about an hour, and at the close he had won the balance of my bounty, except what I had given to the chaplain for safe keeping, and a pair of pants, and a blouse, and a flannel shirt, and a pair of shoes, which I had on my saddle. I was rather glad to get rid of some of my extra baggage, and when he put on the clothes he had won from me, blessed if I wasn't rather proud of him. A man could wear any kind of clothes in the Confederate army, and my rebel looked real comfortable in my clothes, and I felt that it was a real kind act to allow him to win a blue suit that I did not need.

If the men of both the armies, and the people of both sections of the distracted country could have seen us two soldiers together, there in the judges stand, peacefully playing poker, while the battles were raging in the East and in the West, that would have felt that an era of good feeling was about to dawn on the country. After we had played enough poker, and I had lost everything I had that was loose, I suggested that he sing a song, so he sung the "Bonnie Blue Flag." I did not think it was right for him to work in a rebel song on me, but it did sound splendid, and I forgot that there was any war, in listening to the rich voice of my new friend.

When he got through he asked me to sing something. I never *could* sing, anyway. My folks had always told me that my voice sounded like a corn sheller, but he urged me at his own peril, and I sung, or tried to, "We'll Hang Jeff Davis to a Sour Apple Tree." I had no designs on Mr. Davis, honestly I hadn't, and it was the farthest thing from my thoughts to hurt the feelings of that young man, but before I had finished the first verse he took his handkerchief out and placed it to his eyes. I stopped and apologized, but he said not to mind him, as he was better now. He told me, afterwards, in the strictest confidence, that my singing was the worst he ever heard, and gave it as his opinion that if Jeff Davis could hear me sing he would be willing, even anxious, to be hung. If I had been sensitive about my musical talents, probably there would have been hard feelings, and possibly bloodshed, right there, but I told him I always knew I couldn't sing, and he said that I was in luck.

Well, we fooled around there till about ten o'clock in the morning, and decided that we would part, and each seek our respective commands, so I put some more horse liniment on his sprained ankle, and he saddled my horse for me, and after expressions of mutual pleasure at meeting each other, and promises that after the war we would seek each other out, we mounted, he gave three cheers for the Yanks, and I gave three cheers for the Johnnies, he divided his plug of tobacco with me, and I gave him the bottle of horse liniment, he turned his horse towards the direction his gray coats had taken the night before, while I turned my horse towards the hole in the woods our fellows had made, and we left the race track where we had fought so gamely, eat so heartily, and played poker so disastrously, to me. As we were each about going into the woods, half a mile apart, he waved his handkerchief at me, and I waved mine at him, and we plunged into the forest.

After riding for an hour or so, alone in the woods, thinking up a good lie to tell about where I had been, and what I had been doing, I heard horses neighing, and presently I came upon my regiment, just starting out to hunt me up. The colonel looked at me and said, "Kill the fat prodigal, the calf has got back."

CHAPTER 3

I am Wounded in the Canteen

The last chapter of this history left me facing my regiment, which had started out to hunt me up, after my terrible fight with that Confederate. The colonel rode up to me and shook me by the hand, and congratulated me, and the major and adjutant said they had never expected to see me alive, and the soldiers looked at me as one returned from the grave, and from what I could gather by the looks of the boys, I was something of a hero, even before I had told my story. The colonel asked me what had become of all the baggage I had on my saddle when I went away, and I told him that I had thrown ballast over-board all over the Southern Confederacy, when I was charging the enemy, because I found my horse drew too much water for a long run.

He said something about my being a Horse-Marine, and sent me back to my company, telling me that when we got into camp that night he would send for me and I could tell the story of my capture and escape. I rode back into my company, and you never saw such a change of sentiment towards a raw recruit, as there was towards me, and they asked me questions about my first fight. The corporal who had placed me on picket, and stampeded at the first fire, was unusually gracious to me, and said when he saw a hundred and fifty rebels come charging down the road, yelling and firing, he knew it was no place for his small command, so he lit out.

He said he supposed of course I was shot all to pieces. I didn't tell him that it was me that did all the yelling, and that there was only one rebel, and that he was perfectly harmless, but I told him that he miscalculated the number of the enemy, as there were, all told, at least five hundred, and that I had killed fourteen that I knew of, besides a number had been taken away in ambulances, wounded. The boys opened their eyes, and nothing was too good for me during that march. We went into camp in the pine woods late in the afternoon, and after supper the colonel sent for me, and I went to his tent. All the officers were there, and as many soldiers as dared crowd around. The colonel said the corporal had reported where he left me, and how the enemy had charged in force, and he supposed that I had been promptly killed. That he felt that he could not hold his position against such immense odds, so he had fallen back slowly, firing as he did so, until the place was too hot for him, and now he wanted to hear my story. I told the colonel that I was new at the business, and maybe I did not use the best judgment in the world, by remaining to fight against such odds, but I meant well.

I told him I did not wish to complain of the corporal, who no doubt was an able fighter, but it did seem to me that he ought at least to have waited till the battle had actually commenced. I said that the first charge, which stampeded the corporal and his men, was not a marker to what took place afterwards. I said when the enemy first appeared, I dismounted, got behind a tree, and poured a murderous fire into the ranks of the rebels, and that they fell all around. I could not tell how many were killed, but probably ten, as I fired eleven shots from, my carbine, and I usually calculated on missing one out of ten, when shooting at a mark. Then they fell back and I mounted my horse and rode to their right flank and poured it into them red hot from my revolver, and that I saw several fall from their horses, when they stampeded, and I drew my sabre and charged them, and after cutting down several, I was surrounded by the whole rebel army and captured.

They tied me to the wheel of a gun carriage, and after trying to pump me as to the number of men I had fighting against them, they left me to hold a council of war, when I untied myself, mounted my horse, and cut my way out, and took to the woods. I apologized to the colonel for running away from the enemy, but told him it seemed to me, after the number I had killed, and the length of time I had held them at bay, it was no more than right to save my own life, as I had use for it in my business.

During my recital of the lie I had made up, the officers and soldiers stood around with mouths open, and when I had concluded my story, there was silence for a moment, when the colonel stepped forward and took me by the hand, and in a few well chosen remarks congratulated me on my escape, and thanked me for so valiantly standing my ground against such fearful odds, and he said I had reflected credit upon my regiment, and that hereafter I would be classed as a veteran instead of a recruit. He said he had never known a man to come right from the paths of peace, and develop into a warrior with a big "W" so short a time. The other officers congratulated me, and the soldiers said I was a bully boy. The colonel treated to some commissary whisky, and then the business of the evening commenced, which I found to be draw poker.

I sat around for some time watching the officers play poker, when the chaplain, who was a nice little pious man, asked me to step outside the tent, as he wished to converse with me. I went out into the moon-light with him, and he took me away from the tents, under a tree, and told me he had been much interested in my story. I thanked him, and said I had been as brief as possible. He said, "I was interested, because I used to be something of a liar myself, before I reformed, and studied for the ministry." It occurred to me that possibly the chaplain did not believe my simple tale, and I asked him if he doubted my story. "That is about the size of it," says he. I told him I was sorry I had not told the story in such a manner that he would believe it, because I valued the opinion of the chaplain above all others. He said he had known a good many star liars in his time, some that had national reputations, but he had never seen one that could hold a candle to me in telling a colossal lie, or aggregation of lies, and tell them so easy.

I thanked him for his good opinion, and told him that I flattered myself that for a recruit, right fresh from the people, who had never had any experience as a military liar, I had done pretty well. He said I certainly had, and he was glad to make my acquaintance. I asked him to promise not to give it away to the other officers, which he did, and then I told him the whole story, as it was, and that I was probably the biggest coward that ever lived, and that I was only afraid that my story of blood-letting would encourage the officers to be constantly putting me into places of danger, which I did not want to be in. I told him I believed this war could be ended without killing any more men, and cited the fact that I had been a soldier nearly forty-eight hours, and nobody had been killed, and the enemy was on the run. I told the chaplain that if there was one thing I didn't want to see, it was blood.

Others might have an insatiable appetite for gore, but I didn't want any at all I was willing to do anything for this government but fight; and if he could recommend to me any line of action by which I could pull through without being sent out to do battle with strangers who could shoot well, I should consider it a favour. What I wanted was a soft job, where there was no danger. The chaplain looked thoughtful a moment, and then took me over to his tent, where he opened a bottle of blackberry brandy. He took a small dose, after placing his hand on his stomach and groaning a little. He asked me if I did not sometimes have a pain under my vest. I told him I never had a pain anywhere. Then he said I couldn't have any brandy. He said the brandy came from the sanitary commission, and was controlled entirely by the chaplains of the different regiments, and the instructions were to only use it in case of sickness.

He said a great many of the boys had pains regularly, and came to him for relief. He smacked his lips and said if I felt any pain coming on, to help myself to the brandy. It is singular how a pain will sometimes come on when you least expect it. It was not a minute before I began to feel a small pain, not bigger than a man's hand, and as I looked at the bottle the pain increased, and I had to tell the chaplain that I must have relief before it was everlastingly too late, so he poured out a dose of brandy for me. I could see that I was becoming a veteran very fast, as I could work the chaplain for sanitary stores pretty early in the game. Well, the chaplain and me had pains off and on, for an hour or two, and became good friends.

He told me of quite a number of methods of shirking active duty, such as being detailed to take care of baggage, acting as orderly, and going to surgeon's call. He said if a man went to surgeon's call, the doctor would report him sick, and he could not be sent out on duty. The next day we went back to our post, where the regiment was stationed, and where they had barracks, that they wintered in, and remained there several weeks, drilling. I was drilled in mounting and dismounting, and soon got so I could mount a horse without climbing on to him from a fence. But the drill became irksome, and I decided to try the chaplain's suggestion about going to surgeon's call. I got in line with about twenty other soldiers, and we marched over to the surgeon's quarters.

I supposed the doctor would take each soldier into a private room, feel of his pulse, look at his tongue, and say that what he needed was rest, and give him some powders to be taken in wafers, or in sugar. But all he did was to say "What's the matter?" and the sick man would tell him, when the doctor would tell his assistant to give the man something, and pass on to the next. I was the last one to be served, and the interview was about as follows:

Doc.—What's the matter?

Me—Bilious.

Doc.—Run out your tongue. Take a swallow out of the black bottle.

That seems very simple, indeed, but it nearly killed me. When he told me to run out my tongue, I run out perhaps six inches of the lower end of it, the doctor glanced at it as though it was nothing to him anyway, and then he told me to take a swallow out of the bottle. In all my life I had never taken four doses of medicine, and when I did the medicine was disguised in preserves or something. The hospital steward handed me the bottle that a dozen other sick soldiers had drank out of, and it was sticky all around the top, and contained something that looked like castor oil, for greasing a buggy. He told me to take a good big swallow, and I tried to do so.

Talk about the suffering brought on by the war, it seems to me nobody ever suffered as I did, trying to drink a swallow of that castor oil out of a two quart bottle, that was dirty. It run so slow that it seemed, an age before I got enough to swallow, and then it seemed another age before the oil could pass a given point in my neck. And great Caesar's ghost how it *did* taste. I think it went down my neck, and I just had strength enough to ask the steward to give me something to take the taste out of my mouth. He handed me a blue pill. O, I could have killed him. I rushed to the chaplain's tent and took a drink of blackberry brandy, and my life was saved, but for three years after that I was never sick enough to get farther than the chaplain's quarters.

I suppose the meanest trick that was ever played on a raw recruit, was played on me while we were in camp at that place. It seemed to me that some of the boys got jealous of me, because I had become a hero, accidentally. May be some of them did not believe I had killed as many of the enemy as I had owned up to having killed. Anyway every little while some soldier would say that he thought it was a mean man that would go out and kill a lot of rebels and not bury them. He said a man that would do that was a regular pot-hunter, who killed game and left it on the ground to spoil.

They made lots of such uncharitable remarks, but I did not pay much attention to them. I had a tent-mate who took a great interest in me, and he said no soldier's life was safe who did not wear a breast-plate, and he asked me if I did not bring any breast-plate with me. I told him I never heard of a breastplate, and asked him what it was. He said it was a vest made of the finest spring steel, that could be worn under the clothes, which was so strong that a bullet could

"Great Caesar's ghost, how it did taste!"

not penetrate it. He supposed of course I had one, when he heard of the fight I had, and said none of the old boys would go into a fight without one, as it covered the vital parts, and saved many a life. I bit like a bass. If there was anything I wanted more than a discharge, it was a breast-plate. If the chaplain should succeed in getting me a soft job, where there was no danger, I could get along without my breast-plate, but there was no sure thing about the chaplain, so I asked the soldier where I could get a breastplate.

He said the quartermaster used to issue them, but he didn't have any on hand now, but he said he knew where there was one that once belonged to a soldier who was killed, and he thought he could get it for me. I asked him how it happened that the soldier was killed, when he had a breast-plate, and he told me the man was killed by eating green peaches. Of course I couldn't expect a breastplate to save me from the effects of eating unripe fruit, and I felt that if it would save me from bullets it would be worth all it cost, so I told the soldier to get it for me. That evening he brought it around, and he helped me put it on. I learned afterwards that it was an old breast-plate that an officer had brought to the regiment when the war broke out, and that it had been played on raw recruits for two years.

After I had got it on, the soldier suggested that we go out with several other dare devils, and run the guard and go down town and play billiards, and have a jolly time. I asked him if the guard would not shoot at us, and he said the guards would be all right, and if they did shoot they would shoot at the breast-plates, as all the boys had them on. So about six of us sneaked through the guards, went to town and had a big time, and came back along towards morning, each with a canteen of whisky. It was not easy getting back inside the lines, as the moon was shining, but we got by the guards, and then my friends suggested that we take our breast-plates off and put them on behind us, as the guards, if they shot at all, would be firing in our rear.

I took mine off and put it on behind my pants, and just then somebody fired a gun, and the boys said "run," and I started ahead, and the firing continued, and about every jump I could hear and feel something striking my breast-plate behind, which seemed to me to be bullets, and I was glad I had the breast-plate on, though afterwards I found that the boys behind me were firing off their revolvers in the air, and throwing small stones at my breast-plate. Presently a bullet, as I supposed, struck me in the back above the breast-plate, and I could feel blood trickling down my back, and I knew I was wounded.

O, I hankered for gore, before enlisting, and while editing a paper, and now I had got it, got gore till I couldn't rest. The blood run down my side, down my leg, into my boot, and I could feel I was wading in my own blood. And great heaven's, how it did smell. I had never smelled blood before, that I knew of, and I thought it had the most peculiar, pungent, intoxicating odour. I ran towards my quarters as fast as possible, fainting almost, from imaginary loss of blood, and finally rushed into my tent, threw myself on my bunk and called loudly for the doctor and chaplain, and then I fainted. When I came to I was surrounded by the doctor, and a lot of the boys, all laughing, and the chaplain was trying to say something pious, while trying to keep a straight face.

"Have you succeeded in staunching the blood, doc?" I asked, in a trembling voice. He said the blood was quite staunch, but the whisky could never be saved. I did not know what he meant, and I turned to the chaplain and asked him if he wouldn't be kind enough to say something appropriate to the occasion. I told him I had been a bad man, had lied some, as he well knew, and had been guilty of things that would bar me out of the angel choir, but that if he had any influence at the throne of grace, and could manage to sneak me in under the canvass anyway, he could have the balance of my bounty, and all the pay that might be coming to me.

The chaplain held up the breast-plate that had been removed by kind hands, from the back portion of my person, and said I had better take that along with me, as it would be handy to wear when I wanted to stand with my back to the fire in hades. I could not understand why the good man should joke me, on my death bed, and I rolled over with my back to the wall, to weep, unobserved, and I felt the blood sticking to my clothes and person, and I asked the doctor why he did not dress my wound. He said he should have to send the wound to the tin-shop to be dressed, and then they all laughed. This made me indignant, and I turned over and faced the crowd, and asked them if they had no hearts, that they could thus mock at a dying man.

The doctor held up my canteen with a hole in it, made by a stone thrown by one of my companions, and said, "You d——d fool, you are not wounded. Somebody busted your canteen, and the whiskey run down your leg and into your boot, and you, like an idiot, thought it was your life blood ebbing away. Couldn't you tell that it was whis- key by the smell?" I felt of myself, where I thought I was wounded, and couldn't find any hole, and then I took off my boot, and emptied the whisky out, and felt stronger, and finally I got up, and the boys went away laughing at me, leaving the chaplain, who was kind enough to tell me that of all the raw recruits that had ever come to the regiment, he thought I was the biggest idiot of the lot, to let the boys play that ancient breast-plate and canteen joke on me.

I asked him if the boys didn't all wear breast-plates, and he said "naw!" He told me that was the only breast-plate in the whole Department of the Gulf, and it was kept to play on recruits, and that I must keep it until a new recruit came that was green enough to allow the boys to do him up. So I hid the breast-plate under my bunk, and went to bed and tried to dream out some method of getting even with my persecutors, while the chaplain went out, after offering to hold himself in readiness, day or night, to come and pray for me, if I was wounded in the canteen any more.

CHAPTER 3

I am Put in Charge of a Funeral

I had now been fighting the battles of my country for two weeks, and felt that I needed rest, and one day I became so homesick that it *did* seem as though it would kill me. Including the week it had taken me to get from home to my regiment, three weeks had elapsed since I bid good-bye to my friends, and I wanted to go home. I would lay awake nights and think of people at home and wonder what they were doing, and if they were laying awake nights thinking of me, or caring whether I was alive, or buried in the swamps of the South. It was about the time of year when at home we always went off shooting, and I thought how much better it was to go off shooting ducks and geese, and chickens, that could not shoot back, than to be hunting bloodthirsty Confederates that were just as liable to hunt us, and who could kill, with great ease. I thought of a pup I had at home that was just the right age to train, and that he would be spoiled if he was not trained that season.

O, how I did want to train that pup. The news that one of my comrades had been granted a furlough, after three years' service, and that he was going home, made me desperate, and I dreamed that I had waylaid and murdered the fortunate soldier, and gone home on his furlough. The idea of getting a furlough was the one idea in my mind, and the next morning as I took my horse to the veterinary surgeon for treatment,[1] I had a talk with the horse doctor about the possibili-

---

1. I neglected to say, in my account of the battle at the race-track, that when firing with my revolver, at my friend the rebel, I put one bullet-hole through the right ear of my horse. I was so excited at the time that I did not know it, and only discovered it a week later when currying off my horse, which I made a practice of doing once a week, with a piece of barrel-stave, when I noticed the horse's ear was swelled up about as big as a canvas ham. (Continued next page.)

ties of getting a furlough. I had known him before the war, when he kept a livery stable, and as I owed him a small livery bill, I thought he would give it to me straight.

The horse doctor had his sleeves rolled up, and was holding a horse's tongue in one hand while he poured some medicine down the animal's throat out of a bottle with the other hand, which made me sorry for the horse, as I remembered my experience at surgeon's call, in drinking a dose of castor oil out of a bottle, and I was mean-enough to be glad they played it on horses as well as the soldiers. The horse doctor returned the horse's tongue to its mouth, kicked the animal in the ribs, turned and wiped his hands on a bale of hay, and said:

"Well, George, to get a furlough a man has got to have plenty of gall, especially a man who has only been to the front a couple of weeks. There is no use making an application in the regular way, to your captain, have him endorse it and send it to regimental head-quarters, and so on to brigade headquarters, because you would never hear of it again. My idea would be for you to go right to the general commanding the division, and tell him you have got to go home. But you mustn't go crawling to him, and whining. He is a quick-tempered man, and he hates a coward. Go to him and talk familiar with him, and act as though you had always associated with him, and slap him on the shoulder, and make yourself at home. Just make up a good, plausible story, and give it to him, and if he seems irritated, give him to under-stand that he can t frighten you, and just as likely as not he will give you a furlough. I don't say he will, mind you, but it would be just like him. But he does like to be treated familiar like, by the boys."

I thanked the horse doctor and went away with my horse, resolved to have a furlough or know the reason why. The general's headquar-ters were about half a mile from our camp, and after drill that morn-ing I went to see him. I had seen him several times, at the colonel's headquarters, and he always seemed mad about something, and I had thought he was about the crossest looking man I ever saw, but if there was any truth in what the horse doctor had told me, he was easily reached if a man went at him right, and I resolved that if pure, un-adulterated cheek and monumental gall would accomplish anything, I

I took him to the horse doctor, who reduced the swelling so we could find the hole through the horse's ear, and the horse doctor tied a blue ribbon in the hole. He said the blue ribbon would help heal the sore, but later I found that he had put the rib-bon in the ear to call attention to my poor marksmanship, and the boys got so they made comments and laughed at me every time I appeared with the horse.

would have a furlough before night, for a homesicker man never lived than I was. I went up to the general's tent and a guard halted me and asked me what I wanted, and I said I wanted to see "his nibs," and I walked right by the guard, who seemed stunned by my cheek. I saw the general in his tent, with his coat off, writing, and he *did* look savage. Without taking off my hat, or saluting him, I went right up to him and sat down on the end of a trunk that was in the tent, and with a tremendous effort to look familiar, I said:

"Hello, Boss, writing to your girl?"

I have seen a good many men in my time who were pretty mad, but I have never seen a man who appeared to be as mad as the general did. He was a regular army officer, I found afterwards, and hated a volunteer as he did poison. He turned red in the face and pale, and I thought he frothed at the mouth, but maybe he didn't. He seemed to try to control himself, and said through his clenched teeth, in a sarcastic manner, I thought, in imitation of a ring master in a circus:

"What will the little lady have next?"

I had been in circuses myself, and when the general said that I answered the same as a clown always does, and I said:

"The banners, my lord."

I thought he would be pleased at my joking with him, but he looked around as though he was seeking a revolver or a sabre with which to kill me finally he said:

"What do you want, man?"

It was a little tough to be called plain "man," but I swallowed it. I made up my mind it was time to act, so I stood up, put my hand on the shoulder of the general familiarly, and said:

"The fact is, old man, I want a furlough to go home. I have got business that demands my attention; I am sick of this inactivity in camp, and besides the shooting season is just coming on at home, and I have got a setter pup that will be spoiled if he is not trained this season. I came down here two weeks ago, to help put down the rebellion; but all we have done since I got here is to monkey around drilling and cleaning off horses, while the officers play poker for red chips. Let me go home till the poker season is over, and I will be back in time for the fall fighting. What do you say, old apoplexy. Can I go?"

I do not now, and never did know, how I got out of the general's tent, whether he kicked me out, or threw his trunk at me, or whether there was an explosion, but when I got outside there were two soldiers trying to untangle me from the guy ropes of the general's tent, his wash basin and pail of water were tipped over, and a cord that was strung outside with a lot of uniforms, shirts, sabres, etc., had fallen down, and the general was walking up and down his tent in an excited manner, calling me an escaped lunatic, and telling the guards to tie me up by the thumbs, and buck and gag me. They led me away, and from their conversation I concluded I had committed an unpardonable offense, and would probably be hung, though I couldn't see as I had done much more than the horse doctor told me to.

Finally the officer of the day came along and told the guards to get a rail and make me carry it. So they got a rail and put it on my shoulder, and I carried it up and down the camp, as a punishment for insulting the general. I thought they picked out a pretty heavy rail, but I carried it the best I could for an hour, when I threw it down and told the guards I didn't enlist to carry rails. If the putting down of this rebellion depended on carrying fence rails around the Southern Confederacy, and I had to carry the rails, the aforesaid rebellion never would be put down. I said I would fight if I had to, and be a hostler, and cook my own food, and sleep on the ground, and try to earn my thirteen dollars a month, but there must be a line drawn somewhere, and I drew it at transporting fences around the sunny South.

The guards were inclined to laugh at my determination, but they said I could carry the rail or be tied up by the thumbs; and I said they could go ahead, but if they hurt me I would bring suit against the government. They were fixing to tie me up when the colonel of my regiment rode up to see the general, and he got the guards to let up on me till he could see the general. The general sent for me after the colonel had talked with him, and they called me in and asked me how I happened to be so fresh with the general; and I told them about the horse doctors' advice as to how to get a furlough; and then they both laughed, and said I owed the horse doctor one, and I must get even with him.

The colonel told the general who I was, that he had known me before the war, and that I was all right only a little green, and that the boys were having fun with me. The colonel told the general about my first fight the first day of my service, and how I had, single-handed, put to flight a large number of rebels, and the general got up and shook hands with me, and said he forgave me for my impertinence, and gave me some advice about letting the boys play it on me, and said I might go back to my company. He was all smiles, and insisted on my taking a drink with himself and the colonel.

When I was about leaving his tent, I turned to him and said: "Then I don't get any furlough?" "Not till the cruel war is over," said the general, with a laugh, and I went away.

The guards treated me like a gentleman when they saw me taking a drink with the general, and I went back to my regiment, resolved not to go home, and to get even with the horse doctor for causing me to make a fool of myself. However, I was glad I visited the general, for, after getting acquainted with him, he seemed a real nice man, and he kept a better article of liquor than the chaplain.

For several days nothing occurred that was worthy of note, except that the chaplain took a liking to my horse, and wanted to trade a mule for him. I never did like a mule, and didn't really want to trade, but the chaplain argued his case so eloquently that I was half persuaded. He said the horse I rode, from its friskiness, and natural desire to "get there, Eli!" would eventually get me killed, for if I ever got in sight of the enemy the horse would rush to the front, and I couldn't hold him. He said he didn't want to have me killed, and with the mule there would be no danger, as the mule knew enough to keep away from a fight.

The chaplain said he had always rode a mule, because he thought the natural solemnity of a mule was in better keeping with a pious man, but lately he had begun to go into society some, in the town near where we were camped, and sometimes had to preach to different regiments, so he thought he ought to have a horse that put on a little more style, and as he knew I wanted an animal that would keep as far from the foe as possible, and not lose its head and go chasing around after rebels, and running me into danger, as my spiritual adviser he would recommend the mule to me. He warranted the mule sound in every particular, and as a mule was worth more than a horse he would trade with me for ten dollars to boot. He said there was not another man in the regiment he would trade with on such terms, but he had taken a liking to me, and would part with his mule to me, though it broke his heart.

At home there was a sentiment against trading horses with a minister, as men who did so always got beat, but I thought it would be an insult to the chaplain to refuse to trade, when he seemed to be working for my interests, to prevent me from being killed in a fight by the actions of my horse, so I concluded to trade, though it seemed to me that if I couldn't shoot off a horse without hitting its ears, I would fill a mule's ears full of bullets. I spoke to the chaplain about that, and he said there was no danger, because whenever fighting commenced the mule always wore his ears lopped down below the line of fire. He said the mule had been trained to that, and I would find him a great comfort in time of trial, and a sympathizing companion always, one that I would become attached to. I told him there was one thing I wanted to know, and that was if the mule would kick. I had always been prejudiced against mules because they kicked.

He said he knew mules had been traduced, and that their reputations were not good, but he believed this mule was as free from the habit of kicking as any mule he had ever met. He said he would not deny that this mule could kick, and in fact he had kicked a little, but he would warrant the mule not to kick unless something unusual happened. He said I wouldn't want a mule that had no individuality at all, one that hadn't sand enough to protect itself. What I wanted, the chaplain said, was a mule that would treat everybody right, but that would, if imposed upon, stand up for its rights and kick. I told the chaplain that was about the kind of mule I wanted, if I had any mule at all, and we traded. The chaplain rode off to town on my horse, on a canter, as proud as a peacock, while I climbed on to the solemn, lop-eared mule and went out to drill with my company.

I do not know what it was that went wrong with the mule while we were drilling, but as we were wheeling in company front, the mule began to "assert his individuality," as the chaplain said he probably would, and he whirled around sideways and kicked three soldiers off their horses; then he backed up the other way and broke up the second platoon, kicked four horses in the ribs, stampeded the company, and stood there alone kicking at the air. The major rode down to where I was and began to swear at me, but I told him I couldn't help it. He told me to dismount and lead the mule away, but I couldn't dismount until the mule stopped kicking, and he seemed to be wound up for all day.

The major got too near and the mule kicked him on the shin, and then started for the company again, which had got into ranks, kicking all the way, and the company broke ranks and started for camp, the mule following, kicking and braying all the way. I never was so helpless in all my life. The more I spurred the mule, the more it kicked, and if I stopped spurring it, it kicked worse. When we got to camp, I fell off some way, and rushed into the chaplain's tent, and the mule kicked the tent down, and some boys drove the mule away, and while I was fixing up the tent the chaplain came back looking happy, and asked me how

I liked the mule. I never was a hypocrite, anyway, and I was mad, so I said: "Oh, dam that mule!"

Of course it is wrong to use such language, especially in the presence of a minister, but I couldn't help it. I could see it hurt the chaplain, for he sighed and said he was sorry to hear such words from me, inasmuch as he had just got me detailed as his clerk, where I would have a soft thing, and no drilling or fighting. He said he had wanted a clerk, one who was a good-hearted, true man, and he had picked me out, but if I used such language, that settled it. He said he didn't expect to find a private soldier that was as pious as he was, but he did think I would be the best man he could find. I wanted a soft job, with no fighting, as bad as any man ever did, and I told the chaplain that he need not fear as to my swearing again, as it was foreign to my nature, but I told him if he had been on the hurricane deck of a kicking mule for an hour, and seen comrades fall one by one, and bite the dust, and be carried on with marks of mule shoes all over their persons, he would swear, and I would bet on it.

So it was arranged that I was to be the chaplain's clerk, and I moved my outfit over to his tent, and for the first time since I had been a soldier, I was perfectly happy. There was no danger of being detached for guard duty, police duty, drilling, or fighting, and the only boss I had was the chaplain. The chaplain and myself sat that evening in his tent, and ate sanitary stores, drank wine for sickness, and smoked pipes, and didn't care whether school kept or not, and that night I slept on a cot, and had the first good night's rest, and in the morning I awoke refreshed, and with no fear of orderly sergeants, or anybody. I had a soft snap.

The next morning I asked the chaplain what my duties were to be, and he said I was to take care of the tent, write letters for him, issue sanitary stores to deserving soldiers who might need them, ride with him sometimes when he went to town, or to preach, go to funerals with him occasionally, set a good example to the other soldiers, and make myself generally useful. He said I would have to attend to the burial of the coloured people who died, and any such little simple details. He went out and left me pondering over my duties.

I liked it all except the nigger funerals. I had always been a Democrat, at home, and not very much mashed on our coloured brothers, and one thing that prevented me from enlisting before I did was the idea of making the coloured men free. I had nothing against a coloured man, and got to think a great deal of them afterwards, but the idea of acting as an undertaker for the coloured race never occurred to me. I made up my mind to kick on that part of the duties, when the chaplain came in and said the coloured cook of one of the companies was dead, and would be buried that afternoon, and as he had to go to a meeting of chaplains down town, I would have to go and conduct the services, and I better prepare myself with a little speech.

I was in a fix. I told the chaplain that it might not have occurred to him, but honestly, I couldn't pray. He said that didn't make any difference. I told him I couldn't preach hardly at all. He said I didn't need to. All I had to do was to go and find out something about the life of the deceased, what kind of a man he was, and say a few words at the grave complimentary of him, console the mourners, if there were any, and counsel them to try to lead a different life, that they might eventually enter into the glory of the New Jerusalem, or words to that effect. Well, this made me perspire.

This was a tighter place than I was in when I met the rebel. The idea of my conducting the funeral exercises of such a black-burying party, made me tired. The chaplain said a good deal depended on how I got through this first case, as if I succeeded well, it would be a great feather in my cap. His idea, he said, was to try me first on a nigger, and if I was up to snuff, and carried myself like a thoroughbred, there would be nothing too good for me in that regiment.

I went to the orderly sergeant of the company where the man died, to get some points as to his career, in order to work in a few remarks appropriate to the occasion, and I said to the orderly:

"I understand your company cook has gone to that bourne from whence no traveller returns. I thought that was pretty good for a green hand, for a starter."

"Yes," said the orderly, as he looked solemn, "The old son-of-a-gun has passed in his chips, and is now walking in green pastures, beside still waters, but he will not drink any of the aforesaid still waters, if he can steal any whisky to drink."

"You astonish, me," said I to the orderly. "The fact is, the chaplain has sawed off on to me the duty of seeing to the burial of our deceased friend, and I called to gather some few facts as to his characteristics as a man and a brother. Can you tell me of anything that would interest those who may attend?"

"O, I don't know," said the orderly. "The deceased was a liar, a thief, and a drunkard. He would steal anything that was not chained down. He would murder a man for a dollar. He was the worst nigger that ever was. If there was a medical college here that wanted bodies, it would be a waste of money to bury him. But when he was sober he could bake beans for all that was out, and there was no man that could boil corned mule so as to take the taste of the saltpetre out, as he could."

This was not a very good send off for my first funeral, but I clung to the good qualities possessed by the late lamented. Though he might have been a bad man, all was not lost if he could bake beans well, and boil the salt horse or corned mule that soldiers had to eat, so they were appetizing. Many truly good men of national reputation, could not have excelled him in his chosen specialties, and I made a memorandum of that for future use. I made further inquiries in the company, and found that the deceased had a bad reputation, owed everybody, had five wives living that he had deserted, and was suspected of having murdered two or three coloured men for their money. His death was caused by delirium tremens. He had stole a jug of whisky from the major's tent, laid drunk a week, and when the whisky was gone he had tremens, and had gone to the horse doctor for something to quiet his nerves, and the horse doctor had given him a condition powder to take, to be followed with a swallow of mustang liniment, and the man died.

This was the information I got to use in my remarks at the grave of the deceased, and I went back to my tent to think it over. I thought perhaps I had better work in the horse doctor for mal-practice, in my discourse, and thus get even with him for sending me to the general after a furlough. While I was thinking over the things I would say, and trying to forget the bad things about the man, the orderly sent word that the funeral cortege was ready to proceed to the bone yard. I looked down the company street and saw the remains being lifted into a cart, and I went out and put the saddle on my mule, and with a mental prayer that the confounded mule wouldn't get to kicking till the funeral was over, started to do the honours at the grave of the late company cook.

CHAPTER 5

I am Arrested

This last chapter of these celebrated war papers closed with me sad-dling my mule to ride to the funeral of the coloured cook, at which I was to act as chaplain. The mule evidently knew that it was a solemn occasion, for there was a mournful look on its otherwise placid face, the ears drooped more than usual, and there seemed a sweet peace stealing over the animal, which well became a funeral, until I began to buckle up the saddle, when the long-eared brute began to paw and kick and bite, and it took six men to get me into the saddle. I rode down the company street where the cart stood with the remains, and a coloured driver sitting on the foot of the plain pine box, asleep. I woke the driver up with the point of my sabre, when another coloured man came out of a tent with a shovel in one hand, and a hardtack with a piece of bacon in the other. He climbed into the cart, sat down on the coffin and began to eat his dinner. This was my funeral.

All that seemed necessary for a funeral was a corpse, a driver of a cart, and a man with a shovel. I rode up to the orderly's tent and asked him where the mourners were, and he laughed at me. The idea of mourners seemed to be ridiculous. I had never, in all my life, seen so slim a funeral, and it hurt me. In the meantime the nigger with the shovel had woke up the driver of the cart, and he had followed me, with the remains. I told them to halt the funeral right there, until I could skirmish around and pick up mourners enough for a mess, and a choir, and some bearers.

As I rode away to the colonel's tent, the driver of the cart and the man with the shovel were playing "mumbleypeg," with a jack-knife, on the coffin, which shocked me very much, as I was accustomed to living where more respect was paid to the dead. I went to the colonel's tent and yelled "Say!" The colonel, who was changing his shirt, came to the door with his eyes full of soap, rubbing his neck with a towel, and asked what was the row. I told him I would like to have him detail me six bearers, seven or eight mourners, a few singers, and fifteen or twenty men for a congregation. He asked me what on earth I was talking about, and just then the cart with the corpse in was driven up to where I was, the orderly having told the driver to follow me with the late lamented. I pointed to the outfit, and said:

"Colonel, in that box lie the remains of a coloured cook. The chaplain has appointed me to conduct the funeral service, and I find that the two coloured men on the cart are the only ones to accompany the remains to their last resting place. No man can successfully run a funeral on three niggers, one of whom is dead, one liable to go to sleep any minute, and the other with an abnormal appetite for hardtack. It is a disgrace to civilization to give a dead man such a send off, and I want you to detail me some men to see me through. I have loaded myself with some interesting remarks befitting the occasion, and I do not want to fire them off into space, with no audience except these two coons. Give me some mourners and things, or I drop this funeral right where it is."

While I was speaking the general rode up to visit with the colonel, with his staff, and the colonel came out with his undershirt on, and his suspenders hanging down, and he and the general consulted for a minute, and laughed a little, which I thought was disgraceful. Then the colonel sent for the sergeant-major and told, him to detail all the company cooks and officer's servants, to attend the funeral with me, and he said I could divide them off into reliefs, letting a few be mourners at a time. In the meantime, he said, I could move my procession off down by the horse-doctor's quarter's, as he did not want it in front of his tent.

That reminded me that the horse-doctor had prescribed for the deceased, and had given him condition powders, and I asked the colonel to compel the horse-doctor to go with me. It had always seemed to me at home that the attending physician, under whose auspices the person died, should attend the funeral of his patient, and when I told the colonel about it, he called the horse-doctor and told him he would have to go. It took half an hour or so to get the coloured cooks and servants together, but when all was ready to move, it was quite a respectable funeral, except that I could not help noticing a spirit of levity on the part of the mourners.

All the followers were mounted, the officer's servant's on officer's horses, and the cooks on mules, and it required all the presence of mind I possessed to keep the coons from turning the sad occasion into a horse race, as they would drop back, in squads, a quarter of a mile or so, and then come whooping up to the cart containing the remains, and each vowing that his horse could clean out the others. I rode in front of the remains with the horse-doctor, and tried to conduct myself in as solemn a manner as befitted the occasion, and tried to reason with the horse-doctor against his unseemly jokes, which he was constantly getting on.

He told several stories, better calculated for a gathering where bacchanalian revelry was the custom, and I told him that while I respected his calling, he must respect mine. He said something about calling a man on a full hand, against a flush, but I did not pretend to know what he meant. We had to go out of town about two miles, to the cemetery. Unfortunately we were in the watermelon growing section, and the horse-doctor called my attention to the fact that my procession was becoming scarce, when I looked around, and every blessed one of the cooks and servants, and the man with the shovel, had gone on into the field after melons, and I stopped the cart and yelled to them to come back to the funeral.

Pretty soon they all rode back, each with a melon under his arm, and every face looked as though there was no funeral that could prevent a nigger from stealing a watermelon. After several stops, to round up my mourners, from corn fields and horse racing, we arrived at the cemetery, and while the grave was being dug the niggers went for the melons, and if it had been a picnic there couldn't have been much more enjoyment. The horse-doctor took out a big knife that he used to bleed horses, and cut a melon, and offered me a slice, and while I did not feel that it was just the place to indulge in melon, it looked so good that I ate some, with a mental reservation, however. It was all a new experience to me. I had never believed that in the presence of death, or at a funeral, people could be anything but decorous and solemn.

I had never attended a funeral before, except where all present were friends of the deceased, and sorry, but here all seemed different. They all seemed to look upon the thing as a good joke. I had read that in New York and other large cities, those who attended funerals had a horse race on the way back, and stopped at beer saloons and filled up, but I never believed that people could be so depraved. I tried to talk to the coons, and get them to show proper respect for the occasion, but they laughed and threw melon rinds at each other. Finally the colonel and the general, with quite a lot of soldiers, who were out reconnoitring, rode to where we were, and the coons acted a little better, but I could see that the officers were not particularly solemn. They seemed to expect something rich.

They evidently looked upon me as a star idiot, who would make some blunder, or say something to make them laugh: I made up my mind that in my new position I would act just as decorous, and speak as kindly as though the deceased was the president. During all my life I had made it a practice never to speak ill of any person on earth, and if I could not say a good word for a person I would say nothing, a practice which I have kept up until this writing, with much success, and I decided that the words spoken on that occasion should not reflect against the poor man who had passed in his checks, and laid down the burden of life. The grave was completed, and with a couple of picket ropes the body was let down, and there was for a moment a sort of solemnity. I arose, and as near as I can remember at this late day, spoke about as follows:

Friends: We have met here today to conduct the last rites over a man, who but yesterday was among us but who, in an unguarded moment drank too much whisky, and paid the penalty. (There was a smile perceptible on the faces on the officers.) The ignorant man who died, did not know any better, but I see around me men who know better, but who drink more than this man did, and if they are not careful they will go the same way. (There was less smiling among the officers.) It is said of this man that he was bad, that he would steal. I have investigated, and have found that it is true, but that his peculations consisted of small things, of little value, and I am convinced that the habit was not worse with him than with any of us. In war times, everybody steals.

We are all thieves to a certain extent. The soldier will not go hungry if he can jay-hawk anything to eat. The officer will not go thirsty if he can capture whisky, nor will anybody walk if he can steal a horse. The higher a man gets the more he will steal. Shall we harbour unkind thoughts against this dead man for stealing a pair of boots, and honour a general who steals a thousand bales of cotton? (No! no! shouted the cooks and servants, while the officers looked as though they were sorry they attended the funeral.) Friends let us look at the good qualities

I PRONOUNCE A SOLEMN FUNERAL ORATION

of our friend.

I say, without fear of successful contradiction, that a man, how-ever humble his station, who can bake beans as well as the remains could bake them, is entitled to a warm place in the heart of every soldier, and if he goes to the land that is fairer than this,-and who can say that he will not,—he is liable to be welcomed with 'well done, good and faithful servant,' and he will be received where horse doctors can never enter with their condition powders, and where there will never be war any more. To his family, or several families, as the case may be, I would say——

At this point I had noticed an uneasiness on the part of my mourn-ers and bearers, as well as the officers. Nine of the negroes fell down on the ground and groaned as if in pain, and the general and his stall looked off to a piece of woods where a few shots had been fired, and rode away hurriedly, the colonel telling me I had better hurry up that funeral or it was liable to be interrupted. The horse-doctor went to the negroes who were sick, and after examining them he said they had been poisoned by eating melons that had been doctored, and he advised them to get to town as quick as possible.

They scrambled on their horses the best way they could, and just then there was a yell, and out of the woods came half a dozen Union soldiers followed by fifteen or twenty Confederates, and all was confu-sion. The niggers scattered towards town, the driver of the cart taking the lead, trying to catch the general and his start, who were hurrying away, leaving the horse-doctor, myself and the deceased. The horse-doctor seized the shovel and threw a little dirt on the coffin, then mounted his horse, I mounted my mule, and away we went towards town, with the rebels gaining on us every jump. The horse-doctor soon left me, and with a picket I had pulled off the fence of the cem-etery, I worked my passage on that mule. I mauled the mule, and the more I pounded the slower it went.

There was never a more deliberate mule in the world. I forgot all the solemn thoughts that possessed me at the grave, and tried to talk to the mule like a mule-driver, but the animal just fooled along, as though there was no especial hurry. Occasionally I could hear bullets 'zipping' along by me, and the rebels were yelling for all that was out. O, how I did wish I had my old race horse that the chaplain had beat me out of. In my first engagement my horse was too fast, and there was danger that I would catch my friend, the rebel, and I complained of the horse. Now I had a mule that was too slow.

What I wanted was a 'middling' horse, one that was not too confounded fast when after the enemy, and one not so all-fired slow when being pursued. The Johnnies were coming closer, but we were only half a mile from town. Would they chase us clear into town? At that critical moment the blasted mule stopped short, never to go again, and began to kick. What on earth possessed that fool mule to take a notion to stop right there and kick, is more than I shall ever know, but it simply kicked, and I felt that my time had come. The Union soldiers that were being chased by the Confederates passed me, and told me I better light out or I would be captured, but I couldn't get the mule to budge an inch. It just kicked. The good Lord only knows, what that mule was kicking at, or why it should have been scheduled to stop and kick at that particular time, when every minute was precious.

I saw the rebels very near me, and as it was impossible to get the mule to go a step farther, I raised the large, flat, white-washed picket which I had torn on the cemetery fence to maul the mule with, in token of surrender, and the Confederate boys surrounded me, though they kept a safe distance, after my mule had kicked in the ribs of one of their horses. The rebs had gone about as far towards the town as it was safe to go, and they knew the whole garrison would be out after them pretty soon, so they laughed at me for being armed with a whitewashed picket, and asked me if I expected to put down the rebellion by stabbing the enemy with such things. I told them I had been burying a nigger.

One of my captors run the point of his sabre into my mule, to stop its kicking, and then he said to his comrades, "Boys, we came out here with the glorious prospect of capturing a Yankee general and his staff, and instead of getting him, we have broken up a nigger funeral and captured the gospel sharp, armed with a picket fence, and a kicking mule. Shall we hang him for engaging in uncivilized, warfare, by stabbing us with pickets poisoned with whitewash, or shall we take the red-headed slim-Jim back with us as a curiosity." The boys all said not to hang me, but to take me along. I saw that it was all day with me this time. I felt that I was helping put down the rebellion rapidly, as I had been a soldier four weeks, been captured twice, and not a drop of blood had been spilled.

The rebels started back, with me and my mule ahead of them, and they kept the mule ahead by jabbing it with a sabre occasionally. I felt humiliated and indignant at being called slim-Jim, sorrel-top, and elder. They seemed to think I was a preacher. I stood it all until a cuss reached into my pocket and took my *meershaum* pipe and a bag of tobacco, filled the pipe and lit it, then I was mad. I had paid eight dollars of my bounty for that pipe, and I said to the leader: "Boss, I can stand a joke as well as anybody, but when you capture me, in a fair fight, you have no right to jab my mule with a sabre, or call me names.

I am a meek and lowly soldier of the army of the right, and want to so live that I can meet you all in the great hereafter, but by the gods I can whip the condemned galoot that stole my *meershaum* pipe. You think I am pious, and a non-combatant, but I am a fighter from away back, and don't you forget it." The young man who seemed to be in command told me to dry up, and he would get my pipe. He went and took it away from the one who had stolen it, filled it and lit it himself, and said it was a good pipe, and then he passed it around among them all. We moved on at a trot, and were getting far away from my regiment, and I realized that I was a captive, and that I should probably die in Andersonville prison. I looked at the dozen stalwart rebels that were riding behind me, and knew I could not whip them all with one picket off the cemetery fence, and so I resolved to remain a captive, and die for my country, of scurvy, if necessary.

I turned around in my saddle to ask if it wasn't about time for me to have a smoke out of my own pipe, and as I looked up the road we had come over I saw a large body of our own cavalry, coming like the wind toward us. I said nothing, but my face gave me away. I looked so tickled to see the boys coming that the rebels noticed it, and they looked back and saw the soldiers in pursuit, they yelled, "The Yanks are coming!" put spurs to their horses, stabbed my mule and told me to pound it with the picket, and hurry up, and then they passed me, and away they went, leaving me in the road alone between them and my own soldiers, I yelled to the leader to give me back my pipe, and I can hear his mocking laugh to this day, as he told me to "go to hell."

This made me mad, and drawing my picket I dashed after the retreating rebels, knowing that the men of my regiment would soon overtake me, and they would think I had chased the rebels three miles from town, armed only with a picket off the fence, and saved the garrison from capture. The thing worked to perfection, and when our command came up, the horses panting and perspiring, and the boys looking wild, the captain in command asked me how many there was of 'em, and I told him about forty, and he said I had done well to drive them so far, and he charged by me after them. I yelled to the captain to try and kill that long-legged rebel on the sorrel horse, and get my *meershaum* pipe, but he didn't hear me. I hurried along as fast as I could, but before I caught up, there was a good deal of firing, and when I got there flankers were out in the woods, and there was sorrow, for three or four boys in blue had been killed in an ambush, and the rebels had got away across a bayou.

As I rode up on my mule, with the picket still in my hand, I saw the three soldiers of my regiment lying dead under a tree, two others were wounded and had bandages around their heads, and for the first time since I had been a soldier, I realized that war was not a picnic. I could not keep my eyes off the faces of my dead comrades, the best and bravest boys in the regiment, boys who always got to the front when there was a skirmish. To think that I had been riding right amongst the rebels who had done this thing but a few minutes before, and never thought that death would claim anybody so soon. I wondered if those rebels were not sorry they had killed such good boys. I wondered, as I thought of the fathers and mothers, and sisters of my dead companions, whether the rebels would not sympathize with them, and then I thought suppose our fellows had not been killed, and we had killed some of the Confederates, wouldn't it have been just as sorrowful, wouldn't *their* fathers, mothers and sisters have mourned the same.

Then I made a resolve that I would never kill anybody if I could help it; I even decided that if I should meet the rebel that had my *meershaum* pipe, I would not fight him to get it. If he wasn't gentleman enough to give it up peaceably, he could keep it, and be darned. Just then some of our skirmishers came in carrying another dead body, and we were all speculating as to which one of our poor boys had fallen, when we noticed that the dead soldier had on a gray suit, and it was soon found that he was one of the Confederates. He was laid down beside our dead boys, and I don't know but I felt about as bad to see him dead, as it was possible to feel. It is true he had told me, half an hour before, when I asked him for my pipe, to go to hades, but I did not have to go unless I wanted to.

And he was gone first. I saw something sticking out of the breast pocket of the dead Confederate, and could see that it was my pipe. Then I thought of the foolish remark I made to the captain, to kill that long-legged rebel and get my *meershaum*. God bless him, I didn't want anybody to kill him for a bad smelling old pipe, and I wondered if that remark would be registered up against me, in the great book above, when I didn't mean it. I tried to make myself believe that my remark

51

did not have any influence on the man's fate. He just took his chances with his comrades, and was killed, no doubt, and yet it was impossible to get the idea off my mind that I was responsible for his death.

Anyway, I would never touch the confounded old pipe again, and if I ever heard of his mother or sister, after the war was over, I would stand by them as long as I had a nickel. An ambulance was sent for and the dead and wounded were placed in it, and we went back to town, a sad procession. There was no need to detail any mourners for this occasion, and there was no straggling for watermelons. Everybody was full of sorrow. The next day there was a Union funeral in that Southern town, and the three Union boys were laid side by side, while a little, to one side my Confederate was buried, receiving the same kind words from the chaplains. As a volley was about to be fired over the graves, I picked a handful of roses, buds and blossoms, from a rose bush in the cemetery, and went to the grave of the Confederate and tenderly tossed them upon the coffin. The horse doctor saw me do it, and in his rough manner said,

"What you about there? It ain't necessary to plant flowers on the graves of rebels.

"O, no, it isn't necessary, I said, as the volley was fired over the graves, but it will make his mother or his sister feel better to know that there are a few roses in there, and it won't hurt anybody. I will just play that I am the authorized agent of that Confederate soldier's sister.

"O, all right if you say so, said the horse-doctor, as he drew the sleeve of his blue blouse across his eyes, which were wet. The last volley was fired, and the soldiers returned to camp, leaving the dead of two armies sleeping together. As I went in the chaplain's tent and sat down to think, the chaplain handed me something, saying:

"Here's your pipe. They found it on that Confederate soldier that captured you."

I pushed it away and said, "I don't want it. I have quit smoking."

CHAPTER 6

Off on a Raid

The winding up of the last chapter of this history, with its sad incidents, deaths and burials, was unavoidable, but it shall not occur again. The true historian has got to get in all the particulars. I think I never felt quite as downhearted as I did the day or two after the skirmish, when our boys were killed. It had seemed as though there was no danger of anybody getting hurt, as long as they looked out for themselves, but now there was a feeling that anybody was liable to be killed, any time, and why not me? Of course the old veterans of the regiment were the ones who would naturally be expected to take the brunt of the battle, but there was a habit of sending raw recruits into places of danger that struck me as being mighty careless, as well as very bad judgment.

Then there were great preparations being made for an advance movement, or a retreat, or something, and my mind was constantly occupied in trying to find out whether it was to be an advance or a retreat. If it was an advance, I wanted to arrange to be in the rear, and if it was a retreat, it seemed to me as as though the proper place for a man who wanted to live to go home, was in front. And yet what chance was there for a common private soldier to find out whether it was an advance or a retreat. Finally I decided that when the regiment *did* start out, I would manage to be about the middle, so it wouldn't make much difference which way we went.

When that idea occurred to me I pondered over it a good deal and told the chaplain, and he said it was a piece of as brilliant strategy as he had ever heard of, and he was willing to adopt it, only being a staff of-ficer it was necessary for him and me to ride with the colonel, and the colonel most always rode at the head, though his place was about the middle. He said he would speak to the colonel about it. It made my hair stand to see the preparations that were being made for carnage. Ammunition enough was issued to kill a million men, and the doctors were packing bandages and plasters, and physic, and splints and probes, until it made me sick to look at them. When I thought of actual war, my mind reverted to my mule, the kicking brute that was no good, and I decided to get a horse.

I had got so, actually, that I could hear bullets whistle without turning pale and having cold chills run over me, and it seemed as though a horse was none too good for me, so I went to the colonel and told him that a soldier couldn't make no show on a kicking mule and I wanted a horse. I told him I supposed, as chaplain's clerk. I should have to ride with him and his staff on the march, and he didn't want to see as nice a looking fellow as I was riding a kicking mule that would kick the ribs of the officers horses, and break the officers legs. The colonel said he had not thought of that contingency. He had enjoyed seeing me ride the mule, because I was so patient when the mule kicked. He said they used that mule in the regiment to teach recruits to ride.

A man who could stay on that mule could ride any horse in the regiment, and as I had been successful, and had displayed splendid mulemanship, I should be promoted to ride a horse, and he told the quartermaster to exchange with me and give me the chestnut-sorrel horse that the Confederate was shot off of. I went with the quartermaster to the corral, turned out my mule, and cornered the beautiful horse that had been rode so proudly a few days before by my friend, the rebel. It took six of us to catch the horse, and bridle and saddle him, and the men about the corral said the horse was no good. He hadn't eaten anything since being captured, and his eyes looked bad, and he wanted to kick and bite everybody. I told them the poor horse was homesick, that was all that ailed him.

The horse was a Confederate at heart, and he naturally had no particular love for Yankees. I remembered that once or twice when I was riding with the rebels, after they captured me, the young fellow on this horse patted him on the neck and called him "Jeff", so I knew that was his name, so I led him out of the corral away from the other fellows, where there was some grass growing, and made up my mind I would "mash" him. After he had eaten grass a little while, looking at me out of the corner of his eyes as though he didn't know whether to kick my head on, or walk on me, as I sat under a tree, I got up and patted him on the neck and said, "Well, Jeff, old boy, how does the grass fit your stomach?"

You may talk about brute intelligence, but that horse was human. He stopped eating, with his mouth full of grass, looked astonished at being addressed by a stranger without an introduction, and turned a pair of eyes as beautiful and soft as a woman's upon me, and then began to chew slowly, as though thinking. I rubbed his sleek coat with, my bare hands, and did not say much, desiring to have Jeff make the first advances. He looked me over, and finally put his nose on my sleeve, and rubbed me, and looked in my face, and acted as though he would say, "Well, of course this red-headed fellow is no comparison to my dead master, but evidently he's no slouch, and if I have got to be bossed around by a Yankee, as he is the only one that has spoken a kind word to me since I was captured, and he seems to know my name, I guess I will tie to him," and the intelligent animal rubbed his nose all over me, and licked my hand.

I rubbed the horse all over, petted him, took up his feet and looked at them, and spoke his name, and pretty soon we were the best of friends. I mounted him and rode around and it was just like a rocking chair. That poor, dead Confederate had probably rode Jeff since he was a kid and Jeff was a colt, and had broken him well, and I was awfully sorry that the original owner was not alive, riding his horse home safe and sound, to be greeted by his family with loving embraces. But he was dead and buried, and his horse belonged to me, by all the laws of war. And yet I had not become a hardened warrior to such an extent that I could forget the hearts that would ache at his home, and I made up mind that horse would be treated as tenderly as though he was one of my family.

I rode Jeff around for an hour or two, found that he was trained to jump fences, stand on his hind feet, trot, pace, rack, and that he could run like a scared wolf, and everything the horse did he would sort of look around at me with one eye as much as to say, "Boss, you will find I have got all the modern improvements, and you needn't be afraid that I will disgrace you in any society." I was fairly in love with my new horse, and, except for a feeling that I was an interloper with the horse, and sorry for the poor boy that had been shot off him, I should have been perfectly happy.

The chaplain had got in the habit of wearing a nice, blue broadcloth blouse which I had brought from home, which had two rows of brass buttons on it. I had paid about twenty dollars of my bounty for the blouse, and had found that the private soldiers did not wear such elaborate uniforms in active duty, so I kept it in the chaplain's tent. I thought if I was killed and my body was sent home, the blouse would come handy. The chaplain wore it occasionally, and he said any time I wanted to wear any of his clothes to just help myself. An order had been issued to move the following day, with ten days' rations, and some of the boys asked for passes to go down town and have a little blow-out before we started. They wanted me to go along, and so I got a pass, too.

We were to go down town in the afternoon and stay till nine o'clock at night, when we had to be in camp. I saddled up Jeff and looked for my blouse, but it was gone, the chaplain having worn it to visit the chaplain of some other regiment, so I took his coat and put it on, as he had told me to. The coat had the chaplain's shoulder-straps on, but I thought there would be no harm in wearing it, so about a dozen of us privates started for town to have a good time, and I with chaplain's-straps on. It was customary, when soldiers went to town on a pass, to partake of intoxicating beverages more or less, as that was about the only form of enjoyment, and I blush now, twenty-two years afterward, to write the fact that we all got pretty full. It seemed so like home to be able to go into a saloon and drink beer, good old northern beer, and who knew but tomorrow we would be killed. So we ate, drank, and were merry.

One of the boys said when the officers got on a tear, they would ride right into billiard saloons, and sometime shoot at decanters of red liquor behind the bar, and he said a private was just as good as an officer any day, and suggested that we mount our horses and paint the town. We mounted, and rode about town, racing up and down the streets, and finally we came to a billiard saloon, and half a dozen of us rode right in, took cues out of the rack, and tried to play billiards on horse-back. It was a grand picnic then, though it seems foolish now. My horse Jeff would do anything I asked him, and when I rode up to the bar and told him to rear up, he put both forefeet on the bar, and looked at the bartender as much as to say, "set up the best you have got."

The chaplain's shoulder-straps gave the crowd a sort of confidence that everything was all right, and after exhibiting in a saloon for a time, there was something said about horse-racing, and I said my horse could beat anything on four legs, so we adjourned to the outskirts of town for a race, followed by half the people in town. We had a horse-race, and Jeff beat them all, and wherever I went the crowd would cheer the chaplain. They said they liked to see a man in that position who could unbend himself and mix up with the boys. There never was a chaplain more popular than the "Wisconsin preacher" was. It did not occur to me that I was placing the chaplain in an unfavourable position before the public, by wearing his coat.

Nothing occurred to me, that day, except that we were having a high old time. Finally, after dark, one of our boys got into a row with a loafer in a saloon, and picked the loafer up and tossed him through the window, to the sidewalk. This was very wrong, but it couldn't be helped. There was a great noise, cries for the provost guard, and we knew that the only way to get out of the scrape honourably, would be to get out real quick, so we mounted and rode to our camp. My horse was the fastest and I got home first, unsaddled my horse and went to the tent, took off the chaplain's coat and hung it up carefully, and was at work writing a letter, and thinking how my horse acted as though he had been on sprees before, he enjoyed it so, when I heard a noise outside, and it was evident that the provost guard had followed us to camp, and were making complaint to the colonel about our conduct down town.

Finally the guard went away, and shortly the colonel and the adjutant called at our tent and inquired for the chaplain. I told them the chaplain had been away most of the day, and had not returned. The colonel and the adjutant winked at each other, and asked me if he wasn't away a good deal. I told them that he was away some. They asked me if I never noticed that his breath had a peculiar smell. I told them that it was occasionally a little loud. They went away thoughtfully. Now that I think of it I ought to have explained that the peculiarity of the chaplain's breath was caused from eating pickled onions of the sanitary stores, but it did not occur to me at the time. After a while the chaplain came back, asked me if anybody had died during the day, took a drink of blackberry brandy for what ailed him, and we retired. The next morning there was a circus. The little town boasted, a daily paper, and it contained the following:

> The community is prepared to overlook an occasional scene of hilarity among the Federal soldiers stationed in this vicinity, but when a gang of roisterers is led by a chaplain, as was the case yesterday, all right-minded people will be indignant. It is said by our informant that the chaplain of a certain cavalry regiment was the liveliest one of the crowd, that he rode into a billiard room, caused his horse to place its forefeet on the bar, and that he played a better game of billiards on horseback than many

worldly men can play on foot. It is the duty of the command-ing officer to discipline his chaplain. The chaplain also beat the boys several horse races while in town, and they say he is a per-fect horseman, and has one of the finest horses ever seen here, which he probably stole.

I had a boy bring me a paper every morning, and I read the article before the chaplain awoke, and destroyed the paper. Early the next morning the colonel sent for the chaplain, placed him under arrest, and the good man came back to the tent feeling pretty bad. I asked him what was wrong, and he said he was under arrest for conduct un-becoming an officer and a gentleman. He said charges were preferred against him for drunkenness and disorderly conduct, horse-racing, playing billiards on horse-back, riding his horse into a saloon and trying to jump him over the bar, and lots of things too numerous to mention. I felt sorry for him, and told him I had been fearful all along that he would get into trouble by going away from me so much, and associating with the chaplains of the other regiments, but I had never supposed it would come to this.

"Wine is a mocker," said I, becoming warmed up, "and none of us can afford to tamper with it. With me, it does not make so much dif-ference, as I have no reputation but that which is already lost, but you, my dear sir, think of your position. Go to the colonel and confess all, and ask him to forgive you," and I wiped my eyes on my coat sleeve.

"But I was not drunk," said the chaplain, indignantly. "I was not in a saloon, and never saw a game of billiards in my life. I was over to the New Jersey regiment, talking with their chaplain about getting up a revival, among the soldiers," and the good man groaned as he said, "it is a case of mistaken identity."

"Bully, elder," said I. "If you can make the court-martial believe you, you will be all right, and you will not be cashiered. But it looks dark, very dark, for you. May heaven help you."

The chaplain was worried all the morning, and the officers and men joked him unmercifully. At noon the chaplain was released from arrest, as we were to move at four p. m., and he begged so to be al-lowed to accompany the regiment. The colonel told him he could be tried when we got back, and he was happy. There was a great com-motion as the regiment broke up its camp and got ready to move. There was the usual crowd of negresses who had been doing washing for the soldiers, to be paid on pay day, and we were going away, no one knew where, and no one knew when we would meet pay day.

There were saloon-keepers with bills against officers, and standing-off creditors was just about as hard in the army as at home. I couldn't see much difference. But finally everything was ready, the ammunition wagons, wagon train of stores, and a battery of little guns, about three pounders, had been added. I didn't like the battery. It seemed to me hard enough to kill our fellow citizens with revolver balls, without shooting them with cannon.

At 4 p.m. the bugle sounded "forward," and with the clanking of sabres, rattling of hoofs and wagons, we marched outside the picket line, past the cemetery where my deceased friends were buried, and were going towards the enemy. The chaplain and myself were riding behind the colonel, when the colonel asked the good man to ride up to a log that was beside the road, and make his horse put his forefeet upon it, as he did on the bar in the saloon. I felt sorry for the chaplain, and I rode up to the log, and had Jeff put his feet up on it. Then I rode back and saluted the colonel and told him it was I who had done the wicked things the chaplain was accused of, and I told him how the chaplain was using my coat, so I put on his, with the shoulder straps on, and all about it. He laughed at first and then said, "Then you are under arrest. You may dismount and walk and lead your horse until further orders."

I dismounted, like a little man, and for five miles I walked, keeping up with the regiment. Finally the colonel sung out, "gallop, march," and I got on my horse. I reasoned that the order to gallop was "further orders," and that as he knew I couldn't very well gallop on foot he must have meant for me to get on. We galloped for about ten miles, and were ordered to halt, when I dismounted and led my horse up to the colonel, and saluted him.

"Well, you must have had a hard time keeping up with us on foot," said he. I told him it rested me to go on foot.

We were just going into camp for the night, and the colonel said, "Well, as you are rested so much from your walk, you may go out with the foraging party and get some feed for your horse and the chaplain's."

I was willing to do anything for a quiet life, so I fell in with a party of about forty, under a lieutenant, and we rode off into the country to steal forage from a plantation, keeping a sharp lookout for Confederates who might object. I guess we rode away from camp two or three miles, when we came to a magnificent plantation house, and outhouses, negro quarters, etc. The house was on a hill, in a grove of live oaks, and had immense white pillars, or columns in front. As we rode up to the plantation the boys scattered all over the premises. This was the first foraging expedition I had ever been with, and I thought all we went for was to get forage for our horses, so I went to a shock of corn fodder and took all that I could strap on my saddle, and was ready to go, when I passed a smoke house and found some of the boys taking smoked hams and sides of bacon.

I asked one of the boys if they had permission to take hams and things, and he laughed and said, "everything goes," and he handed me a ham which I hung on to my saddle. Then the lieutenant told me to go up in front of the house and stand guard, and prevent any soldier from entering the house. I rode up to the house, where there was an old lady and a young married woman with a little girl by her side. They were evidently much annoyed and frightened, though too proud to show it, and I told them they need have no fear, as the men were only after a little forage for their horses.

The old lady looked at the ham on my saddle and asked me if the horses eat meat, and I said, "No, but sometimes the men eat horses." I thought that was funny. The young woman was beautiful, and the child was perfectly enchanting. They were on the opposite side of the railing from me, and my horse kept working up towards them, rubbing his nose on the pickets, and finally his nose touched the clasped hands of the mother and child. The little girl laughed and patted the horse on the nose, while the mother drew back. It was almost dark and the horse was almost covered with corn fodder, but the little girl screamed and said:

"Mamma, that is Jeff, papa's horse!"

The mamma looked at me with a wild, hunted look, then at the horse, rushed down the steps and threw her arms around the neck of the horse and sobbed in a despairing manner:

"O, where is my husband? Where is he? Is he dead?

"My son, my son!" cried the old lady.

"Bring me my papa, you bad man!" said the little child, and I was surrounded by the three.

Gentle reader, I have been through many scenes in my life, and have been many times where it was not the toss of a copper whether death or life was my portion, and I had some nerve to help me through, but I never was in a place that tried me like that one. I had been captured by the father of this little child, the husband of this beautiful, proud woman, the son of this charming old lady. I had seen him brought in, dead, had seen him buried, and had thrown a bunch of roses in his grave. Now I was surrounded by these mourners, mourners when they should know the worst. Cold chills run all over me, and cold perspiration was on my brow.

"Is he dead?" they all shouted together.

I hate a liar, on general principles, and yet there are times when a lie is so much easier to tell than truth. I did not want to be a murderer, and I knew, by the dreadful light in the eyes of that lovely wife, as she looked up at me from the neck of the horse, her face as white as snow, that if I told the truth she would fall dead right where she was. If I told the truth that blessed old lady's heart would be broken, and that little child's face would not have any more smiles, during the war, for mamma and grandma, and, with a hoarse voice, and choking, and trying to swallow something that seemed as big as a baseball in my throat, I deliberately lied to them. I told them the young man who rode this horse had been captured, after a gallant fight, unharmed, and sent north. That he was so brave that our boys fell in love with him, and there was nothing too good for him in our army, and that he would be well taken care of, and exchanged soon, I had no doubt, and bade them not to worry, but to look at the discomforts and annoyances of war as leniently as possible, and all would be well soon.

"Thank heaven! Take all we have got in welcome," said the old lady, as a heavenly smile came over her face. "My boy is safe."

"O, thank you, sir," said the little mother, as a lovely smile chased a dimple all around her mouth, and corralled it in her left cheek, while a pair of navy-blue eyes looked up at me as though she would hug me if I was not a Yankee, eyes that I have seen a thousand times since, in dreams, often with tears in them.

"You are a darling good man," said the little girl, dancing on the gravel path. The mother blushed and said,

"Why, Maudie, don't be so rude;" and there was a shout:

"Fall in!"

The lieutenant rode up to me and asked, as he noticed the glad smiles on the faces of the ladies, if this was a family reunion, and, apologizing for being compelled to raid the plantation, we rode away. I was afraid they would mention the news I had brought them, and the lieutenant would tell the truth, so I was glad to move. I was glad to go, for if I had remained longer I would have cried like a baby, and given them back the horse, and walked to camp. As we moved away, I took out my knife and cut the string that held the smoked ham on my saddle, and had the satisfaction of hearing it drop on the path before the house. I could not give back the husband of the blue-eyed woman, the son of the saintly Southern mother, the father of the sweet child, but I *could* leave that ham.

As we rode back to camp that beautiful moonlight night, I did not join in the singing of the boys, or the jokes. I just thought of that happy home I had left, and how it would be stricken, later, when the news was brought them, and wondered if that fearful lie I had been telling, them was justifiable, under the circumstances, and it would be laid up against me, charged up in the book above. That night I slept on the ground on some corn fodder and dreamed of nothing but blue-eyed mamma's and golden-haired Maudie's and white-haired angel grandmothers.

CHAPTER 7

I Nearly Kill an Old Man

When our foraging party got back to camp, and I unloaded the corn fodder from my horse, I was about as disgusted with war as a man could be. The faces of those people I had met at the plantation rose up before me, and I could imagine how they would look when they heard that the Confederate soldier who was their all, was dead. I hoped that they would never hear of it. While I was thinking the matter over, and grooming my horse, the chaplain came along and took nearly all the fodder I had brought in, and fed it to his horse, and asked me where the chickens and hams, and sweet potatoes were. I told him I didn't get any. Then he spoke very plainly to me, plainer than he had ever spoken before, and told me that fodder for horses was not all that soldiers got when they went out foraging. He said I wanted to snatch anything that was lying around loose, that could be eaten. I asked him if the government did not furnish rations enough for him to live comfortably, in addition to the sanitary stores. He said sometimes he yearned for chicken.

Then I told him his salary was sufficient to buy such luxuries. He was hot, and talked back to me, and told me he didn't propose to be lectured by no red-headed private as to his duties, or his conduct, and he wanted me to understand that I was expected to forage for him as well as myself, and not to let another soldier come into camp with a better assortment of the luxuries afforded by the country, than I did. He said that he picked me out as a man that would fill the bill, and do his duty. I told him if he had selected me from all the men in the regiment as being the most expert sneak thief, he had made a mistake, and I would be teetotally d——d if I would go through the country stealing hens and chickens for any chaplain that ever lived, and he could put that in his pipe and smoke it. It was pretty sassy talk for a private

63

soldier to indulge in towards a chaplain, but I was so disgusted to hear a man who should discountenance anything unsoldierly, talk so flippantly about taking from the women and children of the country what little they had to live on, because we had the power, their men folks being away in the army, that I got on my ear, as it were.

I told him that I was not much mashed on war, and hoped I would never have to fire a gun at a human being, but now that I was into the business, I would fight if I had to, or do any duty of a soldier, but I would be cussed if I would rob hen-roosts, and he didn't weigh enough to compel me to. Then he said I could go back to my company, as he didn't want a man around him that hadn't sand enough to do his duty. I asked him if I hadn't better wait till after supper, it being after dark, but he said I could go right away, and he would have another man detailed to take my place. I was discharged, because I struck against stealing hens. I saddled my horse, took my share of the fodder, and started for my company to return to duty as a soldier.

On the way to my company I saw a half a dozen soldiers, covered with mud, and their horses covered with foam, ride up to the colonel's tent, and I stopped to see what was the matter. A sergeant gave the colonel a dispatch, which he tore open, read it, looked excited, and then he turned to me and said, "Ride to every commanding officer of a company and say with my compliments, that 'Boots and Saddles' will be sounded in ten minutes, and every man must be in line, mounted, within five minutes after the call is sounded, then come back here." Well, I was about as excited as the colonel, and I rode to every captain's tent and gave the command. Some of the captains, who were just sitting down to supper, asked, "What you giving us," thinking it was some foolishness on my part. One captain said if I came around with any more such orders he would run a sabre through me and turn it around a few times; another said to his lieutenant, "That is the chaplains idiot, that the boys play jokes on; some corporal has probably told him to carry that message."

I got all around the companies, and went back to the colonel, and told him that I had delivered his invitation, but the most of the captains sent regrets in one way and another, and one was going to jab me with a sabre. He called the bugler, and told him to blow "Boots and Saddles," and in five minutes to sound, "To Horse;" then he turned to me and said, "You will be my orderly tonight, and you will have the liveliest ride you ever experienced. Buckle up your saddle girth and lead my horse out here." I told the colonel I should have to buckle up my own belt a few holes, as I hadn't had any supper, when he told his servant to bring me out what was left of his supper, which he did, one small hard tack.

I eat pretty hearty, and let my horse fill himself all he could on corn stalks, and in a short time the bugle calls were echoing through the woods, men were saddling up and mounting, and picking up camp utensils in the dark, and swearing some at being ordered out in that unceremonious manner when they had got all ready to have a night's rest. There was not near as much swearing as I had supposed there would be, but there was enough. The chaplain came rushing up to where I was with his coat off, and asked me what was the matter, and the colonel having gone to the major's tent, I answered him that we were going to have the liveliest ride he ever experienced, and not to forget it, and that probably before morning we would have the biggest fight of the season.

"Come and help me catch my horse," said the chaplain, "I turned him loose so he could roll over, and he has stampeded."

"Go catch your own horse," said I with lofty dignity, "and steal your own chickens. I am serving on the start of the commanding officer, sir. I am the colonel's orderly."

I thought that would break the chaplain all up, but it didn't. "The devil you say," remarked the chaplain, as he went off in the darkness, whistling for his horse. Gentle reader, did you ever ride on horseback fifty miles in one night, on an empty stomach, after having ridden thirty miles during the day? If you never have accomplished such a feat, you don't know anything about suffering. O, to this day I can feel my stomach freeze itself to my backbone. We started soon after orders were given on a gallop, and if we walked our horses a minute during the whole night, I did not know it.

We marched by "fours," but I had the whole road to myself, as I rode behind the colonel. I wanted to know where we were going and what for, and once, when the colonel fell back to where I was, while he was taking a drink out of a canteen, I said, "This is a little sudden, ain't it?" My idea was to draw him out, and get him to tell me all about the destination of the expedition, and its object. The colonel got through drinking, and as he knocked the cork into the canteen, he said, "Yes, this *is* a little spry." That was all he said, and evidently he wanted me to draw my own inference, which I did.

Pretty soon the orderly sergeant of the company that was on the advance, directly behind the colonel, rode up to me and asked me if

I had any idea where we were going. He said he had seen me talking with the colonel, and thought maybe he had told me the programme. He added that he thought it was a shame that men couldn't be allowed a little rest. I told him that I had just been talking with the colonel about it, but I had no authority to communicate what he said.

However, I would assure the orderly that we were going to have the liveliest ride he ever experienced. I knew I was safe in saying that, and the orderly remarked that he had about come to that conclusion himself, and he left me. I had never expected to rise, on pure merit, to that proud position of colonel's orderly, and I made up my mind if that night's ride did not founder me, or drive my spine up into the top of my hat, or glue the two sides of my empty stomach together, so they would never come apart, that I would try to conduct myself so that the commanding officers would all cry for me and want me on their starts.

I argued, to myself, as we rode along, that the position of colonel's orderly could not be so very unsafe, as it did not stand to reason that a colonel would go into any place that was particularly dangerous, as long as he could send other officers. I knew that colonels in action should ride behind their regiments, and wondered if this colonel knew his place, or would he be fool enough to go right ahead of his men? I was going to speak to him about it, if we ever stopped galloping long enough, but everything was jarred out of my head.

A fellow can think of a good many things, riding on a gallop at night, and I guess I thought of about everything that night. There were few interruptions of the march. There were about four stops, two being caused by horses falling down and being run over by those behind them, and two by carbines going off accidentally. One man was dismounted and run over by half the horses in the regiment, and when he was pulled out from under the horses he asked for a chew of tobacco, and saying he was marked for life by horse shoes, he kicked his horse in the ribs for falling down, climbed on and said the procession might move on.

He was all cut to pieces by horse's hoofs, but he was full of fight the next morning. Another soldier had his big toe shot off by the accidental discharge of a carbine, and when the regiment stopped, and the colonel asked him if he wanted to stop there and wait for an ambulance to overtake him, he said, not if there is going to be a fight. I don't use a big toe much, anyway, and if there is a fight ahead, I want to be there, if I haven't got a toe left on my feet. The colonel smiled and said, all right, boy. I never saw fellows who were so anxious to fight, and I wondered how much money it would take to induce me to go into a fight when I was crippled up enough to be excused. Along toward morning everybody felt that we were so far into the enemy's lines that there must be some object in the long ride, and the probabilities of a fight seemed to be settled in every man's mind. Uphill and down we galloped, until it seemed to me I should fall off my horse and die.

About half an hour before daylight the command was halted, and the officers of each company were sent for, and they surrounded the colonel, separated from the men, and he said: "There is a town ahead, about four miles, garrisoned by confederate troops. We are to charge it at daylight, drive the enemy out the other side of town, kill as many as possible, and when they go out they will be attacked by another Union regiment that has been sent around to the rear. There is a railroad there, and a bridge across a river, Confederate stores of ammunition, provisions, cotton, etc. The stores are to be burned, the railroad bridge destroyed, the track torn up, engines, if there are any, are to be ditched, and everything destroyed except private residences. You understand?"

The officers said they did, and they went back to their companies and ordered the men to get a bite to eat. When the officers had gone I was pretty scared, and I said, "Colonel, suppose the rebels do not get out of that town." The colonel was chewing a hard-tack when he answered. Daylight was just streaking up from the East, and he held a piece of the hard-tack up to the light to pick a worm out of it, after which he answered: "If they don't get out, we will, those of us who are not killed. I always like to eat hard-tack in the dark, then I can't see the worms."

To say that I was reassured would be untrue. I admired a man who could mingle business with pleasure, as he did when talking of possible death and worms in hard-tack, but death was never an interesting subject to me. I wanted to talk with the colonel more, and asked him if colonels often get killed, and if an orderly was exactly safe in his immediate vicinity, but he leaned against a tree and went to sleep, and I stood near, as wide awake as any man ever was. I wondered whose idea it was to send us fifty miles into the Confederacy to destroy provisions and railroads.

Did they suppose the Confederates didn't want anything to eat. I thought it was a mean man or government that would burn up good wholesome provisions because they couldn't eat them themselves. And who owned this railroad that was going to be torn up? Why burn a bridge that probably cost several hundred thousand dollars. As I was thinking these things over and finding fault with the persons responsible for such foolishness, the chaplain, who had not showed up during the night, came up to where I was, without any hat, leading his horse, which was lame. The first thing he asked me how I would trade horses. They all wanted my Jen, but he was not in the market. The chaplain said he had caught up with the regiment about midnight, and had rode at the rear, with the horse-doctor. He said this expedition was foolish, and had no object except to try the endurance of the horses and men. I told him that we were going to have a fight in less than an hour, and burn a town, and probably we would all be killed. The chaplain turned pale and looked faint.

I had read about hell, and seen pictures of it, from the imagination of some eminent artist, but the hell I had read of, and seen pictured, was not a marker to the experience of the next three hours. In a few minutes the colonel woke up, and the regiment mounted and moved on. An advance guard was put further out than before, with orders to charge the rebel picket almost into town, and then hold up for the rest of us.

As we neared the town it was just light enough to see. The advance captured the picket post without a shot being fired, and moved right into town, followed by the regiment, and we actually rode right into the camp of the boys in gray, and woke them up by firing. They scattered, coatless and shoeless, firing as they ran, and in five minutes they were all captured, killed, gone out of town, or were in hiding in the buildings. Then began the conflagration. Immense buildings, filled with goods, or bales of cotton, were fired, and soon the black smoke and falling walls made a scene that was enough to set a recruit crazy. A train came in just as the fire was at its greatest, and a squad of men was sent to burn it, and the colonel told me to go and capture the engineer and bring him to the headquarters.

I rode up as near to the engine as my horse would go and told the engineer I wanted him. He turned a cock somewhere, and a jet of steam came out towards me that fairly blinded me and the horse, and I couldn't see the engine any more. My horse turned tail, the engineer threw a lump of coal and hit me on the head, and I went away and told the colonel the engineer wouldn't come, and beside had scalded me with steam, and hit me with a lump of coal. The colonel said the engineer could be arrested for such conduct.

Pretty soon the train was on fire, and one of our boys clubbed the

"You are a darling good man", said the little girl.

engineer, got on the engine and run it on to a side track and ditched it, and brought the engineer up to headquarters, where I had quite a talk with him about squirting steam and throwing lumps of coal at peaceable persons. Then the railroad, bridge was set on fire, and it looked cruel to see the timbers licked up by flames, but when the burning trestle fell into the river below, it was a grand, an awful sight. I came out of the fight alive, but with a lump on my head as big as a hen's egg, so big I couldn't wear my hat, and a firm determination to whip that engineer who threw the lump of coal when I could catch him alone.

We cooked a late breakfast on the embers of the ruins, and after eating, I noticed a sign, "Printing Office," in front of a residence just outside the burnt district, and asked permission to go there and print a paper, with an account of the fight, and the destruction of the town. Permission was granted, and I went to the office and found an old man and two daughters, beautiful girls, but intensely bitter rebels. The old man was near eighty years old, and he said he could whip any dozen Yankees. I told him I would like to use his type and press, but he said if I touched a thing I did it at my peril, as he should consider the type contaminated by the touch of a Yankee. The girls felt the same way, but I talked nice to them, and they didn't kick much when I took a "stick" and began to set type. I worked till dinner time, when they asked me to take dinner with them, which I did.

During the conversation I convinced them that I was practically a non-combatant, and wouldn't hurt anybody for the world. I worked till about the middle of the afternoon, when I noticed that the girls, who had been up on the house, looked tickled about something, and presently I heard some firing at the edge of the town, some yelling, more firing, bugle calls among our soldiers, and finally there was an absence of blue coats, and I looked for my horse, and found the old man leading him away. I halted the old man, and he stopped and told me that the Confederates had come into town from the East and driven our cavalry out on the other side, and I would be a prisoner in about five minutes, and he laughed, and the girls clapped their hands, and I felt as though my time had come.

I had never killed an old man in my life, but I made up my mind to have my horse or kill him in his traces, so I drew my revolver and told him to let go the horse or he was a dead man. It was a question with me whether I could hold my hand still-enough to kill him, if he didn't let go the horse, and I hoped to heaven he would drop the bridle. He looked so much like my father at home that it seemed like killing a near relative, and when I looked at the two beautiful daughters on the gallery, looking at us, pale as death, I almost felt as though it would be better to lose the horse and be captured, then to put a bullet through the gray head of that beautiful old man.

How I wished that he was a young fellow, and had a gun, and had it pointed at me. Then I could kill him and feel as though it was self-defence. But the rebels were yelling and firing over the hill, and my regiment was going the other way on important business, and it was a question with me whether I should kill the old man, and see his life-blood ebb out there in front of his children, or be captured, and perhaps shot for burning buildings. I decided that it was my duty to murder him, and get my horse.

So I rested my revolver across my left forearm, and took deliberate aim at his left eye, a beautiful, large, expressive gray eye, so much like my father's at home that I almost imagined I was about to kill the father who loved me. I heard, a scream on the gallery, and the blonde girl fainted in the arms of her brunette sister.

The sister said to me, "Please don't kill my father."

He was not ten feet from me, and I said, "Drop the horse or you die."

The old man trembled, the girl said: "Pa, give the man his horse," the old man dropped the bridle and walked towards the house. I mounted the horse and rode off towards the direction my regiment had taken, thanking heaven that the girl had spoken just in time, and that I had not been compelled to put a bullet through that noble-looking gray head.

The face haunted me all the way, as I rode along to catch my regiment, and when I overtook it, and rode up to the colonel, and asked him what in thunder he wanted to go off and leave me to fight the whole southern Confederacy for, he said, "O, get out! There were no rebels there. That was the Indiana regiment that started out day before yesterday, to get on the other side of the town. The fellows were shooting some cattle for food. What makes you look-so pale?" I was thinking of whether a man ever prospered who killed old people.

CHAPTER 8

I Capture a Rebel Ram

After overtaking my regiment, and enjoying a feeling of safety which I did not feel in the presence of that violent old man who laid savage hands on my horse, and the girls, I began to reflect. Of course the old man was not armed, and I was, but how did I know but those Confederate girls had revolvers concealed about their persons, and might have killed me. To feel that I was once more safe with my regiment, where there was no danger as long as they did not get into a fight, was bliss indeed, and I rode along in silence, wondering when the cruel war would be over, and what all this riding around the country, burning buildings and tearing up railroad tracks amounted to, anyway.

I didn't enlist as a section hand, nor a railroad wrecker, and there was nothing in my enlistment papers that said anything about my being compelled to commit arson. The recruit-officer who, by his glided picture of the beauties of a soldier's life, induced me to enlist as a soldier, never mentioned anything that would lead me to believe that one of my duties would be to touch a match to another man's bales of cotton, or ditch a locomotive belonging to parties who never did me any harm, and who had a right to expect dividends from their railroad stock. If I had the money, that was represented in the stuff destroyed by our troops that day, I could run a daily newspaper for years, if it didn't have a subscriber or a patent medicine advertisement. And who was benefitted by such wanton destruction of property.

As we rode along I told the colonel I thought it was a confounded shame to do as we had done, and that such a use of power, because we had the power, was unworthy of American soldiers. He said it was a soldier's duty to obey orders and not talk back, and if he heard any more moralizing on my part he would send me back to my company,

72

where I would have to do duty like the rest. I told him I was one of the talking backest fellows he ever saw, and that one of my duties as a newspaper man was to criticise the conduct of the war. Then he said I might report to the captain of my company. It seemed hard to go into the ranks, after having had a soft job with the chaplain, and again as colonel's orderly, but I thought if I got my back up and showed the captain that I was no ordinary soldier, but one who was qualified for any position, that maybe he would be afraid to monkey too much with me.

I knew the captain would be a candidate for some office when the war was over, and if he knew I was on to him, and that I should very likely publish a paper that could warm him up quite lively, he would see to it that I wasn't compelled to do very hard work. So I rode back to my company and told the captain that the colonel and the chaplain had got through with me, and I had come back to stay, and would be glad to do any light work he might have for me. The captain heaved a sigh, as though he was not particularly tickled to have me back, and told me to fall in, in the rear of the company. I asked if I couldn't ride at the head of the company. He said no, there was more room at the rear. I tried to tell him that I was accustomed to riding at the head of the regiment, but he told me to shut up my mouth and get back there, and I got back, and fell in at the tail end of the company, with the cook and an officer's servant, and the orderly sergeant came back and wanted to know if the company had got to have me around again. Here was promotion with a vengeance.

From the proud pinnacle from which I had soared, as chaplain's clerk, and colonel's orderly, I had dropped with one fell swoop to the rear end of my company, and nobody wanted me, because I had kicked against stealing hens in one instance, and burning buildings and tearing up railroads in the other. We rode all day, and at night laid down in the woods and slept, after eating the last of our rations. I slept beside a log, and before going to sleep and after waking, I swore by the great horn spoons I would not steal anything more while I was in the army, nor do any damage to property. In the morning the soldiers had scarcely a mouthful to eat, and an order was read to each company that for three or four days it would be necessary to live off the country, foraging for what we had to eat.

I asked the captain what we would do for something to eat if we didn't find anything in the country to gobble up. He said we would starve. That was an encouraging prospect for a man who had taken a solemn oath not to steal any more. I told the captain I did not intend to steal any more, as I did not think it right. Then he said I better begin to eat the halter off my horse, because leather would be the only thing I would have to stay my stomach.

The first day I did not eat a mouthful, except half of a hard-tack that I had a quarrel with my horse to get. In throwing the saddle on my horse, one solitary hard-tack that was in the saddle-bag, fell out upon the ground, and the horse picked it up. I did not know the hard-tack was in the saddle, and when it fell upon the ground I was as astonished as I would have been had a clap of thunder come from the clear sky, and when the horse went for it, my stomach rebelled and I grabbed one side of the hard-tack while the horse held the other side in his teeth. Something had to give, and as the horse's teeth nor my hands would give, the hard-tack had to, and I saved half of it, and placed it in the inside pocket of my vest, as choice as though it were a thousand dollar bill.

I have listened to music, in my time, that has been pretty bad, and which has sent cold chills up my back, and caused me pain, but I never heard any bad music that seemed to grate on my nerves as did the noise my horse made in chewing the half of my last hard-tack, and the look of triumph the animal gave me was adding insult to injury. Several times during the day I took that piece of hard-tack from my pocket carefully, wiped it on my coat-sleeve, and took a small bite, and the horse would look around at me wickedly, as though he would like to divide it with me again.

People talk about guarding riches carefully, and of placing diamonds in a safe place, but no riches were ever guarded as securely as was that piece of hard-tack, and riches never took to themselves wings and new, regretted more than did my last hard-tack. Each bite made it smaller, and finally, the last bite was taken, with a sigh, and nothing remained for me to eat but the halter. Some of the boys went out foraging, and were moderately successful, while others did not get a thing to eat. The country was pine woods, with few settlers, and those that lived there were so poor that it seemed murder to take what they had. One of the men of our company came back with about two quarts of corn meal, that night, and I traded him a silver watch for about a pint of it. I mixed it up in some water, and after the most of the men had fallen asleep, I made two pancakes of the wet meal, and put them in the ashes of the camp-fire to bake, but fell asleep before it was done, and when I woke up and reached into the ashes for the first pancake, it was gone.

Some Union soldier, whom it were base flattery to call a thief, had watched me, and stole my riches as I slept, robbed me of all I held dear in life. With trembling hands I raked the ashes for my other pancake, hopelessly, because I thought that, too, was gone, but to my surprise I found it. The villain who had pursued me as I slept, had failed to discover the second pancake, and I was safe, and my life was saved. I have seen a play in a theatre in which a miser hides his gold, first in one place, then in another, looking to the right and to the left to see if anybody was watching him. I was the same kind of a miser about my pancake. If I hid it in the woods I might fail to find the place, in the morning, where I had hid it, and besides, some soldier that was peacefully snoring near me, apparently, might have one eye on me, and commit burglary.

If I put it in my pocket, and went to sleep, I might have my pocket picked, so I concluded to remain awake and hold it in my hands. There appeared to be nothing between me and death by starvation, except that cornmeal pancake, and I sat there for an hour, beside the dying embers of the campfire, trying to make up my mind who stole my other pancake, and what punishment should be meted out to him if I ever found him out. I would follow him to my dying day. I suspected the captain, the colonel, the chaplain, and six hundred soldiers, any one of whom was none too good to steal a man's last pancake if he was hungry.

To this day I have never found out who stole my pancake, but I have not given up the search, and if I live to be as old as Methuselah, and I find out the fellow that put himself outside my pancake that dark night in the pine woods, I will gallop all over that old soldier, if he is older than I am. That is the kind of avenger that is on the track of that pancake-eater. I sat there and nodded over my remaining pancake, clutched in my hands, and finally started to my feet in alarm. Suppose I should fall asleep, and be robbed? The thought was maddening. I have read of Indians who would eat enough at one sitting to last them several days, and the thought occurred to me that if I ate the pancake my enemies could not get it away from me, and perhaps it would digest gradually, a little each day, and brace me up until we got where there were rations plenty. So I sat there and deliberately eat every mouthful of it, and looked around at the sleeping companions with triumph, laid down and slept as peacefully on the ground as I ever slept in bed.

There may be truth in the story about Indians eating enough to last them a week, but it did not work in my case, for in the morning I was hungry as a she wolf. The pancake had gone to work and digested itself right at once, as though there was no end of food, and my stomach yearned for something. I walked down by the quartermaster's wagons, about daylight, and there was a four-mule team, each with a nose bag on, with corn in it. The mules were eating corn, unconscious of a robber being near.

At home, where I had lived on good fresh meat, bread, pie, everything that was good, nobody could have made me believe that I would steal corn from a government mule, but when I heard the mules eating that corn a demon possessed me, and I meditated robbery. I did not want to take all the corn I wanted from one mule, so I decided to take toll from all of them. I went up to the first one, and reached my hand down into the nose bag beside the mule's mouth and rescued a handful of corn, then went to another to do the same, but that mule kicked at the scheme. I went to two others, and they laid their ears back and began to kick at the trace chains, so I went back to my first love, the patient mule, and took every last kernel of corn in the bag, and as I went away with a pocket full of corn the mule looked at me with tears in its eyes, but I couldn't be moved by no mule tears, with hunger gnawing at my vitals, so I hurried away like a guilty thing.

While I was parching the corn stolen from the mule, in a half of a tin canteen, over the fire, the chaplain came along and wanted to sample it. He was pretty hungry, but I wasn't running a free boarding house for chaplains any more, and I told him he must go forage for himself. He said he would give his birthright for a pocket full of corn. I told him I didn't want any birthright, unless a birthright would stay a man's stomach, but if he would promise to always love, honour and obey me, I would tell him where he could get some corn. He swore by the great bald headed Elijah that if I would steer him onto some corn he would remember me the longest day he lived, and pray for me. I never was very much, mashed on the chaplain's influence at the throne, but I didn't want to see him starve, while government mules were living on the fat of the land, so I told him to go down to the quartermaster's corral and rob the mules as I had done.

He bit like a bass, and started for the mules. Honestly, I had no designs on the chaplain, but he traded me a kicking mule once, and got a good horse of me, because I thought he wanted to do me a favour. As he was familiar with mules, I supposed he would know how to steal a little corn. Pretty soon I heard a great commotion down there, and presently the chaplain came out with a mule chasing him, its ears laid back, and blood in its eyes. The chaplain was white as a sheet, and yelling for help. Before I could knock the mule down with a neck-yoke, the animal had grabbed the chaplain by the coat tail, with its mouth, taking some of his pants, also, and perhaps a little skin, raised him up into the air, about seven feet, let go of him, and tried to turn around and kick the good man on the fly as he came down.

We drove the mule away, rescued the chaplain, tied his pants together with a piece of string, cut off the tail of his coat which the mule had not torn off, so it was the same length as the other one, and made him look quite presentable, though he said he *knew* he could never ride a horse again. It seems that instead of reaching into the nose bag, and taking a little corn, he had unbuckled the nose bag and taken it off. I told him he was a hog, and ought to have known better than take the nose bag off, thus leaving the mule's mouth unmuzzled, while the animal was irritated. He accused me of knowing that the mule was vicious, and deliberately sending him there to be killed, so rather than have any hard feelings I gave him a handful of my parched corn.

A few Sundays afterwards I heard him preach a sermon on the sin of covetousness, and I thought how beautifully he could have illustrated his sermon if he had turned around and showed his soldier audience where the mule eat his coat tail. Soon we saddled up and marched another day without food. Reader, were you ever so hungry that you could see, as plain as though it was before you, a dinner-table set with a full meal, roast beef, mashed potatoes, pie, all steaming hot, ready to sit down to? If you have not been very hungry in your life, you cannot believe that one can be in a condition to see things. The man with delirium tremens can see snakes, while the hungry man, in his delirium, can see things he would like to eat.

Many times during that day's ride through the deserted pine-woods, with my eyes wide open, I could see no trees, no ground, no horses and men around me, but there seemed a film over the eyes, and through it I could see all of the good things I ever had eaten. One moment there would be a steaming roast turkey, on a platter, ready to be carved. Again I could see a kettle over a cook-stove, with a pigeon pot-pie cooking, the dumpings, light as a feather, bobbing up and down with the steam, and I could actually smell the odour of the cooking pot-pie.

It seems strange, and unbelievable to those who have never experienced extreme hunger or thirst, that the imagination can picture eatables and streams of running water, so plain that one will almost reach for the eatables, or rush for the imaginary stream, to plunge in and quench thirst, but I have experienced both of those sensations for thirteen dollars a month, and nary a pension yet. It is such experiences that bring gray hairs to the temples of young soldiers, and cause eyes to become hollow and sunken in the head.

Today, your Uncle Samuel has not got silver dollars enough in his treasury to hire me to suffer one day of such hunger as to make me see things that were not there, but twenty-two years ago it was easy to have fun over it, and to laugh it off the next day. When we stopped that day, at noon, to rest, the company commissary sergeant came up to the company, with two men carrying the hind quarter of an animal that had been slaughtered, and he began to cut it up and issue it out to the men. It was peculiar looking meat, but it was meat, and every fellow took his ration, and it was not long before the smell of broiled fresh meat could be "heard" all around. When I took my meat I asked the sergeant what it was, and where he got it. I shall always remember his answer. It was this:

"Young man, when you are starving, and the means of sustaining life are given you, take your rations and go away, and don't ask any fool questions. If you don't want it, leave it."

Leave it? Egad, I would have eaten it if it had been a Newfoundland dog, and I took it, and cooked it, and ate it. I do not know, and never did, what it was, but when the quartermaster's mule teams pulled out after dinner, there were two "spike teams;"—that is, two wheel mules and a single leader, instead of four-mule teams. After I saw the teams move out, each mule looking mournful, as though each one thought his time might come next, I didn't want to ask any questions about that meat, though I know there wasn't a beef critter within fifty miles of us. I have had my children ask me, many times, if I ever eat any mule in the army, and I have always said that I did not know. And I don't. But I am a great hand to mistrust.

It was on this hungry day, when filled with meat such as I had never met before that I did a thing I shall always regret. The captain came down to the rear of the company and said, so we could all hear it. "I want two men to volunteer for a perilous mission. I want two as brave men as ever lived. Who will volunteer? Don't all speak at once. Take plenty of time, for your lives may pay the penalty!"

I had been feeling for some days as though there was not the utmost confidence in my bravery, among the men, and I had been studying as to whether I would desert, and become a wanderer on the face of the earth, or do some desperate deed that would make me solid with the boys, and when the captain called for volunteers, I swallowed a large lump in my throat, and said, "Captain, *here is your mule*. I will go!" Whether it was that confounded meat I had eaten that had put a seeming bravery into me, or desperation at the hunger of the past few days, I do not know, but I volunteered for a perilous mission. A little Irishman named McCarty spoke up, and said, "Captain, I will go anywhere that red headed recruit will go."

So it was settled that McCarty and myself should go, and with some misgivings on my part we rode up to the front and reported. I thought what a fool I was to volunteer, when I was liable to be killed, but I was in for it, and there was no use squealing now. We came to a cross road, and the captain whispered to us that we should camp there, and that he had been told by a reliable contraband that up the cross road about two miles was a house at which there was a sheep, and he wanted us to go and take it. He said there might be rebels anywhere, and we were liable to be ambushed and killed, but we must never come back alive without sheep meat.

Well, we started off. McCarty said I better ride a little in advance so if we were ambushed, I would be killed first, and he would rush back and inform the captain. I tried to argue with McCarty that I being a recruit, and he a veteran, it would look better for him to lead, but he said I volunteered first, and he would waive his rights of precedence, and ride behind me. So we rode along, and I reflected on my changed condition. A few short weeks ago I was a respected editor of a country newspaper in Wisconsin, looked up to, to a certain extent, by my neighbours, and now I had become a sheep thief.

At home the occupation of stealing sheep was considered pretty low down, and no man who followed the business was countenanced by the best society. A sheep thief, or one who was suspected of having a fondness for mutton not belonging to him, was talked about. And for thirteen dollars a month, and an insignificant bounty, I had become a sheep thief. If I ever run another newspaper, after the war, how did I know but a vile contemporary across the street would charge me with being a sheep thief, and prove it by McCarty.

Maybe this was a conspiracy on the part of the captain, whom I suspected of a desire to run for office when we got home, to get me in his power, so that if I went for him in my paper, he could charge me with stealing sheep. It worked me up considerable, but we were out of meat, and if there was a sheep in the vicinity, and I got it, there was one thing sure, they couldn't get any more mule down me. So we rode up to the plantation, which was apparently deserted. There was a lamb about two-thirds grown, in the front yard, and McCarty and myself dismounted and proceeded to surround the young sheep. As we walked up to it, the lamb came up to me bleating, licked my hand, and then I noticed there was a little sleigh-bell tied to its neck with a blue ribbon.

The lamb looked up at us with almost human eyes, and I was going to suggest that we let it alone, when McCarty grabbed it by the hind legs and was going to strap it to his saddle, when it set up a bleating, and a little boy come rushing out of the house, a bright little fellow about three years old, who could hardly talk plain. I wanted to hug him, he looked so much like a little black-eyed baby at home, that was too awfully small to say "goodbye, papa" when I left. The little fellow, with the dignity of an emperor, said, "Here, sir, you must not hurt my little pet lamb. Put him down, sir, or I will call the servants and have you put off the premises."

McCarty laughed, and said the lamb would be fine 'atin for the boy's, and was pulling the little thing up, when the tears came into the boy's eyes, and that settled it. I said, "Mac, for heaven's sake, drop that lamb. I wouldn't break that little boy's heart for all the sheep-meat on earth. I will eat mule, or dog, but I draw the line at children's household pets. Let the lamb go."

"Begorra, yer right," said McCarty, as he let the lamb down. "Luk at how the shep runs to the little bye. Ah, me little mon, yer pet shall not be taken away from yez," and a big tear ran down McCarty's face. The boy said there was a great big sheep in the back yard we could have, if we were hungry, and we went around the house to see. There was an old black ram that looked as though he could whip a regiment of soldiers, but we decided that he was our meat. McCarty suggested that I throw a *lariat* rope around his horns, and lead him, whiles, he would go behind and drive the animal. That looked feasible, and taking a horse-hair picket rope off my saddle, with a slip noose in the end, I tossed it over the horns of the ram, tied the rope to the saddle, and started.

The ram went along all right till we got out to the road, when he held back a little. Mac jabbed the ram in the rear with his sabre, and he came along all right, only a little too sudden. That was one of the mistakes of the war, Mac's pricking that ram, and it has been the source of much study on my part, for twenty-two years, as to whether the Irishman did it on purpose, knowing the ram would charge on my horse, and butt my steed in the hind legs. If that was the plan of the Irishman, it worked well, for the first thing I knew my horse jumped about eighteen feet, and started down the road towards camp, on a run, dragging the ram, which was bellowing for all that was out.

I tried to hold the horse in a little, but every time he slackened up the ram would gather himself and run his head full tilt against the horse, and away he would go again. Sometimes the ram was flying through the air, at the end of the rope, then it would be dragged in the sand, and again it would strike on its feet, and all the time the ram was blatting, and the confounded Irishman was yelling and laughing.

We went into the camp that way, and the whole regiment, hearing the noise, turned out to see us come in. As my horse stopped, and the ram was caught by a coloured man, who tied its legs, I realized the ridiculousness of the scene, and would have gone off somewhere alone and hated myself, or killed the Irishman, but just then I saw the captain, and I said, "Captain, I have to report that the perilous expedition was a success. There's your sheep," and I rode away, resolved that that was the last time I should ever volunteer for perilous duty. The Irishman was telling a crowd of boys the particulars, and they were having a great laugh, when I said:

"McCarty, you are a villain. I believe you set that ram on to me on purpose. Henceforth we are strangers."

"Be gob," said the Irishman, as he held his sides with laughter, "yez towld me to drive the shape, and didn't I obey?"

I AM WOUNDED BY A LOCOMOTIVE AND A PIECE OF COAL

CHAPTER 9

I Am Willing to Resign

The next day we arrived at a post where rations were plenty, and where it was announced we should remain for a week or two, so we drew tents and made ourselves as comfortable as possible. It did seem good to again be where we did not have to depend on our own resources, of stealing, for what we wanted to eat. To be able to draw from the commissary regular rations of meat, tea, coffee, sugar, baker's bread, and beans, was joy indeed, after what we had gone through, and we almost made hogs of ourselves. There was one thing—those few days of starvation taught us a lesson, and that was, when ordered on a trip with two days' rations, to take at least enough for six days, especially of coffee and salt pork or bacon. With coffee and a piece of old smoked bacon, a man can exist a long time.

I remember after that trip, wherever I went, there was a chunk of bacon in one of my saddle-bags that nobody knew anything about, and many a time, on long marches, when hunger would have been experienced almost as severe as the time written about last week, I would take out my chunk of bacon, cut off a piece and spread it on a hard-tack, and eat a meal that was more strengthening than any meal Delmonico ever spread. It was at this post that the boys in the regiment played a trick that caused much fun throughout all the army. There were a few men in each company who had the chills and fever, or ague, and the surgeon gave them each morning, a dose of whisky and quinine.

It was interesting to see a dozen soldiers go to surgeon's call, take their "bitters," and return to their quarters. The boys would go to the surgeon's tent sort of languid, and drag along, and after swallowing a good swig of whisky and quinine they would walk back to their quarters swinging their arms like Pat Rooney on the stage, and act as though they could whip their weight in wild cats. I got acquainted with the hospital steward, and he said if the boys were not careful they would all be down with the ague, and that an ounce of prevention was worth more than a pound of cure. I thought I would take advantage of his advice, so I fell in with the sick fellows the next morning, and when the doctor asked, "What's the matter?" I said "chills," and he said, "Take a swallow out of the red bottle."

I took a swallow, and it *was* bitter, but it had whisky in it, more than quinine, and the idea of beating the government out of a drink of whisky was pleasure enough to overcome the bitter taste. I took a big swallow, and before I got back to my quarters I had had a fight with a mule-driver, and when the quartermaster interfered I had insulted him by telling him I knew him when he carried a hod, before the war, and I shouted, "Mort, more mort!" until he was going to lather me with a mule whip, but he couldn't catch me. As I run by the surgeon's tent, somebody remarked that I had experienced a remarkably sudden cure for chills.

The whisky was not real good, but as I had heard the hospital steward say they had just put in a requisition for two barrels of it, to be prepared for an epidemic of chills, I thought the boys ought to know it, so that day I went around to the different companies and told the boys how to play it for a drink. There are very few soldiers, in the best regiment, that will not take a drink of whisky when far away from home, discouraged, and worn out by marching, and our fellows looked favourably upon the proposition to all turn out to surgeon's call the next morning.

I shall never forget the look on the face of the good old surgeon, as the boys formed in line in front of his tent the next morning. The last time I saw him, he was in his coffin, about five years ago, at the soldier's home, and a few of the survivors of the regiment that lived here had gone out to the home to take a last look at him, and act as mourners at the funeral. He looked much older than when he used to ask us fellows the conundrum, "What's the matter?" but there was that same look on his white, cold face that there was the morning that nearly the whole regiment reported for "bitters."

There must have been four hundred men in line, and it happened that I was the first to be called. When he asked me about my condition, and I told him of the chills, he studied a minute, then looked at me, and said, You are bilious, David, give him a dose of castor oil. I know I turned pale, for it was a great come down from quinine and whisky to castor oil, for a healthy man, and I kicked. I told him I had the shakes awfully, and all I wanted was a quinine powder. I knew they had put all their quinine into a barrel of whisky, so I was safe in asking for dry quinine. The good old gentleman finally relented on the castor oil, and told David to give me a swallow of the quinine bitters, but there was a twinkle in his eye, as he noticed what a big swallow I took, and then he said, "You will be well tomorrow; you needn't come again." I dropped out of the ranks, with my skin full of quinine and whisky, and watched the other fellows.

There were men in the line who had never been sick a day since they enlisted, big fellows that would fight all day, and stand picket all night, and who never knew what it was to have an ache. And it was amusing to see them appear to shake, and to act as though they had chills. Some of them could not keep from laughing, and it was evident that the doctor had his doubts about there being so many cases of chills, but he dosed out the quinine and whisky as long as there was a man who shook. As each man took his dose, he would show two expressions on his face. One was an expression of hilarity at putting himself outside of a good swig of whisky, and the other was an expression of contempt for the bitter quinine, and an evident wish that the drug might be left out.

When all had been served, they lingered around the surgeon's quarters, talking with each other and laughing, others formed on for a stag quadrille, and danced, while a nigger fiddled. Some seemed to feel as though they wanted someone to knock a chip off their shoulders, old grudges were talked over, and several fights were prevented by the interference of friends who were jolly and happy, and who did not believe in fighting for fun, when there was so much fighting to be done in the way of business. The old doctor walked up and down in front of his tent in a deep study. He was evidently thinking over the epidemic of ague that had broken out in a healthy regiment, and speculating as to its cause.

Suddenly an idea seemed to strike him, and he walked up to a crowd of his patients, who were watching a couple of athletes, who had just taken their quinine, and who had put on boxing gloves and were pasting each other in the nose. "One moment," said the old doctor. The boys stopped boxing, and every last "sick" man listened respectfully to what the old doctor said; "Boys," said he, "you have got it on me this time. I don't believe a confounded one of you have got ague at all. You 'shook me' for the whisky. After this, quinine will be dealt out raw, without any whisky, and now you can shake all you please." Some one proposed three cheers for the boys that had made Uncle Sam stand treat, and the cheers were given, and the boys separated to talk over the event. The next morning only the usual number of sick were in attendance at surgeon's call. The healthy fellows didn't want to take quinine raw.

About this time an incident occurred that was fraught with great importance to the country and to me, though the historians of the war have been silent about it in their histories, whether through jealousy or something else I do not know, and modesty has prevented me from making any inquiries as to the cause. The incident alluded to was my appointment as corporal of my company. I say the incident was "fraught" with importance. I do not know the meaning of the word fraught, but it is frequently used in history in that connection, and I throw it in, believing that it is a pretty good word.

The appointment came to me like a stroke of paralysis. I was not conscious that my career as a soldier had been such as to merit promotion, I could not recall my particularly brilliant military achievement that would warrant my government selecting me from the ranks and conferring honours upon me, unless it was my lassoing that ram and dragging him into camp, when we were out of meat. But it was not my place to inquire into the cause that had led to my sudden promotion over the rank and file. I thought if I made too many inquiries it would be discovered that I was not such an all-fired great soldier after all. If the government had somehow got the impression that I was well calculated to lead hosts to victory, and it was an erroneous impression, it was the governments' place to find it out without any help on my part. I would accept the position with a certain dignity, as though I knew that it was inevitable that I must sooner or later come to the front.

So when the captain informed me that he should appoint me corporal, I told him that I thanked him, and through him, the Nation, and would try and perform the duties of the exacting and important position to the best of my ability, and hoped that I might not do anything that would bring discredit upon our distracted country. He said that would be all right, that he had no doubt the country would pull through.

That evening at dress parade the appointment was read, and I felt elated. I thought it singular that the regiment did not break out into cheers, and make the welkin ring, though they may not have had any welkin to ring. However, I thought it was my duty to make a little speech, acknowledging the honour conferred upon me, as I had read that generals and colonels did when promoted. I took off my hat and said, "Fellow soldiers." That was the end of my speech, for the captain turned around and said to the orderly sergeant, "Stop that red-headed cusses mouth some way," and the orderly told me to dry up. Everybody was laughing, I supposed, at the captain. Anyway, I felt hurt, and when we got back to camp the boys of all the companies surrounded me to offer congratulations, and I was called on for a speech. Not being in the ranks, nobody could prevent me from speaking, so I got up on a barrel, and said:

Fellow Soldiers:—As I was about to remark, when interrupted by the captain, on dress parade, this office has come to me entirely unsought. It has not been my wish to wear the gilded trappings of office and command men, but rather to fight in the ranks, a private soldier. I enlisted as a private, and my ambition has been to remain in the ranks to the end of the war. But circumstances over which I have no control has taken me and placed me on the high pinnacle of Corporal, and I must bow to the decree of fate. Of course, in my new position there must necessarily be a certain gulf between us. I have noticed that there has been a gulf between me and the officers, and I have thought it wrong. I have thought that privates and officers should mingle together freely, and share each others' secrets, privations and rations. But since being promoted I can readily see that such things cannot be. The private has his position and the officer has his, and each must be separate. It is not my intention to make any radical changes in the conduct of military affairs at present, allowing things to go along about as they have, but as soon as I have a chance to look about me, certain changes will be made. All I ask is that you, my fellow soldiers, shall stand by me, follow where I shall lead and—

At this point in my address the head of the barrel on which I stood fell in with a dull thud, and I found myself up to the neck in cornedbeef brine. The boys set up a shout, some fellow kicked over the barrel, and they began to roll it around the camp with me in it.

This was a pretty position for a man just promoted to the proud position of Corporal. As they rolled me about and yelled like Indians, I could see that an official position in that regiment was to be no sine-

WE WENT INTO CAMP THAT WAY

cure. All official positions have more or less care and responsibility, but this one seemed to me to have too much. Finally they spilled me out of the barrel, and I was a sight to behold. My first idea was to order the whole two hundred fellows under arrest, and have them court-martialled for conduct unbecoming soldiers; but on second thought I concluded that would seem an arbitrary use of power, so I concluded to laugh it off.

One fellow said they begged pardon for any seeming disrespect to an official; but it had always been customary in the regiment to initiate a corporal who was new and too fresh with salt brine. I said that was all right, and I invited them all up to the chaplain's tent to join me in a glass of wine. The chaplain was away, and I knew he had received a keg of wine from the sanitary commission that day, so we went up to his tent and drank it, and everything passed off pleasantly until the chaplain happened in. The boys dispersed as soon as he came, and left me to fight it out with the good man.

He was the maddest truly good man I have ever seen. I tried to explain about my promotion, and that it was customary to set em up for the boys, and that there was no saloon near, and that he had always told me to help myself to anything I wanted; but he wouldn't be calm at all. I tried to quote from Paul's epistle about taking a little wine for the stomachache; but he just raved around and called me names, until I had to tell him that if he kept on I would, in my official capacity as corporal, place him under arrest. That seemed to calm him a little, for he laughed, and finally he said I smelled of stale corned-beef, and he kicked me out of his tent, and I retired to my quarters to study over the mutability of human affairs, and the unpleasant features of holding official position.

That night I dreamed that General Grant and myself were running the army in splendid shape, and that we were in-receipt of constant congratulations from a grateful country, for victories. He and I seemed to be great chums. I dreamed of engagements with the enemy, in which I led men against fearful odds, and always came out victorious. I woke up before daylight and was wondering what dangerous duty I would be detailed to lead men upon, when the orderly poked his head in my tent and told me I was detailed to take ten picked men, at daylight, for hard service, and to report at once.

I felt that my time had come to achieve renown, and I dressed myself with unusual care, putting on the blouse with two rows of buttons, which I had brought from home. I borrowed a pair of Corporal's chevrons and sewed them to the sleeves of my blouse, and was ready to die, if need be. I placed a Testament I had brought from home, inside my blouse, in a breast pocket, as I had read of many cases where a Testament had been struck with a bullet and saved a soldier's life. I placed all my keepsakes in a package, and told my tent mate that I was going out with ten picked men, and it was possible I might never show up again, and if I fell he was to send the articles to my family. I wondered that I did not feel afraid to die.

I was no professor of religion, though I had always tried to do the square thing all around, but with no consolation of religion at all, I felt a sweet peace that was indescribable. If it was my fate to fall in defence of my country, at the head of ten picked men, so be it. Somebody must die, and why not me. I was no better than thousands of others, and while life was sweet to me, and I had anticipated much pleasure in life, after the war, in shooting ducks and holding office, I was willing to give up all hope of pleasure in the future, and die like a thoroughbred. I was glad that I had been promoted, and wondered if they would put "Corporal" on my tombstone.

I wondered, if I fell that day at the head of my men, if the papers at the North, and particularly in Wisconsin, would say "The deceased had just been promoted, for gallant conduct, to the position of Corporal, and it will be hard to fill his place." With these thoughts I sadly reported to the orderly. The ten picked men were in line. They were four of them Irishmen, two Yankees, two Germans, a Welshman and a Scotchman. The orderly gave me a paper, sealed in an envelope. I turned to my men, and said, "Boys, whatever happens today, I don't want to see any man show the white feather. The world will read the accounts of this day's work with feelings of awe, and the country will care for those we leave behind."

We started off, and it occurred to me to read my instructions. I opened the envelope with the air of a general who was accustomed to receive important messages. I read it, and almost fainted, It read "Report to the quartermaster, at the steamboat landing, to unload quartermaster's stores from steamer *Gazelle*." Ye gods! And this was the hard service that I was to lead ten picked men into. They had picked out ten stevedores, to carry sacks of corn, and hard-tack boxes, and barrels of pork, and that was the action I was to engage in as my first duty as corporal.

I almost cried. We rode down to the landing, where a dozen teams were waiting to be loaded. It was all I could do to break the news to my picked men that they were expected to lug sacks of corn instead of fight, and when I did they kicked at once. One of the Irishmen said he would be teetotally d——d if he enlisted to carry corn for mules, and he would lay in the guard-house till the war was over before he would lift a sack. There was a strike on my hands to start on. I was sorry that I had permitted myself to be promoted to Corporal. Trouble from the outset. One of the Yankees suggested that we hold an indignation meeting, so we rode up in front of a cotton warehouse and dismounted. The Scotchman was appointed chairman, and for half an hour the ten picked men discussed the indignity that was attempted to be heaped upon them, by compelling them to do the work of niggers.

They argued that a cavalry soldier's duty was exclusively to ride on horseback, and that there was no power on earth to compel them to carry sacks of corn. One of the Dutchmen said he could never look a soldier in the face again after doing such menial duty, and he would not submit to it. The Scotch chairman said if he had read the articles of war right there was no clause that said that the cavalry man should leave his horse and carry corn. I was called upon for my opinion, and said that I was a little green as to the duties of a soldier, but supposed we had to do anything we were ordered to do, but it seemed a little tough. I told them I didn't want any mutiny, and it would be a plain case of mutiny if they refused to work.

One of the Irishmen asked if I would help carry sacks of corn, and I told him that as commander of the expedition it would be plainly improper for me to descend to a common day labourer. I held it to be the duty of a corporal to stand around and see the men work. They all said that was too thin, and I would have to peel on my coat and work if they did. I told them I couldn't lift a sack of corn to save me, but they said if that was the case I ought not to have come. The quartermaster was looking around for the detail that was to unload the boat, and he asked me if I had charge of the men detailed to unload. I told him that I *did* have charge of them when we left camp, but that they had charge of me now, and said they wouldn't lift a pound. He thought a minute, and said, "I don't like to see you boys carrying corn sacks, and rolling pork barrels. Why don't you chip in and hire some niggers."

The idea seemed inspired. There were plenty of niggers around that would work for a little money. One of the Irishmen moved that the Corporal hire ten niggers to unload the quartermasters stores, and the motion was carried unanimously. I would have voted against it, but the Scotchman, who was chairman, ruled that I had no right to vote. So I went and found ten niggers that agreed to work for fifty cents each, and they were set to work, the quartermaster promising not to tell in camp about my hiring the work done. One of my Dutchmen moved that, inasmuch as we had nothing to do all day, that we take in the town, and play billiards, and whoop it up until the boat was unloaded.

That seemed a reasonable proposition, and the motion carried, after an amendment had been added to the effect that the Corporal stay on the boat and watch the niggers, and see that they didn't shirk. So my first command, my ten picked men, rode off up town, and I set on a wagon and watched my hired men. It was four o clock in the afternoon before the stuff was all loaded, and after paying the niggers five dollars out of my own pocket, some of my bounty money, I went up to town to round up my picked men to take them to camp. I found the Scotchman pretty full of Scotch whisky. He had found a countryman who kept a tailor shop, who had a bag pipe, and they were having a high old time playing on the instrument, and singing Scotch songs. I got him on his horse, and we looked for the rest.

The two Germans were in a saloon playing pee-nuckel, and singing German songs, and their skins were pretty full of beer and cheese. They were got into the ranks, and we found the Irishmen playing forty-five in a saloon kept by a countryman of theirs, and they had evidently had a shindig, as one of them had a black eye and a scratch on his nose, and they were full of fighting whisky. The Yankees had swelled up on some kind of benzine and had hired a hack and taken two women out riding, and when we rounded them up each one had his feet out of the window of the hack, and they were enjoying themselves immensely. The Welshman was the only one that was sober, but the boys said there was not enough liquor in the South to get him drunk. When I got them all mounted they looked as though they had been to a banquet.

We started for camp, but I did not want to take them in until after dark, so we rode around the suburbs of the town until night drew her sable mantle over the scene. They insisted on singing until within half a mile of camp, and it would no doubt have been good music, only the Scotchman insisted on singing "The March of the Cameron Men," while the Irishmen sung "Lots of fun at Finnegan's Wake," and the German's sung "*Wacht am Rhine.*" The Yankees sung the "Star Spangled Banner," and the Welshman sung something in the Welsh language which was worse than all.

All the songs being sung together, of course I couldn't enjoy either of them as well as a corporal ought to enjoy the music of his command. Arriving near camp, the music was hushed, and we rode in, and up to the captain's tent, where I reported that the corn was unloaded, all right. He said that was all right. Everything would have passed off splendidly, only one of the Irishmen proposed "three cheers" for the dandy corporal of the regiment, and those inebriated, picked men, gave three cheers that raised the roof of the colonel's tent nearby, because I had hired niggers to do the work, and let the men have a holiday. I dismissed them as quick as I could, but the colonel sent for me, and I had to tell him the whole story. He said I would demoralize the whole regiment in a week more, and I better let up or he would have to discipline me. I offered to resign my commission as corporal, but he said I better hold on till we could have a fight, and maybe I would get killed.

CHAPTER 10

My Chance Arrives

As I could get no one to accept my resignation as corporal, which I tendered after my first service in that capacity, unloading a steamboat, I decided to post myself as to the duties of the position, so I borrowed a copy of *Hardee's Tactics*, and studied a good deal. Every place in the book that mentioned the word "corporal," had a particular and thrilling interest for me, and I soon got so it would have been easy for me to have done almost anything that a corporal would have to do. But I was not contented to study the duty of a corporal. I read about the "school of the company," and the "school of the regiment," and "battalion drills," and everything, until I could handle a regiment, or a brigade, for that matter, as well as any officer in the army, in my mind.

This led me to go farther, and I borrowed a copy of a large blue book the colonel had, the name of which I do not remember now, but it was all military, and told how to conduct a battle successfully. I studied that book until I got the thing down so fine that I could have fought the battle of Gettysburg successfully, and I longed for a chance to show what I knew about military science and strategy. It seemed wonderful to me that one small red-head could contain so much knowledge about military affairs, and I felt a pity for some officers I knew who never had studied at all, and did not know anything except what they had picked up.

I fought battles in my mind, day and night. Some nights I would lay awake till after midnight, planning campaigns, laying out battle-fields, and marching men against the enemy, who fought stubbornly, but I always came out victorious, and then I would go to sleep and dream that the President and secretary of war had got on to me, as it were, and had offered me high positions, and I would wake up in the morning the same red-headed corporal, and cook my breakfast.

Sometimes I thought it my duty to inform the government, in some round about way, what a bonanza the country had in me, if my talent could only be utilized by placing me where I would have a chance to distinguish myself, and bring victory to our arms. I reflected that Grant, and Sherman, and Sheridan, and all of the great generals, were once corporals, and by study they had risen.

There was not one of them that could dream out a battle, and a victory any better that I could. All I wanted was a chance. Just give me men enough, and turn me loose in the Southern Confederacy, with that head of mine, and the result would be all an anxious nation could desire.

My first chance came sooner than I expected. The next day a part of the regiment went out on a scout, to be gone a couple of days, and my company was along. I was unusually absorbed in thought, and wondered if I would be given a chance to do anything. It seemed reasonable that if any corporal was sent out with a squad of men, to fight, it would be an old corporal, while if there was any duty that was menial, the new corporals would get it. The second day out we stopped at noon to let our horses rest, when little scouting parties that had been sent out on different roads during the forenoon, began to come in.

Many of them had picked up straggling rebels, and brought them to camp, and they were carefully guarded, and the major, who was in command of our party, was asking them questions, and pumping them to find out all he could. I went over and looked at them, and they were quite a nice looking lot of fellows, some being officers, with plenty of gold lace on their gray suits. They were home from the Confederate army on a leave of absence, probably recruiting. After talking with a rebel officer for a time the major turned to the adjutant and said, "send me a corporal and ten men."

The adjutant started, on, and I followed him. I used to know the adjutant when he taught a district school, before the war, and I asked him as a special favour to let me be the corporal. He said the detail would be from my company, and if I could fix it with the orderly sergeant of my company it was all right. I rushed to my company and found the orderly, and got him to promise if there was a detail from the company that day, I could go. Before the words were out of his mouth the detail came, and in five minutes I reported to the major with ten men. The major simply told me that a certain rebel captain, from Lee's army, was reported to be at home, and his plantation was about four miles east, and he described it to me. He told me to ride

95

out there, surround the house, capture the captain, and bring him into camp.

No general ever received his orders in regard to fighting a battle, with a feeling of greater pride and responsibility than I did my orders to capture that rebel. We started out, and then for the first time I noticed that there was another corporal in the squad with, me, and at once it occurred to me that he might claim a part of the glory of capturing the rebel. I had heard of the jealousy existing between generals, and how the partisans of different generals filled the newspapers, after a battle, with accounts of the part taken by their favourites, and that the accounts got so mixed, up that the reader couldn't tell to whom the credit of success was due, and I decided to take prompt measure with this supernumerary corporal, who had evidently got in by mistake, so I told him he might go back to the regiment.

He said he guessed not. He had been detailed to go on the scout, and he was going, if he knew himself, and he thought he did. He said when it come right down to rank, he was an older corporal than I was, and could take command of the squad if he wanted to. I told him he was mistaken as to his position. That if the major had wanted him to take charge of the expedition, he would have given him the instructions, but as the major had given me the instructions, in a low tone of voice, nobody but myself knew where we were going or what we were going for, and that I was responsible, and the first intimation I had from him that he wanted to mutiny, or relieve me from my command, I would have him shot at once. I told him he could go along, but he must keep his mouth shut, and obey orders. He said he would obey, if he felt like it.

We moved on, and I would have given a month's pay if that corporal had not been there. In a short time we were in sight of the house, and at a cross road I told the corporal to take one man and stop there, until further orders, and if any rebel came along, to capture him. He was willing enough to stay there, because there was a patch, of musk melons just over the fence. I moved my remaining eight men to a high piece of ground near the house, and halted, to look over the field of battle. Pulling a spy glass from my pocket, which I had borrowed from the sutler, I surveyed, as near like a general as possible, the situation. On one side of the house was a ravine, which I decided must be held at all hazards, and after studying my copy of tactics a moment, I sent an Irishman over there to hold the key to the situation, and told him he might consider himself the Iron Brigade.

The lay of the ground reminded me much of pictures I had seen of the battle of Bull Run, and the road on which I had left the corporal and one man, was the road to Washington, on which we would retreat, if overcome by the enemy. To the right of the ravine, which was held by the Iron Brigade, I noticed a hen-house with a gate leading back to the nigger quarters, and I called a soldier and told him to make a detour behind a piece of woods, and at a signal from me, the waving of my right arm, to charge directly to the gate of the hen-house, and hold it against any force that might attempt to carry it, and to let no guilty man escape.

Fifteen years afterwards General Grant used those self-same words, *Let no guilty man escape,* and they became historic, but I will take my oath I was the first commander to use the words, when I sent that man to hold the gate of the hen-house. That man I denominated the First Division. Farther to the right was a field of sweet potatoes, in which was a coloured man digging the potatoes. I sent a Dutchman to hold that field, with their right resting on the left of the First Division, located at the gate of the hen-house, whose right was supposed to rest on the left of the Iron Brigade, the Irishman who commanded the ravine.

Then I turned my attention to the left of the battle-field, placed one man at the milk-house, with his left resting on the right of the Irishman, and a man at the smoke-house. This left three men, one of whom I appointed an *aide de camp,* one an orderly and the other I held as a reserve, at a cotton gin. When I had got my army into position, I sat under a tree and reflected a little, and concluded that the Iron Brigade was in rather too exposed a position, so I sent my *aide de camp* to order the Iron Brigade to move forward, under cover of the ravine, and take a position behind a mule-shed. The *aide* soon returned and reported that the Iron Brigade had taken off his shirt and kanoodled a negro woman to wash it for him, and would not be able to move until the shirt was dry.

This altered my plans a little, but I was equal to the emergency, and ordered my reserve to make a detour and take the mule-shed, and hold it until relieved by the Iron Brigade, which would be as soon as his shirt was dry, and then to report to me on the field. Then I took my aide and orderly, and galloped around the lines, to see that all was right. I found that the First Division, holding the gate of the hen-house, was well in hand, though he had killed five chickens, and had them strapped on his saddle, and was trying to cut off the head of another with his sabre. He said he thought I said to let no guilty hen escape. I found the Iron Brigade dismounted, his shirt hung on a line to dry, and the coloured woman had been pressed into the Federal service, and was frying a chicken for the Brigade. I told him to get his shirt on as soon as it was dry, and move by forced marches, to relieve the force holding the mule-shed, and the Iron Brigade said he would as soon as he had his dinner.

I found the Division composed of the Dutchman, stubbornly holding the sweet-potato field, and he was eating some boiled ham and corn-bread he had sent the nigger to the house after, and he had a bushel of sweet-potatoes in a sack strapped to his saddle. The force at the milk-house had a fine position, and gave me a pitcher of butter-milk, which I drank with great gusto. I do not know as there is anything in butter-milk that is stimulating, but after drinking it my head seemed clearer, and I could see the whole battle-field, and anticipate each movement I should cause to be made. I was so pleased with the butter-milk, on the eve of battle, that I ordered the Second Division to fill my canteen with it, which he did. Then I rode back to my headquarters, where I started from, having ridden clear around the beleaguered plantation. Presently the reserve returned to me and reported that he had been relieved by the Iron Brigade at the mule-shed, whose shirt had become dry, and who had given the reserve a leg of fried chicken, and a corn dodger. I took the leg of chicken away from my reserve, eat it with great relish, and prepared for the onslaught, the reserve picking some persimmons off a tree and eating them for lunch.

I was about to order the different divisions and brigades of my army to advance from their different positions, and close in on the enemy, when a coloured man came out of the house and moved toward me, signalling that he would fain converse with me. I struck a dignified attitude, by throwing my right leg over the pommel of the saddle, like a hired girl riding a plow-horse to town after a doctor, and waited. When he came up to me, he said, "Massa wants to know what all dis darn foolishness is about. He says if you all don't go away from here he will shoot de liver outen you all." I told the negro to be calm, and not cause me to resort to extreme measures, and I asked him if his master was at home.

He said he was, and he was a bad man wid a gun. He had killed plenty of men before the war, and since the war he had killed more Yankees than enough to build a rail-fence around the plantation. I did not exactly like the reports in regard to the enemy. I told the coloured man to take a flag of truce to his master, and tell him I would like an interview. The coloured man went to the house, and I sent for the Iron Brigade to report to me at once, in light marching order, and the Irishman came riding up without any shirt on. I caused the Brigade to put on his shirt, when I sent him to the house, to follow the nag of truce and feel of the enemy.

He went to the house, and was evidently invited in, for he disappeared. I waited half an hour for him, and as he did not show up, I called the Second Division, and sent the Dutchman to the house. The Second Division went in, and did not come out. I ordered the whole right wing of my army to deploy to my support, and the fellow at the hen-house gate came, and I sent him in after the Irishman and the Dutchman. He didn't come back, and I sent an orderly after the force stationed at the milk-house, and he came, and I sent him, with the same result. It was evident I was frittering away my command, with no good result, so I looked at my tactics, and decided to hold a council of war.

My *aide*, orderly, and reserve, three besides myself, composed the council of war. We three were in favour of ordering up the other corporal and man from the cross-roads, but I opposed it. I did not want the other corporal to have any finger in the pie. So I decided that the four of us would go in a body to the house and demand the surrender of the rebel captain. We rode down the lane where the other men had gone, and it was a question whether we ever came back alive. I thought they had a trap door in the house, which probably let the soldiers down suddenly into a dungeon. Certainly unless there was something of the kind my men would have come back. As we dismounted at the door; and walked up the steps, the door opened and a fine looking rebel officer appeared smiling.

"Come in, Captain, with your men, and join me in a glass of wine," said the rebel.

I had never been called "Captain" before, and it touched me in a tender spot. The rebel evidently thought I looked like a captain, and I was proud. He had probably watched my manoeuvres, and the way I handled my men, and thought I was no common soldier.

"Well, I don't care if I do," said I, and we walked into a splendid old room, and were bidden to be seated.

"Hello, Corp," said my Iron Brigade, as he took his legs down from a table, and poured out a glass of whisky from a bottle near him, "This is the divil's own place for an aisy life."

"*Gorporal,*" said my Dutch fellow soldier, as he poured out a glass of schnapps, "*Led me indroduce you mit dot repel. He is a tasy, und don'd you forgot aboud it. Mishder repel, dot ish der gorporal fun my gumpany.*"

The rebel smiled and said he was glad to see me, and hoped I was well, and would I take wine, or something stronger. I took a small glass of wine, but the rest of the fellows took strong drink, and my Iron Brigade was already full, and the Dutchman was getting full rapidly. Finally I told the rebel officer that I did not like to accept a man's hospitality when I had such an unpleasant duty to perform as to arrest him, but circumstances seemed to make it necessary. He said that was all right. In times of war we must do many things that were unpleasant.

We took another drink, and then I told him I was sorry to inconvenience him, but he would have to accompany me to camp. He said certainly, he had expected to be captured ever since he saw that the house was surrounded, and while at first he had made up his mind to take his rifle and kill us all from the gallery of the house, he had thought better of it, and would surrender without bloodshed. What was the use of killing any more men? The war was nearly over, and why not submit, and save carnage. I told him that was the way I felt about it.

Then he said if I would wait until he retired to an adjoining room and changed his linen, he would be ready. I said of course, certainly, and he went out of a door. I waited about half an hour, until it seemed to me the rebel had had time to change all the linen in the state of Alabama. The Iron Brigade had gone to sleep on a lounge, and the German troop was full as a goat, and some of the others were beginning to feel the hospitality.

"I beg your pardon for intruding," said I, as I opened the door and walked into the room the rebel had entered. "Great Scott, he is gone!"

My army, all except the Iron Brigade and the Dutchman, followed me, and the room was empty. A window was up, through which he had escaped. We searched the house, but there was no rebel captain. On going to the front door I found that the horse belonging to the iron brigade was gone, and that the saddle girths of all the other horses had been unbuckled, so we would be delayed in following him. The Irishman was awakened, and when he found his horse was gone, he sobered up and went to the pasture and borrowed a mule to ride.

It took us half an hour to fix our saddles, so we could ride, and then we sadly started for camp. How could I face the major, and report to him that I had met the rebel captain, talked with him, drank with him, enjoyed his hospitality, and then let him escape? I felt that my military career had come to an inglorious ending. "We rode slow, because the Iron Brigade was insecurely mounted on a slippery bare-backed mule. As we neared the corporal and one man, that I had left to guard the cross-roads, I noticed that there was a stranger with them, and on riding closer what was my surprise to find that it was the rebel captain, under arrest. So the confounded corporal, whom I had left there so he would be out of the way, and not get any of the glory of capturing the rebel, had captured him, and got *all* the glory. I was hurt, but putting on a bold military air, like a general who has been whipped, I said:

"Ah, corporal, I see my plan has worked successfully. I arranged it so this prisoner would run right into the trap."

"Yes," said the corporal, throwing away a melon rind that he had been chewing the meat off of, "I saw his nibs coming down the road, and I thought maybe he was the one you wanted, so I told him to halt or I would fill his lungs full of lead pills, and he said he guessed he would halt. He said it was a nice day, and he was only trying one of the Yankee cavalry horses, to see how he liked it." "Here, you murdherin' divil, get down aff that harse," said the Iron Brigade, who had got awake enough to see that the rebel was on his horse. "Take this mule, and lave a dacent gintleman's harse alone."

The rebel smiled, dismounted, gave the Irishman his horse, mounted the mule, and we started for camp. I was never so elated in my life as I was when I rode into camp with that rebel captain beside me on the mule. The object of the expedition had been accomplished, a little different, it is true, from what I had expected and planned, but who knew that it was not a part of my plan to have it turn out as it did? I reflected much, and wondered if it was right for me to report the capture of the Confederate and say nothing about the part played by the other corporal. That corporal was no military strategist, like me. It was just a streak of luck, his capturing the rebel.

He was leaning against the fence where I left him, eating melons, and the rebel came along, and the corporal quit chewing melon long enough to obey my orders and arrest the fellow. By all rules of military law I was entitled to the credit, and I would take it, though it made me ashamed to do so. However, generals did the same thing. If a major-general was in command, and ordered a brigadier-general to do a thing and it was a success, the major-general got the credit in the newspapers. So I rode into camp and turned my prisoner over to the major as modestly as possible, with a few words of praise of my gallant command. Hello, Jim, said the major to the rebel.

Hello, Maje, said the rebel.

"Better take off them togs now, and join your company, said the major.

"I guess so," said the rebel, and he took off his rebel uniform, and the major handed him a blue coat and pair of pants, and he put them on.

I was petrified. The fact was, the rebel was a sergeant in our regiment, who had been detailed as a scout, and had been making a trip into the rebel lines as a spy. I had made an ass of myself in the whole business, and he would tell all the boys about it. I went back to my company crushed.

Chapter 11

I am Attacked With Rheumatism

After the episode, related last week, in which I foolishly organized a regular battle, to capture a supposed rebel, who turned out to be a member of my own regiment, I expected to be the laughing stock of all the soldiers, and that my commission as corporal would be taken away from me, and that I would be reduced to the ranks, and when, the next morning, the colonel sent for me to come to his tent, it was a stand-off with me whether I would take to the woods and desert, in disgrace, and never show up again, or go to the colonel, face the music, and admit that I had made an ass of myself. Finally I decided to visit the colonel.

On the way to his tent I noticed that our force had been augmented greatly. The road was full of wagons, the fields near us were filled with infantry and artillery, and there were fifty wagons or more loaded with pontoons, great boats, or the frame-work of boats, which were to be covered with canvass, which was water-proof, and the boats were to be used for bridges across streams. The colonel had not told me anything about the expected arrival of more troops, and it worried me a good deal. May be there was a big battle coming off, and I might blunder into it unconscious of danger, and: get the liver blowed out of me by a cannon. I felt that the colonel had not treated me right in keeping me in ignorance of all this preparation.

I went to the colonel's tent and there was quite a crowd of officers, some with artillery uniforms, several colonels, and one general with a star on his shoulder straps, and a crooked sword with a silver scabbard, covered with gold trimmings. I felt quite small with those big officers, but I tried to look brave, and as though I was accustomed to attending councils of war. The colonel smiled at me as I came in which braced me up a good deal.

General, this is the sergeant I spoke to you about, said the colonel, as he turned from a map they had been looking at. I felt pale when the colonel addressed me as sergeant, and was going to call his attention to the mistake, when the general said:

Sergeant, the colonel tells me that you can turn your hand to almost anything. What line of business have you worked at previous to your enlistment?

"Well, I guess there is nothing that is usually done in a country village that I have not done. I have clerked in a grocery, tended bar, drove team on a threshing machine, worked in a slaughter house, drove omnibus, worked in a-saw-mill, learned the printing trade, rode saw-logs, worked in a pinery, been brakeman on a freight train, acted as assistant chambermaid in a livery stable, clerked in a hotel, worked on a farm, been an auctioneer, edited a newspaper, took up the collection in church, canvassed for books, been life-insurance agent, worked at bridge-building, took tintypes, sat on a jury, been constable, been deck-hand on a steamboat, chopped cord-wood, run a cider-mill, and drove a stallion in a four-minute race at a county fair."

"That will do," said the general. "You will be placed in charge of a pioneer corps, and you will go four miles south, on the road, where a bridge has been destroyed across a small bayou, build a new bridge strong enough to cross artillery, then move on two miles to a river you will find, and look out a good place to throw a pontoon bridge across. The first bridge you will build under an artillery fire from the rebels, and when it is done let a squad of cavalry cross, then the pontoon train, and a regiment of infantry. Then light out for the river ahead of the pontoon train, with the cavalry. The pioneer corps will be ready in fifteen minutes."

The colonel told me to hurry up, but I called him out of his tent and asked him if I was really a sergeant, or if it was a mirage. He said if I made a success of that bridge, and the command got across, and I was not killed I would be appointed sergeant. He said the general would try me as a bridge-builder, and if I was a success he would try me, no doubt, in other capacities, such as driving team on a threshing machine, and editing a newspaper.

When, I went on after my horse, being pretty proud. The idea of being picked out of so many non-commissioned officers, and placed in charge of a pioneer corps, and sent ahead of the army to rebuild a bridge that had been destroyed, with a prospect of being promoted or killed, was glory enough for one day, and I rode back to headquarters feeling that the success of the whole expedition rested on me. If I built a corduroy bridge that would pass that whole army safely over, artillery and all, would anybody enquire who built the bridge. Of course, if I built a bridge that would break down, and drown somebody, everybody would know who built it. The twenty men were mounted, and ready, and the general told me to go to the quartermaster and get all the tools I wanted, and I took twenty axes, ten shovels, two log chains, and was riding away, when the general said:

"When you get there, and look the ground over, make up your mind exactly at what hour and minute you can have the bridge completed, and send a courier back to inform me, and at that hour the head of the column will be there, and the bridge must be ready to cross on."

I said that would be all right, and we started out. In about forty minutes we had arrived, at the bayou, and I called a private soldier who used to do logging in the woods, and we looked the thing over. The timber necessary was right on the bank of the stream.

"Jim," I said to the private, "I have got to build a bridge across this stream strong enough to cross artillery. I shall report to the general that he can send, along his artillery at seventeen minutes after eight o clock this evening. Am I right?"

"Well," said Jim, as he looked at the standing timber, at the stream, and spit some black tobacco juice down on the red ground, "I should make it thirty-seven minutes after eight. You see, a shell may drop in here and kill a mule, or something, and delay us. Make it thirty-seven, and I will go you."

We finally compromised by splitting the difference, and I sent a courier back to the general, with my compliments, and with the information that at precisely eight o clock and twenty-seven minutes he could start across. Then we fell to work. Large, long trees were cut for stringers, and hewn square, posts were made to prop up the stringers, though the stringers would have held any weight. Then small trees were cut and flattened on two sides, for the road-bed, holes bored in them and pegs made to drive through them into the stringers. A lot of cavalry soldiers never worked as those men did. Though there was only twenty of them, it seemed as though the woods were full of men.

Trees were falling, and axes resounding, and men yelling at mules that were hauling logs, and the scene reminded me of logging in the Wisconsin pineries, only these were men in uniform doing the work.

About the middle of the afternoon we had the stringers across, when there was a half dozen shots heard down the stream, and bullets began "zipping" all around the bridge, and we knew the rebels were onto the scheme, and wanted it stopped. I got behind a tree when the bullets began to come, to think it over. My first impulse was to leave the bridge and go back and tell the general that I couldn't build no bridge unless everything was quiet. That I had never built bridges where people objected to it.

I asked the private what we had better do. He said his idea was to knock off work on the bridge for just fifteen minutes, cross the stream on the stringers, and go down there in the woods and scare the life out of those rebels, drive them away, and make them think the whole army was after them, then cross back and finish the bridge. That seemed feasible enough, so about a dozen of us squirreled across the stringers with our carbines, and the rest went down the stream on our side, and all of us fired a dozen rounds from our Spencer repeaters, right into the woods where the rebels seemed to be.

When we did so, the rebels must have thought there was a million of us, for they scattered too quick, and we had a quiet life for two hours. We had got the bridge nearly completed, when there was a hissing sound in the air, a streak of smoke, and a powder magazine seemed to explode right over us. I suppose I turned pale, for I had never heard anything like it. Says I, "Jim, excuse me, but what kind of a thing is that?"

Jim kept on at work, remarking, O, nothing only they are a shellin on us. And so that was a shell. I had read of shells and seen pictures of them in *Harper's Weekly*, but I never supposed I would hear one. Presently another came, and I wanted to pack up and go away. I looked at my pioneers, and they did not pay any more attention to the shells than they would, to the braying of mules. I asked Jim if there wasn't more or less danger attached to the building of bridges, in the South, and he, the old veteran, said:

"Corp, don't worry as long as they hain't got our range. Them 'ere shell are going half a mile beyond us, and we don't need to worry. Just let 'em think they are killing us off by the dozen, and they will keep on sending shells right over us. If we had a battery here to shell back, they would get our range, and make it pretty warm for us. But now it is all guess work with them, and we are as safe as we would be in Oshkosh. Let's keep right on with the bridge."

I never can explain what a comfort Jim's remarks were to me. After

A PRETTY POSITION FOR A MAN JUST PROMOTED TO THE PROUD POSITION OF CORPORAL

listening to him, I could work right along, driving pegs in the bridge, and pay no attention to the shells that were going over us. In fact, I lit my pipe and smoked, and began to figure how much it was going to cost the Confederacy to "celebrate" that way.

It was costing them at the rate of fourteen dollars a minute, and I actually found myself laughing at the good joke on the rebels. Pretty soon a courier rode up, from the general, asking if the shelling was delaying the bridge. I sent word back that it was not delaying us in the least; in fact, it was hurrying us a little, if anything, and he could send along his command twenty-seven minutes sooner than I had calculated, as the bridge would be ready to cross on at eight o'clock sharp. At a quarter to eight, just as the daylight was fading, and we had lighted pine torches to see to eat our supper, an orderly rode up and said the general and staff had been looking for me for an hour, and were down at the forks of the road.

I told the orderly to bring the general and staff right up to the headquarters, and we would entertain them to the best of our ability, and he rode off. Then we sat down under a tree and smoked and played seven up by the light of pine torches, and waited. I was never so proud of anything in my life, as I was of that bridge, and it did not seem to me as though a promotion to the position of sergeant was going to be sufficient recompense for that great feat of engineering. It was as smooth as though sawed plank had covered it, and logs were laid on each side to keep wagons from running off. I could see, in my mind, hundreds of wagons, and thousands of soldiers, crossing safely, and I would be a hero.

My breast swelled so my coat was too tight. Presently I heard someone swearing down the road, the clanking of sabres, and in a few moments the general rode into the glare of the torch-light. I had struck an attitude at the approach of the bridge, and thought that I would give a good deal if an artist could take a picture of my bridge, with me, the great engineer, standing upon it, and the head of the column just ready to cross. I was just getting ready to make a little speech to the general, presenting the bridge to him, as trustee of the nation, for the use of the army, when I got a sight of his face, as a torch flared up and lit the surroundings. It was pale, and if he was not a madman, I never saw one. He fairly frothed at the mouth, as he said, addressing a soldier who had fallen in the stream, during the afternoon, and who was putting on his shirt, which he had dried by a fire:

"Where is the corporal, the star idiot, who built that bridge?"

I couldn't have been more surprised if he had killed me. This was a nice way to inquire for a gentleman who had done as much for the country as I had, in so short a time. I felt hurt, but, summoning to my aid all the gall I possessed, I stepped forward, and, in as sarcastic a manner as I could assume, I said:

"I am the sergeant, sir, who has wrought this work, made a highway in twelve hours, across a torrent, and made is possible for your army to cross."

"Well, what do you suppose my army wants to cross this confounded ditch for? What business has the army got in that swamp over there? You have gone off the main road, where I wanted a bridge built, and built one on a private road to a plantation, where nobody wants to cross. This bridge is of no more use to me than a bridge across the Mississippi River at its source. You, sir, have just simply raised hell, that's what you have done."

Talk about being crushed! I was pulverized. I felt like jumping into the stream and drowning myself. For a moment I could not speak, because I hadn't anything to say. Then I thought that it would be pretty tough to go off and leave that bridge without the general's seeing what a good job it was, so I said:

"Well, general, I am sorry you did not give me more explicit instructions, but I wish you would get down and examine this bridge. It is a daisy, and if it is not in the right place we can move it anywhere you want it."

That seemed to give the general an idea, and he dismounted and examined it. He said it was as good a job as he ever saw, and if it was a mile down the road, across another bayou, where he wanted to cross, he would give a fortune. I told him if he would give me men enough and wagons enough, I would move it to where he wanted it, and have it ready by daylight the next morning. He agreed, and that was the hardest nights work I ever did. Every stick of timber in my pet bridge had to be taken off separately, and moved over a mile, but it was done, and at daylight the next morning I had the pleasure of calling the general and telling him that the bridge was ready. I thought he was a little mean when he woke up and rubbed his eyes, and said:

"Now, you are sure you have got it in the right place this time, for if that bridge has strayed away onto anybody's plantation this time, you die."

The army crossed all right, and I had the proud pleasure of standing by the bridge until the last man was across, when I rode up to my regiment and reported to the colonel, pretty tired.[1] He was superintending the laying of a pontoon bridge across a large river, a few miles from my bridge, and he said:

"George, the general was pretty hot last night, but he was to blame about the mistake in the location, and he says he is going to try and get you a commission as lieutenant."

I felt faint, but I said, "How can he recommend a star idiot for a commissioned office?"

"O, that is all right," said, the colonel, "some of the greatest idiots in the army have received commissions." As he spoke the rebels began to shell the place where the pontoon bridge was being built, and I went hunting for a place to borrow an umbrella to hold over me, to ward off the pieces of shell. Then a battery of our own opened on the rebels, so near me that every time a gun was discharged I could, feel the roof of my head raise up like the cover to a band box. It was the wildest time I ever saw.

Cavalry was swimming the river to charge the rebel battery, shells were exploding all around, and it seemed to me as though if I was to lay a pontoon bridge I would go off somewhere out of the way, where it would be quiet. Finally my regiment was ordered to swim the river, and we rode in. The first lunge my horse made he went un-

---

1. A few weeks ago I met a member of my old regiment, who is travelling through the South as agent for a beer bottling establishment in the North. He was with me when we built the corduroy bridge twenty-two years ago. As we were talking over old-times he asked me if I remembered that bridge we built one day in Alabama, in the wrong place, and moved it during the night. I told him I wished I had as many dollars as I remembered that bridge. "Well," said my comrade, "on my last trip through Alabama I crossed that bridge, and paid two bits for the privilege of crossing. A man has established a toll-gate at the bridge, and they say he has made a fortune. I asked him how much his bridge cost him, and he said it didn't cost him a cent, as the Yankees built it during the war. He said they cut the timber on his land, and when he got out of the Confederate army he was busted, and he claimed the bridge, and got a charter to keep a toll- gate." My comrade added that the bridge was as sound as it was when it was built. He said he asked the toll-gate keeper if he knew the bridge was first built a mile away, and he said he knew the timber was cut up there, and he wondered what the confounded Yankees went away off there to cut the timber for, when they could get it right on the bank. Then my comrade told the toll-gate keeper that he helped build the bridge, the rebel thanked him, and wanted to pay back the two bits. Someday I am going down to Alabama and cross on that bridge again, the bridge that almost caused me to commit suicide, and if that old rebel—for he must be an old rebel now—charges me two bits toll, I shall very likely pull off my coat and let him whip me, and then as likely as not there will be another war.

der water about a mile, and when we came up I was not on him, but catching hold of his tail I was dragged across the river nearly drowned, and landed on the bank like a dog that has been after a duck I shook myself, we mounted and without waiting to dry out our clothes we went into the fight, before I could realize it, or back out. Scared! I was so scared it is a wonder I did not die. That was more excitement than a county fair. Bullets whizzing, shells shrieking, smoke stifling, yelling that was deafening. It seemed as though I was crazy.

I must have been or I could never, as a raw recruit, with no experience, have ridden right toward those guns that were belching forth sulphur and pieces of blacksmith shop. I didn't dare look anywhere except right ahead. All thought of being hit by bullets or anything was completely out of my mind. Occasionally something would go over me that sounded as though a buzz saw had been fired from a saw mill explosion.

Presently the firing on the rebel side ceased, and it was seen they were in retreat. I was never so glad of anything in my life. We stopped, and I examined my clothes, and they were perfectly dry. The excitement and warmth of the body had acted like a drying-room in a laundry. Then I laid down under a fence and went to sleep, and dreamed I was in hades, building a corduroy bridge across the Styx, and that the devil reprimanded me for building it in the wrong place. When I awoke I was so stiff with rheumatism that I had to be helped up from under the fence, and they put me in an ambulance with a soldier who had his jaw shot off. He was not good company, because I had to do all the talking. And in that way we moved towards the enemy.

CHAPTER 12

We Meet Under Happier Stars

It was at this time that the hardest duty that it was my lot to perform during my service, fell to me, and the only wonder to me is that I am alive today to tell of it. If I ever get a pension it will be on account of night sweats, caused by the terrible and trying work that was assigned to me. One day the colonel sent for me, and I knew at once that there was something unusual in the wind. After seating myself in his tent he opened the subject by asking me if I wasn't something of a hand to be agreeable to the ladies. I told him, with many blushes, that if there was one thing on this earth that I thought was nicer than everything else, it was a lady, and that a good woman was the noblest work of God.

He said he was on to all of that, but it wasn't a good woman that he was after. That startled me a little. I had heard the officers had a habit of fooling around a good deal with certain females, and I told the colonel that any duty that I was assigned to I would perform to the best of my poor ability, but I could not go around with the girls as officers did, because I couldn't afford it, and it was against my principles, anyway. He showed me a picture of a beautiful woman, and asked me if I would know her if I saw her again. I told him I could pick her out of a thousand. He said she was a smuggler. She had a pass from a general, who seemed to be under her influence to a certain extent, for some reason, and went in and out of the lines freely.

The general didn't want to order her arrest, because she would squeal on him, but he wanted her arrested all the same, and the idea was to have some corporal in charge of a picket post take the responsibility of arresting her without orders, refuse to recognize her pass, take the quinine and other medicines, and money away from her, and then be arrested himself for exceeding his authority. He said they wanted a corporal who had every appearance of being a big-headed idiot, and yet who knew what he was about, who knew something about women, and who could do such a job up in shape, and never let the woman know that the general or anybody had anything to do with her arrest. The idea was to catch her in the act of smuggling quinine through the lines to the rebels, by the act of a fresh corporal who took the matter into his own hands, and who claimed that the pass she had from the general was a forgery.

When the general could, when the woman was brought before him, be indignant at the corporal for insulting a woman, and order him arrested, and he could also go back on the woman, and have her sent away, after which he would release the corporal, and perhaps promote him, and all would be well. It was as pretty a scheme as I ever listened to, and I consented to do the duty, though I wouldn't do it again for a million dollars. The colonel told me to take four men and go to a particular place on an unfrequented road, near a school house, and put out a picket. The female would be along during the afternoon, on horseback, and when she showed her pass, one of the men must take hold of her horse and hold him, while I kicked about the pass, made her dismount, and searched her for quinine. I turned ashy pale when the colonel said that, and I said to him:

"Colonel, for heaven's sake don't compel me to search a woman. I have a family at home, and they will hear of it. My political enemies will use it against me at home when I run for office, after the war. Let me bring her here to your tent, and you search her."

"No, that would spoil all," said the colonel. "We want her searched right there at the little school house, by a corporal without apparent authority, and every last quinine pill taken off of her. If she was brought here she would cry, and rave, and we should weaken, because we know her, and have been entertained at her house. You are supposed to be a heartless corporal, with no sentiment, no mercy, no nothing, just a delver after smuggled quinine. Besides, I too, have a family, and I don't want to search no females. By the way, one of the general's staff saw her last night, and drew the cartridges from her revolver, and put in some blank cartridges. If the worst comes, she will draw her revolver on you, and perhaps fire at you, but there are no balls in her revolver, so you needn't be afraid."

"But suppose she has two revolvers," I asked, "and one is loaded with bullets?"

"I don't think she has," said the colonel. "But we have to take some chances, you know. Now go right along. Treat her like a lady, disbelieve everything she says and insist on searching her. The general says she wears an enormous bustle, and probably that is full of quinine. Use your judgement, but get it all. Pretend to be an ignorant sort of a corporal who feels that the success of the war depends on him, act as though you outranked the general, and tell her you would not let her pass with that quinine if the general himself was present. Just display plenty gall and when you have go the quinine, bring the girl here, and I will abuse you, and you take it like a little man, and all will be well. If she bites and scratches, some of you will have to hold her, but the best way will be to argue with her, and persuade her by honied words, to come down with the quinine. Go!"

"One word, colonel, before I go," I said. "About how many men should you think it would take to hold this woman? You suggested three, but if one holds her horse, it seems to me, from my knowledge of female kicking, biting and scratching, that I would need one man for each arm and foot, one to hold her head and choke her, if necessary, and one with a roving commission to work around where he would be apt to make himself useful. What do you say if I take five men!"

"All right, take six," said the colonel. "One may be disabled, or have his jaw kicked off, or something. But don't detail anybody to search her. Do that yourself, and do it like a gentleman. And above all things, do not let her kanoodle you with soft words and looks of love, because she is full of 'em. If she can't scare you, with her indignation at the outrage of arresting and searching her, she will try to capture you and make you love her. You must be as firm as adamant. Now hurry up."

I picked out six men, four of whom were young Americans, rather handsome, and very polite, regular mashers.

Then I had an Irishman named Duffy, and a German named Holz-meyer, who was a butcher. We went out on the road, to the school house, and I put the Irishman on picket, and instructed the German about taking the horse by the bridle at the proper time. Then the rest of us got behind the school house and waited. For two hours we wait-ed, and I had a chance to think over the situation. Here I was, putting down the rebellion, laying for a woman, who was loaded. At home, I was a polite man, and full of fun, a person any lady might be proud to meet and talk with, but here I was expected to do something, for thirteen dollars a month, to put down the rebellion, which there was not money enough in the whole state of Wisconsin to hire me to do.

Was it such a crime to carry a little quinine to a sick friend? Suppose a rebel was sick with ague, and I had quinine, would I see him shake himself out of his boots and not give him medicine? No, I would divide my last quinine powder with him. So would any soldier. If it was not treason to give one rebel a quinine powder, when he was sick, why should it be treason to take along enough for a whole lot of sick rebels? Did our government want to put down the rebellion by keeping medicines away from a sick enemy? Were we to gloat over the number of rebels who died of disease, that we could save by sending them medicines?

It seemed to me, if I was in command of the army, instead of arresting women for carrying medicine to their sick brothers, I would load up a wagon with medicine and send it to them, and say, "Here, you fellows, fire this quinine down your necks, and get well, and then if you want to fight any more, come out on the field and we will give you the best turn in the wheel-house." It seemed to me that would be the way to win the enemy over, and that they would be thankful, take the medicine, get well, and then say, "Boys, these Yankees are pretty good fellows after all. Let's quit fighting, and call it quits." But I was not running the war, and had got to obey orders, if I broke heartstrings and corset strings.

I would have given anything to have got out of the job. The idea of arresting a woman and searching her, and seeing her cry, and have her think me a hard-hearted wretch, was revolting, and I found myself wishing she would take some other road. May be she looked like somebody that I knew at home, and maybe she had a big brother in the Confederate army who would look me up after the war and everlastingly maul the life out of me for insulting his sister. I made up my mind if anything of that kind happened I would tell on the general and the colonel, and get them whipped, too.

"Phat the divil is it coming," said the Irishman. "Corporal of the guaod, the quane of all the South is coming down the road, riding a high stepper. Phat will I do, I dunno?"

"Stop her," I yelled with my teeth chattering.

"Halt right fhere yez are," said the Irishman, with a look on his face that showed he was—well, that he was an Irishman, and had an eye for beauty. The German had taken the horse by the bit, and I stepped out from behind the school house.

Great heavens, but she was a beautiful woman, and she sat on her horse like a statue. I had never seen a more beautiful woman. She was a brunette, with large black eyes, and her face was flushed with the exercise of riding.

She smiled and showed two rows of the prettiest teeth that ever were put into a female mouth, and one ungloved hand, with which she handed me the pass had a dimple at every knuckle, and was as white as paper, and soft as silk. I know it was soft, because it touched my red, freckled hand when I took the pass. I did not blame the general for being in love with her, or for wanting to saw off the unpleasant duty of breaking up her smuggling, on to a poor orphan like me. She said:

"Captain, I have a pass from the general, to go through the lines at any time, unmollested."

"It is no good," I said, examining it. "This pass is evidently a forgery."

"But, my dear captain," she said, with a smile that I would give ten dollars for a picture of, "The pass is not a forgery. I have used it for months."

"I am not a dear captain, only a cheap corporal," I said, with an attempt to be at my ease, which I wasn't.

"There has been at least a wagon load of quinine smuggled through the lines on this pass, and it has got to stop; you cannot go."

"The dickens you say," said she as she drew her revolver, and sung out, "let go that horse," and firing at the German.

"*Kritz-dunnerwetter*," said the German, as he got down by the horse's forefeet, and held on to the bridle, "*vot vor you choot a man ven he holt your horse?*"

"*Madame*," I said, "your revolver is loaded with blank cartridges, and you can do no harm. Try another one on the Irishman."

"Hold on," said the Irishman, "and don't experiment on a poor man who has a wife and six children. Shoot the corporal."

But I had reached up and taken the revolver from her, and she was weak as a kitten. Her nerve had forsaken her, and when I told her to dismount she was like a rag, and had to be helped down. If she was beautiful before, now that she had started her tear mill, she was ravishingly radiant, and I felt like a villain. She leaned on my shoulder, and it was the loveliest burden a soldier ever held. I seated her on the steps of the schoolhouse, and I thought she would faint, but she didn't. She was evidently taken by surprise, and wanted a little time to think it over, and form a plan. So did I.

As I looked her over, and thought what I was expected to do, I wondered where it would be best to commence. She began to recover, smiled at me and asked me to have the other soldiers go away, so she could talk with me. I wished she wouldn't smile like that, because it unnerved me. She asked me what I was going to do with her, what caused me to suspect her, if I would not believe her if she told me she was not a smuggler, if I had orders to arrest her, and all that.

I said, "*Madame*, my orders are to arrest all quinine smugglers, and you are one. I am Hawkshaw, the detective. For months I have shadowed you, and I know you have concealed about your person a whole drug store. In that innocent looking bustle I feel that there is quinine for the million. Your heaving bosom contains, besides love for your friends and hatred of your enemies, a storehouse of useful medicines, contraband of war. In your stockings there is much that would interest the seeker after the truth, your corset that fits you so beautifully is liable to be full of revolver cartridges, while in your shoes there may be messages to the rebels. I shall search you from Genesis to Revelations, and may the Lord have mercy on both of us. To begin, please let me examine the hat you have on."

With some reluctance she took off a sort of half-stovepipe hat, and covered her face with her handkerchief while I looked into it. I found a package of newly printed confederate bonds, and a quantity of court plaster. That settled it. She cried a little, and wanted to go into the schoolhouse. I went in with her, and two of my soldiers.

I told her that it was a duty that was pretty tough, but it was necessary for her to disrobe, as I must have every article she had. She cried, and said if I searched her, or molested her, I would do it at my peril, and that I wouldn't know how to go to work to take off her clothes, anyway, and that I ought to be ashamed of myself. I told her I felt as ashamed as any gentleman could, and though I knew little about the details of the female apparel, I had some general ideas about bustles, polonaise, socks, skirts, and so forth, and while I might be awkward, and uncouth, and nervous, as long as there were buttons to unbutton, hooks to unhook, and safety-pins to unpin, I thought I could eventually get to the quinine, if she would give me time, and I did not faint by the wayside, but my idea was that it would save all trouble, her modesty would not receive a shock, nor mine either, if she would go behind the little pulpit in the schoolhouse, out of sight of us, take off her clothes, and hand them over the pulpit to us to examine.

She said she would die first, besides, she knew we would peek around the pulpit at her. I was getting very nervous, and perspiring a good deal, and wishing it was over, and I swore, upon my honour, that if she would go behind the pulpit and disrobe, she should be as safe from intrusion as though she was in her own room. She swore she would not, and I went up to her to commence unraveling the mystery. Her dress hooked up in the back, which I always *did* think a great nuisance, and I began to unhook it. I wondered that she stood so quietly and let me unhook it, but after it was unhooked from the neck to the small of her back, and I was wishing I was dead, she said:

"There, now that you have got my dress unhooked, a feat I never could accomplish myself, I will go behind the pulpit and take off my dress, if you will promise not to look, and that you will help me hook up my dress when this cruel quinine war is over."

I told her by the great Jehosephat, and the continental congress, I would help her, and that I would kill anybody who looked, and she went behind the schoolhouse pulpit, where a country preacher, very likely, preached on Sundays, and bent over out of sight, and it wasn't half a minute before she handed the dress over to me. In the pockets I found several papers of some kind of medicine, and a few small bottles, sealed up with red sealing-wax.

"Now, the bustle, please, I said, in a voice trembling with emotion.

"Take your old bustle," she said, as she whacked it on the top of the pulpit.

Well, if anybody had told me that a bustle could be made to hold stuff enough to fill a bushel-basket, I would not have believed it. We filled three nose-bags, such as cavalrymen feed horses in, with paper packages and bottles of quinine. There were thirty bottles of pills, and salves and ointments, and plasters.

"This is panning out first rate," I said, with less emotion. The emotion was somehow getting out of me, and the affair was becoming more of a mercantile transaction. It was like a young druggist going from the side of his beloved, to the drug store, to take an inventory. "Now hand out that other lot."

She evidently knew what I referred to, for she handed out over the pulpit a package just exactly the shape of what I had supposed, in my guileless innocence, was a portion of the female form. That is, I had suspected it was not all human form, but didn't know. That was also full of medicines, of which quinine was the larger part, though there was about a pint of gun caps.

"Speaking about stockings," I said, "please take them off and hand them over."

She kicked about taking off her shoes and stockings, and said no gentleman would compel a lady to do that. I said I would wait about two minutes, and then, if it was too much trouble for her to take them off, I would come around the pulpit and help. Bless you, I wouldn't have gone for the world, as I was already more than satisfied with what I had found. She said I needn't trouble myself, as she guessed she could take off her shoes without my help. I heard her unlacing her shoes, and pretty soon two dainty shoes and two very long stockings, came over the pulpit, the heel of one shoe hitting me in the ear. As I picked up the shoes I heard the crumpling of a letter behind the pulpit, and I told her I must have all the messages she had. She said it was only a letter to one she loved. I told her I must have it, and she handed it over. I read, "My darling husband," and handed it back, saying I would not pry into her family secrets. She began to cry, and insisted on my reading it, which I did. It was to her husband, an officer in the Confederate army, and was about as follows:

My Darling Husband:—This life of deception is killing me. I want to do all in my power to help our cause, but I am each day more nervous, and liable to detection. The Yankee officers are frequently at our house, and I have to treat them kindly, but it is all I can do to keep from crying, and I am expected to laugh. I fear that I am suspected of smuggling, as the subject is frequently brought up in conversation, and I feel my face burn, though I try hard not to show it. I think of you, away off in Virginia, with your armless sleeve, our children in New Orleans, and I wonder if we will ever be united again.

O, God, when will this all end. I have no fault to find with the Federal troops. The officers are very kind and through one fatherly general I am allowed to pass into our lines. I feel that I am betraying his kindness every trip I make, and only the urgent need that our dear boys have for medicines could induce me to do as I do. After this trip I shall go to New Orleans,[1]

---

1. Eighteen months after the lady rode away from me, "leaving" her quinine, I was in New Orleans, to be mustered in as Second Lieutenant, having received a commsssion. I had bought me a fine uniform, and thought I was about as cunning a looking officer as ever was. I was walking on Canal street, looking in the windows, and finally went into a store to buy some collars. A gentleman came in with a gray uniform on, and one sleeve empty. (Continued over page.)

"JIM, EXCUSE ME, WHAT KIND OF A THING IS THAT?"
"NOTHIN', ONLY THEY ARE A SHELLIN' ON US."

where I fear Madge is sick, as shew as not at all well the last I heard from her. Pray earnestly, my dear husband, every day, as I do, that this trouble may end soon, some way, and I beg of you not to have a feeling of revenge in your heart towards your enemies, on account of the loss of your arm, as there are thousands of federals similarly afflicted. I shall love you more, and I will wrap your empty sleeve about my neck, and try never to miss the strong arm that was my support. *Adieu.*

Your loving wife.

That letter knocked me out in one round. I had begun to enjoy the unpacking of the smuggled goods, and the discomfiture of my female smuggler, but when I read that loving letter, breathing such a Christian spirit, and thought of the poor wife-mother behind the pulpit unravelling herself, I was ashamed, and I said to myself, "she shall not take off another rag. So I handed back the letter and the dress, and all of the things she had taken off, and I said:

"Put everything right back onto yourself, and come out at your leisure, and we took the medicines and went out of the schoolhouse. Presently She came out, and I told her it was my duty to take her back to headquarters, but if she had no objections to my taking the letter to the general, with the medicines, she could go back to the house where she boarded, and I thought if she took the first boat for New Orleans, it would be all right, and I would see that the letter was sent through the lines to her husband. I helped her on her horse, and I said:

He was evidently a Confederate officer. He asked me if I did not belong to a certain cavalry regiment, and if my name was not so and so. I told him he was correct. He told me there was a lady in an adjoining store that wanted to see me. I did not know a soul, that is, a female soul, in New Orleans, but I went with him. Any lady that wanted to see me, in my new uniform, could see me. As we entered the store a lady left two little girls and rushed up to me, threw her arms around my neck and —(say, does a fellow have to tell everything, when he writes a war history?) Well, she was awfully tickled to see me, and she was my smuggler, the Confederate was her husband, and the children were hers. The officer was as tickled as she was, and they compelled me to go to their house to dinner, and I enjoyed it very much. We talked over the arrest of the "female smuggler," and she said to her husband, "Pa, it was an awfully embarrassing situation for me and this Yankee, but he treated me like a lady, and the only thing I have to find fault about, is that he forgot to help me hook up my dress, and I rode clear to town with it unhooked." The Confederate had been discharged at the surrender, and I was on my way to Texas, to serve another year, hunting Indians. I left them very happy, and as I went out of their door she wrapped his empty sleeve around her waist, drew the children up to her, and said, "Mr. Yankee, may you always be very happy."

121

"You can escape. Your horse is better than ours, and though you are a prisoner, we would not shoot at you if you tried to escape. I hope your prayers will have the effect you desire, and that the trouble will soon be over. I hope you will and the children well, and that the husband will be spared to be a comfort to you."

She bowed her head, as she sat in the saddle, and the look of defiance which she had shown, was gone, and one of thankfulness, peace, hope, purity, took its place. She handed me the letter, and asked:

"Can I go?"

I told, her she was free to go. She turned her horse; towards town, touched him with the whip, and he was; away like the wind. I stood for two minutes, watching her, when I was recalled to my senses by the Irishman, who said:

"Fhat are we to do wid the quinane and the gun caps?" We packed the smuggled goods in our saddle-bags and elsewhere, and rode back to headquarters. The colonel and the general were in the colonel's tent, and I took the "stuff" in and reported all the occurrences.

"But where is the lady?" inquired the general, after reading the letter and wiping his eyes.

"As we were about to start back," said I, "after taking the smuggled goods from her, she gave her horse the whip, and rode away. I had no orders to shoot a woman, and I let her go."

"Thank God," said the general. "That's the best way," said the colonel. "She will quit smuggling and go to her children."

CHAPTER 13

I Reveal My Identity

It was not twenty-four hours before the news spread all over my regiment, as well as several other regiments, that a certain corporal had captured a female smuggler, while on picket, had searched her on the spot and found a large quantity of quinine and other articles contraband of war, and there was a general desire to look upon the features of a man, not a commissioned officer who had gall enough to search a female rebel, from top to toe, without orders from the commanding officer, and I was constantly being visited by curiosity-seekers, who wanted to know all about it.

Of course it was not known that I had been ordered to do as I did, and they all wondered why I was not made an example of; and many privates, corporals and sergeants wondered if they would get out of it so easily if they should do as I did. There were a great many women passing through the lines, and I am sure many soldiers decided that the first woman who attempted to pass through would get searched. It was talked among the men, and for a day or two a lady would certainly have stood a poor show to have rode up to a picket post with a pass to go outside.

The soldiers had so long been away from female society that it would have been a picnic for them to have captured a suspicious looking woman who was pretty. I was pointed out, down town, as the man who captured the woman loaded with quinine, and women with rebel tendencies would look at me as though I was a bold, bad man that ought to be killed, and they acted as though they would like to eat me. But I tried to appear modest, and not as though I had done anything I was particularly proud of.

The next evening the colonel sent for me and said he had got something for me to do that required nerve. I told him that my experience in putting down the rebellion had shown me that the whole thing required nerve. That I had been on my nerve until my nerves were pretty near used up, and I asked him if he couldn't let some of the other boys do a little of the nervous work. He said he had one more woman job that he would like to have me undertake.

I was sick of the whole woman business, and told him I did not want to be aggravated any more; that arresting women and searching them, was nothing but an aggravation, and I wanted to be let out. He said in this case I would not have to arrest anybody of the female persuasion, but that I would have to be arrested, and that it would be the greatest joke that ever was. I told him if there was any joke about it he could count me in. Then he went on to say that my success with the female smuggler had excited all the boys to emulate my deeds, and they were all laying for a female smuggler, and that he feared it wouldn't be safe for a woman to be caught on the picket line.

There had got to be a stop put to it, and he and the general had thought of a scheme. He said there was a corporal in one of the companies who had made his brags that he would arrest the first female that came to his picket post, and search her for smuggled goods, and they wanted to make an example of him. He asked me if I wasn't something of a boxer, and I told him for a light weight I was considered pretty good. Then he asked me if I could ride on a side saddle. I told him I could ride anything, from a hobby to an elephant. He said that was all right, and I would fill the bill.

Then he went into details. I was to go to the town with him, and be fitted out with a riding habit of the female persuasion, false hair, side saddle, and a bustle as big as a bushel basket. That I was to ride out on a certain road, where the corporal would be on picket with two men. He would stop me, and search me, I was to cry, and beg, and all that, but finally submit to be searched, and after the corporal had got started to search me, I was to haul off and give him one "biff" in the nose, another if it was necessary to knock him down, paste one of the men in the ear, if he showed any impudence, jump on my horse and come back to town, and leave the corporal to find his mistake.

I didn't half like the idea of dressing up in such a masquering costume, but of course if I could help put down the rebellion that way, it was my duty to do it, and besides, I had a grudge against that corporal, anyway, because he called me a "jay" and a "substitute," and a "drafted man," when I came to the regiment. The colonel took me to the residence of a lady friend who rode on horseback a good deal, and as he let her into the secret, she helped fix me up. All I had to do was to remove my cavalry jacket, and she put the dress on over my head. I always supposed they put on these dresses the same as men put on pants, by walking into them feet first, but she said they went over the head. I felt as though my pants were going to show, but she gave me some instructions about keeping the dress down, and I began to feel a good deal like a woman.

The dress fit me around the waist as though it was made for me, and when it was all buttoned up in front I felt stunning. She and the colonel made a bustle out of newspapers, and a small sofa cushion of eider down was placed where it would do the most good. After the dress was all fixed, she got a wig and put it on my head, and a hat, with a feather in it, and then pinned a veil on the hair, so it reached down to my rose-bud mouth. Then she took a powder arrangement and powdered my face, put on a pair of long gauntlets which she usually wore, and told me to look in the glass. When I looked into the glass I almost fainted. The deception was so good that it would have fooled the oldest man in the world.

The colonel said he was almost inclined to fall in love with me himself, and he did put his arm around me and squeeze me, but I didn't notice any particular feeling, such as I did when his lady friend was fooling around me. That was different. Well, I was an inveterate smoker at that time, so I took my pipe and a bag of tobacco, and put it in a pocket of the dress, and some matches, and we went out doors. The colonel took my tiny number eight boot in his hand and tossed me lightly into the saddle, then he mounted his own horse and we rode around the suburbs of the town, so I could get used to the side-saddle. I got him to stop behind a fence and let me have a smoke out of my pipe, and then I told him I was ready. He gave me a pass, and told me to go out on the road the corporal was on, and if he let me pass out of the lines to go on to a turn in the road, where a squad of our men were on a scout, and to report to the officer in charge, who would bring me in all right, by another road, but if the corporal attempted to search me, to do as I had been told to do.

After I had knocked the corporal down, if I would give a yell, the officer who was outside would come and arrest us all and bring us to headquarters, where the colonel could reprimand the corporal, etc. I threw a kiss to the colonel and started out on the road. It was about a mile to the picket post, and I had time to reflect on my position. This was putting down the rebellion at a great rate. I was an ostensible female, liable to be insulted at any moment, but I would maintain the dignity of my alleged sex if I didn't lay up a cent. I put on a proud, haughty look, full of purity and all that, and as I neared the picket post, I saw the corporal step out into the road, and as I came up he told me to halt. I halted, and handed him my pass, but he said it was a forgery, and ordered me to dismount. I turned on the water, from my eyes, and began to cry, but it run off the bad corporal like water off a duck.

"None of your sniveling around me," said the vile man. "Get down off that horse."

"Sir," I said, with well feigned indignation, "you would not molest a poor girl who has no one to defend her. Let me go I prithe."

I had read that, "Let me go I prithe," in a novel, and it seemed to me to be the proper thing to say, though I couldn't hardly keep from laughing.

"Prithe nothing," said the corporal. "What you got in that bustle?" said the corporal.

"Bustle," I said, blushing so you could have touched a match to my face. "Why speak of such a thing in the presence of a lady. I want you to let me go or I shall think you are real mean, so now. Please, Mr. Soldier, let me go," and I smiled at him and winked with my left eye in a manner that ought to have paralyzed a marble statue. "O, what you giving us," said the vile man. "Get down off that horse and let me go through you for quinine. Do you hear?"

I was afraid if he helped me down he would see my boots or pants, which would be a give-away. So I gathered my dress in my hands and jumped down in pretty good shape. I had sparred with the corporal several times in camp, and I knew I could knock him out easy, and I made up my mind that the first indignity he offered me I would just "lam him one. It was all I could do to keep from pasting him in the nose, when I first landed on the ground, but I had a part to play, and it would not do to go off half cocked. So I looked sad, pouted my lips, and wondered if he would kiss me, and feel the beard where I had been shaved.

"Now, shuck yourself," said he.

"Do what? I asked, with apparent alarm.

"Peel," said he, as he put his hand on my back,

"Sir," I said with my eyes flashing fire, and my heart throbbing, and almost bursting with suppressed laughter, "you are insolent. I am a poor orphan, unused to contact with coarse men. I have been raised a pet, and no vile hand has ever been laid upon me until you just touched me. If you touch me I shall scream. I shall call for help. What would you do, you wicked, naughty man."

"Unbutton," said he as he pointed to my dress in front. "Call for help and be darned. You are a smuggler, and I know it."

"O, my God," said I, with a stage accent, "has it come to this? Am I to be robbed of all I hold dear, by a common Yankee corporal. Has a woman no rights which are to be respected? Am I to be murdered in cold bel-lud, with all my sins upon my head. O, Mr. Man, give me a moment to utter a silent prayer."

"O, hush," said he, "and hold up your hands. There ain't going to be any bel-lud. All I want is to go through you for quinine."

"Spare me, I beseech you," I said, as I held up my hands, and got in position to knock him silly the first move he made. "I am no walking drug store, I am a good girl." Around my awful form I draw an imaginary circle. "Step but one foot within that sacred circle, and on thy head I launch the cu-r-r-r-se of Rome, Georgia."

"Let up on this Shakespeare, and get to business, said the corporal, as he reached up to my neck to unbutton the top button of my dress. He was looking at my dress, and wondering what he would find concealed within, when I brought down both fists and took him with one in each eye, with a force that would have knocked a mule down. He fell backwards, and gave a yell that could have been heard a mile. Then one of his men started for me and I knocked him in the ear, and he fell beside the corporal.

The other man was going to come for his share, when the officer who had been stationed outside the lines rode up with his men and asked what was the matter. The soldier-who was not hit said I had assassinated the corporal. The officer said that was wrong, and women who would go around killing off the Union army with their fists ought to be arrested. Just then the corporal raised up on his elbow and tried to open two of the blackest eyes that ever were seen. Turning to the officer, he said:

"That woman is a smuggler, and she struck me with a brick house!

"Ancient female," said the officer, looking at me and laughing, "why do you go around like a besum of destruction, wiping out armies, one man at a time. You ought to be ashamed of myself, and you should be muzzled.

"Don't call me a female," said I, in my natural hoarse voice. "That is something that I will not submit to."

127

He fell to the ground and gave a yell that could have been heard a mile.

The corporal looked up at me with one eye, the other being al-most closed from the effects of the fall of the brick house. He looked as though he smelled woollen burning, as the old saying is. The officer said he guessed he would take us all to headquarters, and inquire into the affair. The corporal said that there was nothing to inquire into. That this female came along and insisted on going outside of the lines, and when he asked her, in a polite manner, to show her pass, she struck him down with a billy, or some weapon she had concealed about her person.

"You are not much of a liar, either," said I, jumping on to my horse astraddle, like a man.

The corporal looked at me as though he would sink, but he main-tained that he had done nothing that should offend the most fastidi-ous female. The corporal and his men mounted, and we all started for headquarters. I rode beside the officer, and the corporal was right behind me. After we had got started I pulled out my pipe, filled it, lit a match as soldiers usually do, though it was quite unhandy, and began to smoke.

As the tobacco smoke rolled out under my veil, from the alleged rosebud mouth, the scene was one that the corporal and the most of the men had never thought of, though the officer was "on" all right enough. The corporal could hardly believe his eyes, or one eye, for the other one had gone closed. I was a fine enough looking female as we rode through the regiment, except the pipe, which I puffed along just as though I had no dress on. As we rode up to the colonel's tent, it was noised around that a scout had captured a daring female rebel, and she had almost killed a corporal, and the whole regiment gathered around the colonel's tent.

"What is the trouble, corporal?" asked the colonel of my black-eyed friend.

"Well this woman wanted to go outside, and when I objected, she knocked me down with a rail off a fence."

"And you offered her no indignity?" the colonel asked.

"Not in the least," said the corporal.

Then the colonel asked me to tell my story, which I did. The cor-poral said it was a lie, but the other man, whom I did not hit, said I was right.

"Can you disrobe, before these soldiers, without getting off your horse?" asked the colonel, looking at me.

I told him I could and he told me to proceed. I pulled the hat

129

and hair off first and appeared with my red hair clipped short. I then I threw the dress over my head, and appeared in my cavalry pants, all dressed, except my jacket and cap, which the colonel handed me, having brought it from the house where I put on the dress. I put on the jacket, wiped the powder off my face, and the corporal said:

"It's that condemned raw recruit."

All the boys took in the transformation scene, and then the colonel told them that he wanted this to be a lesson to all of them, to let all women who came to the picket posts, or anywhere, who had passes, alone, and not think because one woman had been caught smuggling, that all women were smugglers. In fact he wanted every soldier to mind his own business. Then he dismissed us, and we went to our quarters. On the way, the one-eyed corporal touched me on the arm, and he said:

"Old man, you played it fine on me, but I will get even with you yet."

CHAPTER 14

The Report is an Astonishing One

About this time I received the greatest shock of the whole war. I had prided myself upon my uniform that I brought from home, which was made by a tailor, and fit me first rate. It was of as good cloth and as well made as the uniforms of any of the officers, and I was not ashamed to go out with a party of officers on a little evening tear, because there was nothing about my uniform to distinguish me from an officer, except the shoulder-straps, and many officers did not wear shoulder-straps at all, except on dress parade or inspection. I took great pleasure in riding around town, wherever the regiment was located, looking wise, and posing as an officer.

But the time came when my uniform, which came with me as a recruit, became seedy, and badly worn, and it was necessary to discard it, and draw some clothing of the quartermaster. That is a trying time for a recruit. One day it was announced that the quartermaster sergeant had received a quantity of clothing, and the men were ordered to go and draw coats, pants, hats, shoes, overcoats, and underclothing, as winter was coming on, and the regiment was liable to move at any time.

Something happened that I was unable to be present the first forenoon that clothing was issued, and, when I did call upon the quartermaster-sergeant, there was only two or three suits left, and they had been tumbled over till they looked bad. I can remember now how my heart sank within me, as I picked up a pair of pants that was left. They were evidently cut out with a buzz-saw, and were made for a man that weighed three hundred. I held them up in instalments, and looked at them. Holding them by the top, as high as I could, and the bottom of the legs of the pants laid on the ground. The sergeant charged the pants to my account, and then handed me a jacket, a small one, evidently made for a hump-backed dwarf.

The jacket was covered with yellow braid. O, so yellow, that it made me sick. The jacket was charged to me, also. Then he handed me some undershirts and drawers, so coarse and rough that it seemed to me they must have been made of rope, and lined with sand-paper. Then came an overcoat, big enough for an equestrian statue of George Washington, with a cape on it as big as a wall tent. The hat I drew was a stiff, cheap, shoddy hat, as high as a tin camp kettle, which was to take the place of my nobby, soft felt hat that I had paid five dollars of my bounty money for. The hat was four sizes too large for me. Then I took the last pair of army shoes there was, and they weighed as much as a pair of anvils, and had raw-hide strings to fasten them with.

Has any old soldier of the army ever forgotten the clothing that he drew from the quartermaster? These inverted pots for hats, the same size all the way up, and the shoes that seemed to be made of sole leather, and which scraped the skin off the ankles. O, if this government ever does go to Gehenna, as some people contend it will, sometime, it will be as a penalty for issuing such ill-fitting shoddy clothing to its brave soldiers, who never did the government any harm. I carried the lot of clothing to my tent, feeling sick and faint. The idea of wearing them among folks was almost more than I could bear to think of. I laid them on my bunk, and looked at them, and "died right there."

That hat was of a style older than Methuselah. O, I could have stood it, all but the hat, and pants, and shoes, but they killed me. While I was looking at the layout, and trying to make myself believe that my old clothes that I brought with me were good enough to last till the war was over, though the seat of the pants, and the knees, and the sleeves of the coat were nearly gone, an orderly came through the company and said the regiment would have a dismounted dress parade at sundown, and every man must wear his new clothes.

Ye gods! that was too much! If I could have had a week or ten days to get used to those new clothes, one article at a time, I could have stood it, but to be compelled to put the pants, and jacket, shoes and hat on all at once, was horrible to think of, and if I had not known that a deserter was always caught, and punished, I would have deserted. But the clothes must be put on, and I must go out into the world a spectacle to behold. Believing that it is better to face the worst, and have it over, I put on the pants first.

If I could ever meet the army contractor who furnished those pants to a government almost in the throes of dissolution, I would kill him as I would an enemy of the human race. There was room enough in those pants for a man and a horse. Yes, and a bale of hay. There were no suspenders furnished to the men, and how to keep the pants from falling from grace was a question, but I got a piece of tent rope, cut a hole in the waist band, and run the rope around inside, and tied it around my waist, puckering the top of the pants at proper intervals.

When I think of those pants now, after twenty-two years, I wonder that I was not irretrievably lost in them. I would have been lost if I had not stuck out of the top. But when I looked at the bottoms of the pants I found at least a foot too much. If I had tied the rope around under my arms, or buttoned them to my collar button, they would have been too long at the bottom. I finally rolled them up at the bottom, and they rolled clear up above my knees. But how they did bag around my body. There was cloth enough to spare to have made a whole uniform for the largest man in the regiment.

At that time I was a slim fellow, that weighed less than 125 pounds, and there is no doubt I got the largest pair of pants that was issued in the whole Union army. I only had a small round mirror in my tent, so I could not see how awfully I looked, only in instalments, but to a sensitive young man who had always dressed well, anyone can see how a pair of such pants would harrow up his soul. If the pants were too large, you ought to have seen the jacket. The contractor who made the clothes evidently took the measure of a monkey to make that jacket. It was so small that I could hardly get it on. The sleeves were so tight that the vaccination marks on my arm must have shown plainly. The sleeves were too short, and my hands and half of my forearm riding outside. The body was so tight that I had to use a monkey-wrench to button it, and then I couldn't breathe without unbuttoning one button. It was so tight that my ribs showed so plain they could be counted.

I stuffed some pieces of grain sack in the shoes, and got them on, and tied them, put on that awful hat, the bugle sounded to fall in, and I fell out of my tent towards the place of assembly, with my carbine. If we had been going out mounted, I could have managed to hide some of the pants around the saddle, if I could have got my shoe over the horse's back, but to walk out among men, stubbing my shoes against each other, and interfering and knocking my ankles off, was pretty hard. The company was about formed when I fell out of my tent, and when the men saw me they snickered right out. I have heard a great many noises in my time that took the life out of me.

The first shell that I heard whistle through the air, and shriek, and explode, caused my hair to raise, and I was cold all up and down my spine. The first flock of minnie bullets that sang about my vicinity caused my flesh to creep and my heart's blood to stand still. Once I was near a saw mill when the boiler exploded, and as the pieces of boiler began to rain around me, I felt how weak and insignificant a small, red-headed, freckled-faced man is.

Once I heard a girl say "no," when I had asked her a civil question, and I was so pale and weak that I could hardly reply that I didn't care a continental whether she married me or not, but I never felt quite so weak, and powerless, and ashamed, and desperate as I did when I came out, falling over myself and the men of my company snickered at my appearance. The captain held his hand over his face and laughed. I fell in at the left of my company, and the captain went to the right and looked down the line, and seeing my pants out in front about a foot, he ordered me to stand back. I stood back, and he looked at the rear of the line, and I stuck out worse behind, and he made me move up. Finally he came down to where I was and told me to throw out my chest. I tried to throw it out, and busted a button off, but the pressure was too great, and my chest went back.

Finally the captain told me I could go to the right of the company and act as orderly sergeant on dress parade. He said as our company was on the right of the regiment, they could dress on my pants, and I wouldn't be noticed.

What I ought to have done, was to have committed suicide right there, but I went to the right, trying to look innocent, and we moved off to the field for dress parade. Everything went on well enough, except that in coming to a "carry arms," with my carbine, from a present, the muzzle of the carbine knocked off my stiff hat, and the stock of the carbine went into the pocket of my pants and run clear down my leg, before I could rescue it. A file closer behind me picked up my hat and put it on me, with the yellow cord tassels in front, and before I could fix it, the order came, "First sergeants to the front and centre, march."

Those who are familiar with military matters, know that at dress parade the first sergeants march a few paces to the front, then turn and march to the centre of the regiment, turn and face the adjutant, and each salutes that officer in turn, and reports, "Co. ——, all present or accounted for." That was the hardest march I ever had in all of my army experience. I knew that every eye of every soldier in the six companies at the right of the regiment, would be on my pants, and the officers would laugh at me, and the several hundred ladies and gentlemen from town, who were back of the colonel, witnessing the dress parade, would laugh, too.

A man can face death, in the discharge of his duty, better than he can face the laughter of a thousand people. I seemed to be the only soldier in the whole regiment who had not got a pretty good fit in drawing his new clothes, but I was a spectacle. As I marched to the front, with the other eleven first sergeants, and stood still for them to dress on me, I felt as though the piece of tent rope with which I had fastened my large pants up, was becoming untied, and I began to perspire. What would become of me if that rope *should* become untied? If that rope gave way, it seemed to me it would break up the whole army, stampede the visitors, and cause me to be court-martialled for conduct unbecoming any white man. I made up my mind if the worst came, I would drop my carbine and grab the pants with both hands, and save the day. At the command, right and left face, I turned to the left, and I could feel the pants begin to droop, as it were, so I took hold of the top of them with my left hand, and at the command, march, I started for the centre.

I had got almost past my own company, and there had been no general laugh, but when I passed an Irishman, named Mulcahy, I heard him whisper out loud to the man next to him, "Howly Jasus, luk at the pants." Then there was a snicker all through the company, which was taken up by the next, and by the time I got to the centre, and "front faced," a half of the regiment were laughing, and the officers were scolding the men and whispering to them to shut up. Just then I felt that the one hand that was trying to hold the pants up, was never going to do the work in the world, so I dropped my carbine behind me, said, "Co. E, all present or accounted for," and stood there like a stoughton bottle, holding the waist-band of those pants with both hands, as pale as a ghost. I could see that the adjutant and the colonel and two majors, were laughing, and many of the visitors were trying to keep from laughing.

I think I lived seventy years in five minutes, while the other eleven orderlies were reporting, and when the order came to return to our posts, I whispered to the next orderly to me, and told him if he would pick up my carbine and bring it along, I would die for him, and he picked it up. The dress parade was soon finished, but instead of marching the companies back to their quarters, they were ordered to break ranks on the parade ground, and for an hour I was surrounded with officers and men, who laughed at me till I thought I would die.

The colonel and adjutant finally told me that it was a put up job on me, to make a little fun for the boys. They said I had often had fun at the expense of the other boys, and they wanted to see if I could stand a joke on myself, and they admitted that I had done it well. If I had known it was a joke, I could have lived through it better. The adjutant said he had got a little work for me that evening, and the next morning I could take my clothes down town to the post quartermaster, and exchange them for a suit that would fit me. I went to his tent, and he showed me a lot of company reports, and wanted me to make out a consolidated monthly report, for the assistant adjutant general of the brigade.

I had done some work for him before, and he left a blank signed by himself and colonel, and told me to make out a report and send it to the brigade headquarters, as he was going down town with a party of officers. I made up my mind that I would get even with the adjutant and the colonel, so I took a pen and filled out the blank. My idea was to put all the figures in the wrong column, which I did, and send it to the brigade headquarters. The next morning I went down town with the quartermaster, and got a suit of clothes to fit me, and on the way back to camp I passed brigade headquarters, when I saw our adjutant looking quite dejected.

He called to me and said he had been summoned to brigade head-quarters to explain some inaccuracies in the monthly report sent in the night before, and he wanted me to stay and see what was the trouble, but I acted as though if there was a mistake, it was an error of the head rather than of the feet. Pretty soon the old brigade adjutant, who was a strict disciplinarian, and a man who never heard of a joke, came in from the general's tent, with his brow corrugated. They had evidently been brooding over the report.

"I beg your pardon, adjutant," said he, with a preoccupied look, "but in your report I observe that your regiment contains forty-three enlisted men, and nine hundred and twenty-six company cooks. This seems to me improbable, and the general cannot seem to understand it."

The adjutant turned red in the face, and was about to stammer out something, when the adjutant general continued:

"Again, we observe that your quartermaster has on hand nine hundred bales of condition powders, which is placed in your report as rations for the men, that you only have eleven horses in your regiment fit for duty, that you have the same number of men, while the commissioned officers foot up at nine hundred and twenty-six. Of your sick men there seems to be plenty, some eight hundred, which would indicate an epidemic, of which these headquarters had not been informed previously. In the column headed "officers detailed on other duty" I find four "six-mule teams," and one "spike team of five mules." In the column "officers absent without leave" I find the entry "all gone off on a drunk." This, sir, is the most incongruous report that has ever been received at these head-quarters, from a reputably sober officer. Can this affair be satisfactorily explained, at once, or would you prefer to explain it to a court-martial?"

"Captain," said the adjutant in distress, and perspiring freely, "my clerk has made a mistake, and placed a piece of waste paper that has been scribbled on, in the envelope, instead of the regular report. Let me take it, and I will send the proper report to you in ten minutes."

The adjutant general handed over my report, after asking how it happened that the signature of the colonel and adjutant was on the ridiculous report, and the adjutant and the red-headed recruit went out, mounted and rode away. On the way the adjutant said, "I ought to kill you on the spot. But I won't. You have only retaliated on us for playing them pants on you. I hate a man that can't take a joke."

Then we made out a new report, and I took it to headquarters, and all was well. But the adjutant was not as kitteny with his jokes on the other fellows for many moons.

CHAPTER 15

I am Sent to the Hospital

Up to this time I had never been sick a day in my life, that is, sick enough to ache and groan and grunt, and lay in bed. At home I had occasionally had a cold, and I was put to bed at night, after drinking a quart of ginger tea, and covered up with blankets in a warm room, and I was fussed over by loving hands until I got to sleep, and in the morning I would wake up as fresh as a daisy, with my cold all gone. Once or twice at home I had a bilious attack that lasted me almost twenty-four hours; but the old family doctor fired blue pills down me, and I came under the wire an easy winner.

I did have the mumps and the measles, of course before enlisting, but the loving care I was given brought me out all right, and I looked upon those little sicknesses as a sort of luxury. The people at home would do everything to make sick experiences far from bitter memories. It was getting along towards Christmas of my first year in the army, and though it was the Sunny South we were in, I noticed that it was pretty all-fired cold. The night rides were full of fog and malaria; and one morning I came in from an all-night ride through the woods and swamps, feeling pretty blue.

The mud around my tent was frozen, and there was a little snow around in spots. As I laid down in my bunk to take a snooze before breakfast, I noticed how awfully thin an army blanket was. It was good enough for summer, but when winter came the blanket seemed to have lost its cunning. I was again doing duty as a private soldier, having learned that my promotion to the position of corporal was only temporary. I had been what is called a "lance corporal," or a brevet corporal. It seemed hard, after tasting of the sweets of official position, to be returned to the ranks, but I had to take the bitter with the sweet, and a soldier must not kick. I had never laid down to sleep before without dropping off into the land of dreams right away, but now, though I was tired enough, my eyes were wide open and I felt strange.

At times I would be so hot that I would throw the blanket off, and then I would be so cold that it seemed as though I would freeze. I had taken a severe cold which had settled everywhere, and there was not a bone in my body but what ached; my lungs seemed of no use; I could not take a long breath without a hacking cough, and I felt as though I should die. It was then that I thought of the warm little room at home and the ginger tea, and the soaking of my feet in mustard water and wrapping my body in a soft flannel blanket, and the kindly faces of my parents, my sister, my wife—everybody that had been kind to me. I would close my eyes and imagine I could see them all, and open my eyes and see my cold little tent and shiver as I thought of being sick away from home.

I laid for an hour wishing I was home again; and while alone there I made up my mind I would write home and warn all the boys I knew against enlisting. The thought that I should die there alone was too much, and I was about to yell for help when my tent mate, who had been on a scout, came in. He was a big green Yankee, who had a heart in him as big as a water pail, but he wasn't much, of a nurse. He came in nearly frozen, threw his saddle down in a corner, took out a hard tack and began to chew it, occasionally taking a drink of water out of a canteen. That was his breakfast.

"Well, I've got just about enough of war," said he, as he picked his teeth with a splinter off his bunk, and filled his pipe and lit it. "They can't wind up this business any too soon to suit the old man. War in the summer is a picnic, but in winter it is wearin on the soldier."

Heretofore I had enjoyed tobacco smoke very much, both from my own pipe and Jim's, but when he blew out the first whiff of smoke it went to my head and stomach and all up and down me, and I yelled, in a hoarse, pneumonia sort of voice:

"Jim, for God's sake don't smoke. I am at death's door, and I don't want to smell of tobacco smoke when St. Peter opens the gate."

"What, pard, you ain't sick," said Jim, putting his pipe outside of the tent, and coming to me and putting his great big hand on my forehead, as tender as a woman.

"Great heavens! you have got the yellow fever. You won't live an hour."

That was where Jim failed as a nurse. He made things out worse than they were. He, poor old fellow, thought it was sympathy, and if

139

I had let him go on he would have had me dead before night. I told him I was all right. All I had was a severe cold, on my lungs, and pneumonia, and rheumatism, and chills and fever, and a few such things, but I would be all right in a day or two. I wanted to encourage Jim to think I was not very bad off, but he wouldn't have it. He insisted that I had typhoid fever, and glanders, and cholera. He went right out of the tent and called in the first man he met, who proved to be the horse doctor.

The horse doctor was a friend of mine, and a mighty good fellow, but I had never meditated having him called in to doctor me. However, he felt of my foreleg, looked at my eyes, rubbed the hair the wrong way on my head, and told Jim to bleed me in the mouth, and blanket me, and give me a bran mash, and rub some mustang liniment on my chest and back. I didn't want to hurt the horse doctor's feelings by going back on his directions, but I told him I only wanted to soak my feet in mustard water, and take some ginger tea. He said all right, if I knew more about it than he did, and that he said he would skirmish around for some ginger, while Jim raised the mustard, and they both went out and left me alone. It seemed an age before anybody come, and I thought of home all the time, and of the folks who would know just what to do if I was there.

Pretty soon Jim came in with a camp kettle half full of hot water, and a bottle of French mixed mustard which he had bought of the sutler. I told him I wanted plain ground mustard, but he said there wasn't any to be found, and French mustard was the best he could do. We tried to dissolve it in the water, but it wouldn't work, and finally Jim suggested that he take a mustard spoon and plaster the French mustard all over my feet, and then put them to soak that way. He said that prepared mustard was the finest kind for pigs feet and sausage, and he didn't know why it was not all right to soak feet in. So he plastered it on and I proceeded to soak my feet. I presume it was the most unsuccessful case of soaking feet on record.

The old camp kettle was greasy, and when the hot water and French mustard began to get in their work on the kettle, the odor was sickening, and I do not think I was improved at all in my condition. I told Jim I guessed I would lay down and wait for the ginger tea. Pretty soon the horse doctor came in with a tin cup full of hot ginger tea. I took one swallow of it and I thought I had swallowed a blacksmith's forge, with a coal fire in it. I gasped and tried to yell murder. The horse doctor explained that he couldn't get any ginger, so he had taken cayenne pepper, which, he added, could knock the socks off of ginger any day in the week.

I felt like murdering the horse doctor, and I felt a little hard at Jim for playing French mustard on me, but when I come to reflect, I could see that they had done the best they could, and I thanked them, and told them to leave me alone and I would go to sleep. They went out of the tent and I could hear them speculating on my case. Jim said he knew I had diabetes, and lung fever combined, with sciatic rheumatism, and brain fever, and if I lived till morning the horse doctor could take it out of his wages. The horse doctor admitted that my case had a hopeless look, but he once had a patient, a bay horse, sixteen hands high, and as fine a saddle horse as a man ever threw a leg over, that was troubled exactly the same as I was.

He blistered his chest, gave him a table-spoonful of condition powders three times a day in a bran mash, took off his shoes and turned him out to grass, and in a week he sold him for two hundred and fifty dollar. I laid there and tried to go to sleep listening to that talk. Then, some of the boys who had heard that I was sick, came along and inquired how I was, and I listened to the remarks they made. One of them wanted to go and get some burdock leaves, and pound them into a pulp, and bind them on me for a poultice. He said he had an aunt in Wisconsin who had a milk sickness, and her left leg swelled up as big as a post, and the doctors tried everything, and charged her over two hundred dollars, and never did her any good, and one day an Indian doctor came along and picked some burdock leaves and fixed a poultice for her, and in a week she went to a hop-picker's dance, and was as kitteny as anybody, and the Indian doctor only charged her a quarter.

Jim was for going out for burdock leaves at once, for me, but the horse doctor told him I didn't have no milk sickness. He said all the milk soldiers got was condensed milk, and mighty little of that, and he would defy the world to show that a man could get milk sickness on condensed milk. That seemed to settle the burdock remedy, and they went to inquiring of Jim if he knew where my folks lived, so he could notify them, in case I was not there in the morning. Jim couldn't remember whether it was Atchison, Kan., or Fort Atkinson, Wis., but he said he would go and ask me, while I was alive, so there would be no mistake, and the poor fellow, meaning as well as any man ever did, came in and asked for the address of my father, saying it was of no account, particularly, only he wanted to know. I gave him the address, and then he asked me if he shouldn't get me something to eat. I told him I couldn't eat anything to save me.

He offered to fry me some bacon, and make me a cup of coffee, but the thought of bacon and coffee made me wild. I told him if he could make me a nice cup of green tea, and some milk toast, or poach me an egg and place it on a piece of nice buttered toast, and give me a little currant jelly, I thought I could swallow a mouthful. Jim's eyes stuck out when I gave my order, which I had done while thinking of home, and a tear rolled down his cheek, and he went out of the tent, saying, "All right, pard." I saw him tap his forehead with his finger, point his thumb toward the tent, and say to the boys outside:

"He's got 'em! Head all wrong! Wants me to make him milk toast, poached eggs, green tea, and currant jelly. And I offered him *bacon*. Sow belly for a sick man! There isn't a loaf of bread in camp. Not an egg within five miles. And milk! currant jelly! Why, he might as well ask for Delmonico's bill of fare, but we have got to get 'em. I told him he should have 'em, and, by mighty! he shall. Here, Mr. Horse-doctor, you stay and watch him, and I and Company D here will saddle up and go out on the road to a plantation, and raid it for delicacies."

"You bet your life," says the Company "D" man, and pretty soon I heard a couple of saddles thrown on two horses, and then there was a clatter of horses feet on the frozen ground. I have thought of it since a good many times, and have concluded that I must have dropped asleep. Any way, it didn't seem more than five minutes before the tent nap opened and Jim came in.

"Come, straighten out here, now, you red-headed corpse, and try that toast," said he, as he came in with a piece of hard-tack box for a tray, and on it was a nice china plate, and a cup and saucer, an egg on toast, and a little pitcher of milk, and some jelly.

"Jim," I said, tasting of the tea, which was not much like army tea, "you never made this tea. A woman made that tea, or I'm a goat. And that toast was toasted by a woman, and that egg was poached by a woman. Where am I?" I asked, imagining that I was home again.

"You guessed it the first time, pard," said Jim, as he threw the blanket over my shoulders, as I sat up on the bunk to try and eat. "The whole thing was done by the rebel angel."

"Rebel angel, Jim; what are you talking about? There ain't any rebel angels," and I became weak and laid down again.

"Yes, there is a rebel angel, and she is a dandy," said Jim, as he covered me up. "She is out by the fire making milk toast for you. You see,

I went out to the Brown plantation, to try and steal an egg, and some bread, and milk, but I thought, on the way out, as it was a case of life and death, the stealing of it might rest heavy on your soul when you come to pass in your chips, so I concluded to go to the house and ask for it. There was a young woman there, and I told her the red-headed corporal that captured the female smuggler, was dying, and couldn't eat any hard-tack and bacon, and I wanted to fill him up on white folks food before he died, so he could go to heaven or elsewhere, as the case might be, on a full stomach, and she flew around like a kernel of pop-corn on a hot griddle, and picked up a basket of stuff, and had the nigger saddle a mule for her, and she came right to the camp with me, and said she would attend to everything. She's a thoroughbred, and don't you make no mistake about it."

I must have gone to sleep when Jim was talking about the girl, for I dreamed that there was a million angels in rebel uniforms, poaching eggs for me. Pretty soon I heard a rustle of female clothes, and a soft, cool hand was placed on my forehead, my hair was brushed back, a perfumed handkerchief wiped the cold perspiration from my face, and I heard the rebel angel ask Jim what the doctor said about me. Jim told her what the horse doctor had said about curing a horse that had been sick the same as I was, and then she asked if we had not sent for the regular doc-doctor. Jim said we had not thought of that. She asked what had been done for me, and Jim told her about the French mustard episode, and the cayenne pepper tea.

I thought she laughed, but it had become dark in the tent, and I couldn't see her face, but she told Jim to go after the regimental surgeon at once, and Jim went out. The angel asked me how I felt, and I told her I was all right, but she said I was all wrong. I thanked her for the trouble she had taken to come so far, and she said not to mention it. She said she had a brother who was a prisoner at the-North, and if somebody would only be kind to him if he was sick, she would be well repaid. She said the last she heard of him he was a prisoner of war at Madison, Wis., and she wondered what kind of people lived there, away off on the frontier, and if they could be kind to their enemies. That touched me where I lived, and I raised up on my elbow, and said:

"Why bless your heart, Miss, if your brother is a prisoner in old Camp Randlll, in Madison, he has got a picnic. That town was my home before I came down here on this fool job. The people there are the finest in the world. All of them, from old Governor Lewis, to the poorest man in town, would set up nights with a sick person, whether he was a rebel or not. Your brother couldn't be better fixed if he was at home. The idea of a man suffering for food, clothing, or human sympathy in Madison, would be ridiculous. There is not a family in that town," I said, becoming excited from the feeling that any one doubted the humanity of the people of Wisconsin, "but would divide their breakfast, and their clothes, and their money, with your brother, egad, I wish I was there myself. I will be responsible for your brother, Miss."

She told me to lay down and be quiet, and not talk any more, as I was becoming wild. She said she was glad to know what kind of people lived there, as she had supposed it was a wilderness. In a few minutes Jim came back and said the doctor was playing poker with some other officers, in a captain's tent, and he didn't dare go in and break up the game, but he spoke to the doctor's orderly, and he said I ought to take castor oil.

That didn't please the little woman at all, and she told Jim to go to the poker tent and tell the doctor to come at once, or she would come after him. It was not long before the doctor came stooping in to my pup tent. His idea was to have all sick men attend surgeon's call in the morning, and not go around visiting the sick in tents. He asked me what was the matter, and I told him nothing much. Then he asked me why I wasn't at surgeon's call in the morning. I told him the reason was that I was wading in a swamp, after the rebels that ambushed some of our boys the day before. "Then you've got malaria," said he. "Take some quinine tonight, and come to surgeon's call in the morning."

The little woman, the rebel angel, got her back up at the coolness of the doctor; and she gave him a piece of her mind, and then he called for a candle, and he examined me carefully. When he got through, he said:

"He is going to have a run of fever. He must be sent to the hospital. Jim, go tell the driver to send the ambulance here at once, and you, Jim, go along and see that this fellow gets to the hospital all right. He can't live here in a tent, and I doubt if he will in the hospital."

That settled it. In a short time the ambulance came, and I got in and sat on a seat, and the rebel angel got in with me, and we rode seven miles to the hospital, over the roughest road a sick man ever jolted over, and I would have died, if I could have had my own way about it, but the little woman talked so cheerfully that when we arrived at the great building, I should have considered myself well, only that my mind was wandering.

THE "REBEL ANGEL GIVES THE DOCTOR A PIECE OF HER MIND"

All I remember of my entrance to the hospital was that when we got out of the ambulance Jim was there on his horse, leading the mule belonging to the angel. Some attendants helped me up stairs, and down a corridor, where we met two stretchers being carried out to the dead house with bodies on them, and I had to sit in a chair and wait till clean sheets could be put on one of the cots where a man had just died. The little woman told me to keep up my courage, and she would come and see me often, Jim cried and said he would come every day, a man said, "your bed is ready, No. 197," and I laid down as No. 197, and didn't care whether I ever got up again or not. I just had breath enough left to bid the angel goodbye, and tell Jim to see her safe home. Jim said, "You bet your life I will," and the world seemed blotted out, and for all I cared, I was dead.

CHAPTER 16

I Go Back to My Regiment

Let's see, last week I wound up in the hospital. When Jim, my old comrade, and the rebel angel, left me, I to all intents and purposes. I supposed I was going to sleep, but after I got well enough to know what was going on, I found that for about ten days I had been out of my head. It was not much of a head to get out of, but however small and insignificant a man's head is, he had rather have it with him, keeping good time, than to have it wandering around out of his reach. When I "come to," as the saying is, it only seemed as though I had been asleep over night, but I dreamed more than any able-bodied man could have done in one night. I was what they call unconscious, but I did a great deal of work during that period of unconsciousness.

One thing I did, which I was proud of, was to wind up the war. I arranged it so that all of the bullets that were fired on each side, were made of India-rubber, like those little toy balloons, and war was just fun. The boys on both sides would fire at each other and watch the rubber balloons hit the mark, and explode, and nobody was hurt, and everybody laughed. There was no more blood. Everything was rubber and wind. There was no one killed, no legs shot off, and the men on each side; when not fighting with the harmless missiles, were gathered together, blue and gray, having a regular picnic, and every evening there was a dance, the rebels furnishing the girls.

In my delirium I could see that my rebel angel was dancing a good deal with the boys, and frequently with my comrade, Jim, and I was pretty jealous. I made up my mind that I wouldn't speak to either of them again. I would watch my balloon battles with a good deal of interest, and think how much better and safer it was to fight that way. Every day, when the battle was over, and the two sides would get together for fun, I noticed when the bugle sounded for battle again,

147

that on each side the boys were terribly mixed, there being about as many blue-coated Yankees among the gray rebels as there were rebels among the Yankees, and after awhile it seemed as though all were dressed alike, in a sort of "blue-gray," and then they disappeared, and I recovered my senses.

Frequently, during my delirium and unconsciousness, I would feel my mouth pulled open, and hear a spoon chink against my teeth, and I would taste something bad going down my neck, and then my head would buzz as though a swarm of bees had taken up their abode where my brain used to be. Sometimes I would hear the clanking of a sabre and a pair of Mexican spurs, and feel a great big hand on my head, and I knew that was Jim, but I couldn't move a muscle, or say a word. "I guess he's dead, ain't he doc?" I would hear in Jim's voice, and the doc would say there was a little life left, but not enough, to swear by.

Then the doc would say, "You better come in about 10:30 tomorrow, as we bury them all at that hour, and I guess he'll croak by that time." I tried to speak and tell them that I was alive, and that I was going to get well, but it, wasn't any use. I was tongue-tied. Again I would hear the sweet rustle of a dress, and feel a warm hand on my head, and I knew that the rebel angel had rode her mule to town to see me. Then I would try hard to tell her that I was going to write a letter to the governor of Wisconsin, and ask him to look out particularly for her brother, who was a rebel prisoner at Madison, and take care of him if he was sick, but I couldn't say a word, and after smoothing my hair a little while, she would give my cheek three or four pats, just as a mother pats her child, and she would go away.

One morning, a little after daylight, I woke up and looked around the ward of the hospital. My eyes were weak, and I was hungry as a bear. I had to try two or three times before I could raise my hand to my head, and when I felt of my head it seemed awfully small. I could feel my cheek bones stick out so that you could hang your hat on them. My cheeks were sunken, and my fingers were like pipe-stems. I wondered how a man could change so in one night. I saw two or three fellows over at the other end of the room, and I thought I would get up and go over there and have some fun with them. I wanted to know where my horse was, and where I was. I tried to raise up and couldn't get any further than on my elbow.

From that position I looked around to see what was going on, and tried to attract the attention of some attendant. Finally, I saw four fellows bringing a stretcher along towards my cot. They had evidently been told by the doctor that I would be dead in the morning, and having confidence in the word of the professional man, had come to take me to the dead house, before the other sick man was awake. As they came up to the foot of my cot and sat the stretcher down, I thought I would play a joke on them. I pulled the sheet over my face, and laid still.

One of the men said, "Two of us can lift it, as it is thinner than a lathe." To be considered dead, when I was alive, was bad enough, but to be called "it" was too much. I felt one of the men take hold of my feet, and then I threw the sheet off my face and in a hoarse voice I said, "Say, Mr. Body-snotcher, you can postpone the funeral and bring me a porter-house steak and some fried potatoes." Well, nobody ever saw a couple of men fall over themselves and turn pale, as those fellows did. Before I had given my order for breakfast, the two men had fallen back over the stretcher and the two others were backing on as though a ghost had appeared.

But finally they came toward me and I convinced them that I was not dead. They seemed hurt to know that I was still alive, and one of them went off after the doctor, to enter a complaint, I supposed. The doctor soon came and he was the only one that seemed pleased at my recovery. He ordered some sort of gruel for me, but wouldn't let me have meat and things. I took the gruel under protest but it did strengthen me. I told the doctor I wanted him to send for my horse, because I wanted to go out with the boys, but he said he guessed I wouldn't go out with the boys very soon. He said I might sit up in bed a little while, and when I did so I found that I did not have my clothes on, but was clothed in a hospital night-gown, which was also used for a shroud for burial when a fellow died. He said Jim and the girl would be in about 10 o clock, as he had sent for them, and some of my comrades. I told him if I was going to entertain company, and give a reception, I wanted my pants on, as I was sure no gentleman could give a reception successfully without pants.

The doctor seemed sort of glad to see me taking an interest in human affairs again, and so he let me put my pants and jacket on. I got a butcher to shave me, and when ten o clock came I looked quite presentable for a skeleton. I was sitting up in bed, with a little round zinc frame looking-glass, noting the changes in my personal appearance, when a door opened and Jim entered, dressed up in his best, with the rebel angel on his arm, and followed by six boys from the regiment.

They came in as solemn as any party I ever saw. The angel looked as sad as I ever saw anybody, and I thought she had probably heard that her brother was dead. It did not occur to me that they had come to attend my funeral. They stood there by the door, in that helpless manner that people always stand around at a funeral, waiting for the master of ceremonies to tell them that they can now pass in the other room and view the remains.

I finally caught Jim looking my way, and I waved a handkerchief at him. He gave me one look, and jumped over two cots and came up to me with tears in his eyes, and a package in his hand, and said, "Pard, you ain't dead worth a cent," and then he hugged me, and added, "but there ain't enough left of you for a full size funeral." Then he unrolled the package he had in his hand, and dropped on the bed four silver-plated coffin handles. By that time the girl, and the six boys had seen me, and they came over, and we had a regular visit. They were all surprised to find me alive, as they had been notified that I was on my last legs, and would be buried in the morning, and the captain had detailed the six boys to act as pall-bearers and fire a salute over the grave, while Jim and the girl were to act as mourners.

"Well, it saves ammunition," said Jim. "But how be I going to get these coffin handles off my hands. There is no dependence to be placed on doctors, anyway. When that doctor appointed this funeral, we thought he knew his business, and I told the angel, say I, 'My pard ain't going to be buried without any style, in one of those pine boxes that ain't planed, and has got slivers on.' So I hired the hospital coffin-maker to sandpaper the inside and outside of a box, and black it with shoe-blacking, and I went to a store down town and bought these handles. Of course, pard, I am glad you pulled through, and all that, but I want to say to you, if you had croaked in the night, and been ready to bury this a. m., you would have had a more stylish outfit than anybody, except officers, usually get in this army, and the angel and I would have been a pair of mourners that would have slung grief so your folks to home would have felt proud of you."

The angel was tickled to see me alive, and suggested to Jim and the boys, that it was easy to talk a fellow to death after he had been so sick, and told them to go back to camp, and she would stay with me all day. So the boys shook hands with me, and Jim had an attendant to roll my cot up to a window, so I could see my horse when they rode away. The boys got on their horses and Jim led my horse, and I could see that my pet had been fixed up for the occasion. He had the saddle on, and it was draped with black, a pair of boots were fastened in the stirrups, and my carbine was in the socket. The idea was to have my horse, with empty boot and saddle tied behind the wagon that took me to the cemetery where soldiers wind up their career. It was not a cheerful thing to look at, and to think of, but it did me good to see the old horse, and the boys ride away in good health, and happy at my escape, and it encouraged me to make every effort to get well, so I could ride with the gang.

The rebel angel remained with me till almost night, and superintended my eating. No person who has never had a fever, can appreciate the appetite of a person when the fever "turns." I wanted everything that was ever eaten, and roast beef or turkey was constantly in my mind. As anything of that kind would have made use for Jim's coffin-handles, I had to put up with soups and gruels. The doctor thought that this thin gruel was good enough, but it didn't seem to hit the spot, and so the girl asked the doctor if he thought nice *gumbo* soup and a weak milk punch wouldn't be pretty good for me. He said it would, but nobody in the hospital could make *gumbo* soup, or milk punch.

She said she could, and she told me not to eat a thing until she came back, and she would bring me a dish fit for the gods. She said she knew an old coloured woman in town, who cooked for a lady friend of hers, who had some gumbo, and the lady had a little brandy that was seventy years old, but she said the lady was a rebel, and I must overlook that. I told her I didn't care, as I had got considerably mashed on all the rebels I had met personally. She went out with a smile that would have knocked a stronger man than I was silly, and I turned over and took a nap, the first real sleep I had had in a week. I woke up finally smelling something that was not gruel. O, I had got so sick of gruel.

The angel handed me a glass of milk punch, and told me to drink a swallow and a half. I have drank a great many beverages in my lifetime, but I never swallowed anything that was as good as the milk punch that rebel girl made for me. It seemed to go clear to my toes, and I felt strong. Then she gave me a small soup plate and told me to taste of the *gumbo*. I had never tasted *gumbo* soup before, but I had no difficulty in mastering it. No description can do *gumbo* soup justice, or explain to a person who has never tasted it the rich odour, and palatable taste. The little that I ate seemed to make a man of me again, instead of the weak invalid. Since then I have been loyal to southern *gumbo* soup, and have always eaten it wherever it could be obtained, and I never put a spoonful of it to my lips without thinking of the rebel girl in the hospital, who prepared that dish for me. If I ever become a glutton, it will be on *gumbo* soup, and if I am ever a drunkard, it will be a milk-punch drunkard, and the soup and the punch must be prepared in the South.

Well, my experience after that, in the hospital, was about the same as a hundred thousand other boys in blue, only few of the boys had such care, and such food. The girl kept me supplied with *gumbo* soup and milk punch until I could eat heartier food, and in a couple of days I got so I could walk around the hospital. At home I had never been much of a hand to be around with the sick, but experience had been a good teacher, and I found that going around among the boys, and talking cheerfully did them good and me too. I found men from my own regiment, that I did not know had been sick.

The custom was to make just as little show about sending sick men to the hospital, as possible, hence they were often packed off in the night, and the first their comrades would know of their illness would be a detail to bury them, or a boy would suddenly appear in his company, looking pale and sick, having been discharged from the hospital. If the men had known how many of their comrades were sent to the hospital, it would have demoralized the well ones. For ten days I visited around among the sick men, telling a funny story to a group here and cheering them up, and writing letters home for fellows that were too weak to write. I learned to lie a little bit in writing letters for the boys.

One young fellow who had his leg taken off, wanted me to write to his intended, and tell her all about it, how the leg was taken off, and how he was sick and discouraged, and would always be a cripple and a burden on his friends, etc. I wrote the letter entirely different from the way he told me. I spoke of his being wounded in the leg but that the care he received had made him all right, and that he would probably soon have a discharge, and be home, and make them all happy. I thought to myself that if she loved him as a girl ought to, that a leg or two short wouldn't make any difference to her, and there was no use of harrowing up her feelings in advance, and that he could buy a cork leg before he got home, and maybe she would never find it out.

I might have been wrong, but when he got an answer from that letter he was the happiest fellow I ever saw in this world, and he arranged at my suggestion, to stop over in New York and get a cork leg before he went home. I have never learned whether the girl ever found out that he had a cork leg, but if she did, and blames anybody, she can lay it to me. Lots of the boys that wrote letters for wanted to detail all of their calamities to their mothers and sisters and sweethearts, but I worded the letters in a funny sort of way, so that the friends at home would not be worried, and the answers the boys got would please them very much.

The hardest work I had was a couple of days writing letters for a doctor, to relatives of boys who had died, detailing the sickness, death and burial, and notifying friends that they could obtain the personal effects of the deceased, clothing, money, pipes, knives, etc., by sending express charges.

It always seemed to me that if I had been running the government I would have paid the express charges on the clothing of the boys who had died, if I didn't lay up a cent. Finally I got well enough to go back to my regiment, and one day I showed up at my company, and the first man I met saluted me and said, "Hello, Lieutenant." I told him he did wrong to joke a sick man that way, and I went on to find Jim. He was in our tent, greasing his shoes, and he looked up with a queer expression on his face and said, "Hello, Lieutenant."

"Look a here." I said, as I grasped his greasy hand, "what do you fellows mean by calling me names, I have never done anything to deserve to be made a fool of. Pard, what ails you anyway?"

"Didn't they tell you," said Jim, as he scraped the mud on his other shoe with a stick. "The colonel has sent your name to the governor of Wisconsin to be commissioned as second Lieutenant of the company. All the boys are tickled to death, and they are going to whoop it up for you when your commission comes. But this pup tent will not be good enough for you then, and old Jim will have to pick up another pard. You won't have to cook your bacon on a stick when you get your commission, and you can drink out of a leather covered flask instead of a flannel covered canteen. But by the great horn spoons I shall love you if you get to be a Jigadier Brindle," and the old pard looked as though he wanted to cry like a baby.

"Jim," I said, "I think the fellows are giving us taffy, and that there is nothing in this Lieutenant business. But if there is, you will be my pard till this cruel war is over, and don't you forget it," and I went along the company street towards the colonel's tent, leaning on a cane, and all the boys congratulated me, and I felt like a fool.

"Lieutenant, I am glad to see you back," said the Colonel, as I en-

153

tered his tent, and he showed it in his face. "What is the foolishness, colonel? I asked. The boys are all guying me. Can't I stay a private?"

CHAPTER 17

My First Day as a Commissioned Officer

The last chapter of this history wound up in my interview with the colonel, in which he told me that what the boys had said was true, and that I had a right to to be called "Lieutenant." He said there was a vacancy in the commissioned officers of my company, caused, by some discrepancy in regard to the ownership of a horse which an officer had sold as belonging to him, when investigation showed that there was "U. S." branded on the horse. The colonel said he had looked over the company pretty thoroughly, and while I was not all that he could desire in an officer, there were less objections to me than to many others, and he had recommended the governor of our state to commission me. He said he didn't want me to run away with the idea that my promotion from private to a commissioned office was for any particular gallantry, or that I was particularly entitled to promotion, but I seemed the most available.

It was true, he said, that I had done everything I had been told to do, in a cheerful manner, and had not displayed any cowardice, that he knew of, though I had often admitted to him that I was a coward. He said he thought few men knew whether they were cowards or not, until they got in a tight place, and that most men honestly believed they were cowards, but they didn't want others to know it, and they took pains to conceal the fact. He said he had rather be considered a coward than a dare-devil of bravery, for if he flunked when a chance come to show his metal, it wouldn't be thought much of, and if he pulled through, and made a decent record for bravery, he would get a heap of credit. He said he believed it took a man with more nerve to do some things he had ordered me to do, than it did to get behind

155

a tree and shoot at the enemy, and he was willing to take his chances on me. He congratulated me, and some of the other officers did the same.

I was invited to sit into a game of draw poker with some of the officers. I pleaded that I was not sufficiently recovered from my sickness to play poker, and I went back to my tent to talk with Jim. I was thinking over the new responsibilities that were about to come to me, and figuring on the salary. A hundred and fifty dollars a month! It is cruel to raise the salary of a poor devil from thirteen dollars a month to a hundred and fifty. I wondered how in the world the government was ever going to get that much out of me.

Certainly I couldn't do any more than I had been doing towards crushing the rebellion for thirteen dollars. And what would I do with so much money? In my wildest dreams of promotion I had never hoped to be a commissioned officer. I had thought sometimes, a week or two after I enlisted, that if I was a general I could put down the rebellion so quick the government would have lots of nations left on its hands to spoil, but a few months active service had taken all that sort of nonsense out of me, and I had been contented as a private.

But here I was jumped over everybody, and made an officer unbeknown to me, It made me dizzy. I was not very strong anyway, and this thing had come upon me suddenly I was thinking of the magnificent uniform I would have, and the fancy saddle and bridle, and the regular officer's tent, with bottles of whiskey and glasses, when Jim asked me if I wouldn't just hold that frying-pan of bacon over the fire, while he cooked some coffee. He said we would just eat a little to settle our stomachs, and then go out to Thanksgiving dinner.

"Thanksgiving dinner," I said. "What are you talking about?"

"Don't you know," said Jim, "today is Thanksgiving? The 'angel' told me last night to bring you out to the plantation today, and I was going after you at the hospital if you hadn't showed up. She has received a letter from her brother, who is a rebel prisoner at Madison, and he says a Yankee hotel-keeper at Madison, that you had written to, had called at the pen where they were kept, and had brought him a lot of turkey and fixings, and offered to send him a lot for Thanksgiving, so the rebel boys could have a big feed, and he says he is well and happy, and going to be exchanged soon. And she wants us to come out and eat turkey and possum. I had rather eat gray tom-cat than possum, but I told her we would come. So we will eat a little bacon and bread, and ride out."

"Well, all right Jim," I said. "We will go, but in my weak state I can't be expected to eat possum. If there is anything of that kind to be eat, Jim, you will have to eat it. However, I will do anything the rebel angel asks me to do," I added, remembering her kindness to me when I was sick.

The ride to the plantation, after several weeks confinement, was better than medicine, and I enjoyed every step my proud horse took. The animal acted as though he had been told of my promotion, but it was plain to me that he acted proud, because he had been resting during my sickness. It was all I could do to keep Jim alongside of me. He would fall back every little while and try to act like an orderly riding behind an officer. I had to discipline him before he would come up alongside like a "partner." I mention this Thanksgiving dinner in the army, in order to bring in a little advice the rebel girl gave me, which I shall always remember.

We arrived at the old plantation house where the girl and her mother and some servants were living, waiting for the war to close, so the men folks could come back. The old lady welcomed us cordially, the girl warmly and the servants effusively. The dinner was good, though not elaborate, except the possum. That was elaborate, and next to *gumbo* soup, the finest dish I ever tasted. After we had got seated at the table, the old lady asked a blessing, and it was more like a prayer. She asked for a blessing upon all of the men in both armies, and made us feel as though there was no bitterness in her heart towards the enemies of her people. During the dinner Jim told of my promotion, and the circumstance was commented on by all, and after dinner the rebel angel took me one side, and said she had got a few words of advice to give me. She commenced by saying:

Now that you are to be a commissioned officer, don't get the big head. During this war, we have had soldiers near us all the time, and I have seen some splendid soldiers spoiled by being commissioned. Nine out of ten men that have received commissions in this locality, have been spoiled. I am a few years older than you, and have seen much of the world. You are a kind hearted man, and desire to treat everybody well, whether rich or poor, Yankee or Confederate. If you let this commission spoil you, you are not worthy of it.

You will naturally feel as though you should associate with officers entirely, but you will find in them no better companions than you have found in the private soldiers, and I doubt if you will find as true friends. Do not, under any circumstances, draw away from your old friends, and let a barrier raise up between you and them. My observation teaches me that the only difference between the officers and men in the Union army, is that officers get more pay for doing less duty; they become dissipated and fast because they can better afford it, they drink more, put on style, play cards for money, and think the world revolves around them, and that they are indispensible to success, and yet when they die, or are discharged for cause, private soldiers take their place and become better officers than they did, until they in turn become spoiled. I can think of no position better calculated to ruin a young man than to commission him in a cavalry regiment.

Now take my advice. Do not run in debt for a new uniform and a silver mounted sword, and don't put a stock of whisky and cigars into your tent, and keep open house, because when your whisky and cigars are gone, those who drank and smoked them will not think as much of you as before, and you will have formed habits that will illy prepare you for your work. You will not make any friends among good officers, and you will lose the respect of the men who have known you when you were one of them, but who will laugh at you for getting the big head and going back on those who are just as good as you are, but who have not yet attained the dignity of wearing shoulder straps.

I meet officers every day, who were good soldiers before they were raised from privates, and they show signs of dissipation, and have a hard look, leering at women, and trying to look *blasé*. They try to act as near like foreign noblemen who are officers, as they can, from reading of their antics, but Americans just from farms, workshops, commercial pursuits, and the back woods and country villages of the north, are not of the material that foreign officials are made of, and in trying to imitate them they only show their shallowness. Do not, I beg of you, change one particle from what you have been as a private soldier, unless it is to have your pants fit better, and wear a collar. Of course, you will be thrown among officers more than you have before. Imitate their better qualities, and do not compete with them in vices.

Always remember that when a volunteer army is mustered out,

all are alike. The private, who has business ability, will become rich and respected, after the war, while the officer, who has been promoted through favouritism, and who acquires bad habits, will keep going downhill, and will be glad to drive a delivery wagon for the successful private, whom he commanded and snubbed when he held a proud position and got the big head. Now, my convalescent red-headed Yankee, you have the best advice, I know how to give a young man who has struck a streak of luck. Go back to your friends, and may God bless you.

Well, I had never had any such advice as that before, and as Jim and me rode back to camp that Thanksgiving evening, her words seemed to burn into my alleged brain. I could see how easy it would be for a fellow to make a spectacle of himself. What did a commission amount to, anyway, that a fellow should feel above anybody. When we arrived in camp, and went into our tent to have a smoke, the chaplain came in. I had not seen much of him lately. When I was sick I felt the need of a chaplain considerably. Not that I cared particularly to have him come and set up a howl over me, as though I was going to die, and he was expected to steer me the right way. But I felt as though it was his duty to look after the boys when they were sick, and talk to them about something cheerful.

But he did not show up when I needed him, and when he called at our tent after I was well, there wasn't that cordiality on my part that there ought to have been. He had a package which he unrolled, after congratulating me on my recovery, and it proved to be a new sabre, with silver mounted scabbard and gold sword handle. The chaplain said he had heard that I was to be commissioned, and he had found that sabre at a store down town, and thought I might want to buy it. He said of course I would not want to wear a common government sabre, as it would look too rude..He said he could get that sabre for forty dollars, dirt cheap, and I could pay for it when I got my first pay as an officer.

I could see through the chaplain in a minute. He had thought I would jump at the chance to put on style, and that he could make ten or fifteen dollars selling me a gilt-edged sabre. I thanked him warmly, and a little sarcastically, for his great interest in the welfare of my soul, in sickness and in health, but told him that I was going to try and pull through with a common private's sabre. I told him that the few people I should kill with a sabre, would enjoy it just as well to be run

159

through with a common sabre. My only object was to help put down the rebellion, and I could do it with ordinary plain cutlery, as well as silver-mounted trappings. I said that to smear a silver-mounted sabre all over with gore, would spoil the looks of it.

The chaplain went out, when a drummer for a tailor shop came in with some samples, and wanted to make up a new uniform for me, regardless of expense. I stood him off, and went to bed, tired, and thought I had rather be a private than a general. The next morning it was my turn to cook our breakfast, and I turned out and built a fire, cut off some salt pork, and was frying it, when the orderly sergeant came along and detailed Jim and me, with ten or a dozen others to go to work on the fortifications. The rebels were preparing to attack our position, and the commanding officer had deemed it advisable to throw up some earthworks. I told the orderly that he couldn't detail me to work with a shovel, digging trenches, when I was an officer, but he said he could, until I received my commission and was mustered in. I left my cooking and went to the colonel's tent. He was just rolling out of his bunk, and I said:

"How is it, Colonel? Can an officer be detailed to go and shovel dirt? I have been detailed by the orderly, with a lot of privates, to re-port to the engineer, to throw up fortifications. That does not strike me as proper work for a commissioned officer."

"You will have to go," said the colonel, as he stood on one leg while he tried to lasso his other foot with a pants leg. "It may be three months before your commission will arrive, and then you will have to go to New Orleans to be mustered out as a private and mustered in as an officer. Until that time you will have to do duty as a private."

"Then what the devil did you say anything about my being com-missioned for, until the commission got here," said I, and I went back and finished cooking breakfast for myself and Jim.

Our detail went down to the river, at the left of the line, and reported to the engineer, and were set to work cutting down trees, throwing up dirt, and doing about the dirtiest and hardest work that I had ever done. As a private I could have done anything that was asked of me, but the thought of doing such work, while all the boys were calling me "Lieutenant," was too much. I never was so crushed in my life. How glad I was that I did not buy that gilt-edged sabre of the chaplain.

We had to wear our side arms while at work, fearing an attack at any minute, and I thought how ridiculous I would have looked with that silver-mounted sabre hanging to me, while I was handling a shovel like a railroad labourer. If that detail was made to humiliate me, and reduce my proud flesh, that had appeared on me by my sudden promotion, it had the desired effect, for before night I was as humble an amateur officer as ever lived. I had chopped down trees until my hands were blistered, and had shovelled dirt until my back was broke, and at night returned to my tent too tired to eat supper, and went to bed too weary and disgusted to sleep. And that was my first day as a commissioned officer.

CHAPTER 18

We Have a Grand Attack

I became satisfied, more each day, that my sickness, and experience in the hospital, had spoiled me for a soldier. Being attended to so kindly by a rebel girl and getting acquainted with her people, and hearing her mother pray earnestly that the bloodshed might cease, sort of knocked what little fight there was in me, out, and I didn't hanker any more for blood. It seemed to me as though I could meet any rebel on top of earth, and shake hands with him, and ask him to share my tent, and help eat my rations.

The fact of being promoted to a commissioned office, didn't make me feel half as good as I thought it was going to, and I found myself wishing I could be a he sister of charity, or something that did not have to shoot a gun, or go into any fight. I got so I didn't care whether my commission ever arrived or not. The idea of respectable men going out to hunt each other, like game, became ridiculous to me, and I wondered why the statesmen of the North and South did not get together and agree on some sort of a compromise, and have the fighting stop. I would have agreed to anything, only, of course, whatever arrangement was made, it must be understood that the South had no right to secede.

Then I would think, why, that is all the South is fighting for, and if they concede that they are wrong it is the same as though they were whipped, and of course they could not agree to that. I tried to think out lots of ways to wind the business up without fighting any more, but all the plans I made, maintained that our side was right, and I concluded to give up worrying about it. But I made up my mind that I would not fight any more. I was still weak from sickness, and there was no fight in me. I thought this over a good deal, and concluded that if I was called upon to go into another fight, where there was any chance of anybody being killed, I would just have a relapse, and go to the hospital again till it was over.

I had heard of fellows being taken suddenly ill when a fight was in prospect, and I knew they were always laughed at, but I made up my mind that I had rather be laughed at than to hurt anybody. There was no thought of sneaking out of a fight because of the danger of being killed myself, but I just didn't want to shoot any friends of that girl who had nursed me when I was sick. These thoughts kept coming to me for a week or more, and one evening it was rumoured around that we were liable to be attacked the next day. Some of our regiments had been out all day, and they reported the enemy marching on our position, in force.

The rebels that lived in town could not conceal their joy at the idea that we were to be cleaned out. They would hint that there were enough Confederates concentrating at that point to drive every Yankee into the river, and they were actually preparing bandages and lint, to take care of the Confederates who might be wounded. If we had taken their word for it there wouldn't be a Yankee left in town, when the Confederate boys begun to get in their work. I went to bed that night resolved that I should not be so well in the morning, and would go to surgeon's call, and be sent to the hospital. But I didn't like the way those rebels talked about the coming fight. Egad, if they were so sure our fellows were going to be whipped, maybe I would stay and see about it.

If they thought any of our fellows were going to slink out, when they made their brags about whipping us, they would find their mistake. However, if I didn't feel very well in the morning, I would go to surgeon's call, but I wouldn't go to the hospital. In the meantime, I would just see if I had cartridges enough for much of a row, and rub up the old carbine a little, for luck. Not that. I wanted to shoot anybody dead, but I could shoot their horses, and make the blasted rebels walk, anyway. And so all that evening I was part of the time trying to see my way clear to get out of a regular fight, where anybody would be liable to get hurt, and again I was wondering if my sickness had injured my eyesight so I couldn't take good aim at the buttons on a rebel's coat. I was about half and half.

If the rebels would let us alone, and not bring on a disturbance, I was for peace at any price, but god-blast them, if they come fooling around trying to scare anybody, I wouldn't go to a hospital, not much. I talked with Jim about it, and he felt about as I did. He didn't want any more fighting, and while he couldn't go to the hospital, he was going to try and get detailed to drive a six mule team for the quartermaster, but he cleaned up his gun all the same, and looked over his cartridges to see if they were all right. We got up next morning, got our breakfast, and Jim asked me if I was going to the hospital and I told him I would wait till afternoon. I asked him if he was going to drive mules, and he said not a condemned mule, not until the fight was over. There was a good deal of riding around, orderlies, staff officers, etc.

Artillery was moving around, and about eight o clock some of our boys who had been on picket all night, came in looking tired and nervous, saying they had been shot at all night, and that the rebels had got artillery and infantry till you couldn't rest, and they would make it mighty warm for us before night. Orders come to each company, that no soldier was to leave camp under any circumstances, to go to town or anywhere. I told Jim if he was going to drive mules, he better be seeing the quartermaster sergeant, but he said he never was much gone on mule driving, anyhow. But he said if he looked as sick as I did he would go to the hospital too quick. I told him there wasn't anything the matter with me.

Pretty soon, over to the right, near the river, there was a cannon discharged. It was not long before another went off around to the left, and then a dozen, twenty, a hundred, all along the line. They were rebel cannon, and pretty soon they were answered by our batteries. Then there was a rattling of infantry, and the noise was deafening. I expected at the first fire that our bugler would come out in front of headquarters and blow for heaven's sake, for us to saddle up, but for three hours we loafed around camp and no move was made. It was tiresome. We started to play cards several times, but nobody could remember what was trumps, and we gave that up.

Some of our boys would sneak up on to a hill for a few minutes, against orders, and come back and say that they could see the fight, and it was which and tother. Then a few more would sneak off, and after awhile the whole regiment was up on the hill, looking off to the hills and valleys, watching rebel shells strike our earth works and throw up the dust, and watching our shells go over to the woods where the rebels were. Then I found myself hoping our shells were just paralyzing the Johnnies. Presently the ambulances began to come by us, loaded with wounded, and that settled it.

When there was no fighting, and I was half sick, and felt under obligations to a Confederate girl for taking care of me, I didn't want any of her friends hurt, but when her friends forgot themselves, and come to a peaceable place, and began to kill off our boys, friendship ceased, and I wondered why we didn't get orders to saddle up and go in. We were all on the hill watching things, when the colonel, who had been riding off somewhere, came along. We thought he would order us all under arrest for disobeying orders, but he rode up to us, and pointing to a place off to the right a mile or so, where there was a sharp infantry fight, he said, "Boys, we shall probably go in right there about 3 p.m., unless the rebels are reinforced," and he rode down to his tent.

Well, after about twenty ambulances had gone by us with wounded soldiers, we didn't care how soon we went in there. We watched the infantry and artillery for another hour, as pretty a sight as one often sees. It was so far away we could not see men fall, and it was more like a celebration, until one got near enough to see the dead. Presently the regimental bugle sounded "Boots and saddles," and in a minute every man on the hill had rushed down to his tent, even before the notes had died away from the bugle.

Nothing was out of place. Every soldier had known that the bugle *would* sound sooner or later, and we had everything ready. It did not seem five minutes before every company was mounted, in its street, waiting for orders. Jim leaned over towards me and said, "Hospital?" and I answered, "Not if I know myself," and I patted my carbine on the stock.

I said to him, "Six mule team?" and he whispered back, "Nary six mule team for the old man." Then the bugle sounded the "Assembly," and each company rode up on to the hill and formed in regimental front facing the battle. Every eye was on the place where the colonel had said we would probably "go in." There never was a more beautiful sight, and every man in the cavalry regiment looked at it till his eyes ached. Then came an order to dismount and every man was ordered to tighten up his saddle girth as tight as the horse would bear it, and be sure his stirrup straps were too short rather than too long. To a cavalry man these orders mean business.

Then we mounted again, and a few noticed a flag off to the right signalling. The colonel noticed it and coolly gave the order, "fours right, march." We went off towards the fighting, then right down by our own cannon and formed in line behind the infantry, that was at work with the enemy, the artillery firing over our heads at the confederates in the woods. The noise was so loud that one could not hear his neighbour speak; but above it all came a bugle note, and glancing to the left, another cavalry regiment, and another, formed on our left. Another bugle note, and to the right another cavalry regiment formed, and for half a mile there was a line of horsemen, deafened by the waiting the command of some man, through a bugle. If the rebels had time to notice those four regiments of cavalry, fresh and ready for a gallop, they must have known that it was a good time to get away. Finally, our artillery ceased firing and it seemed still as death, except for the rattling of infantry in front of us.

The rebel artillery had ceased firing also, and a great dust beyond the woods showed that they were getting away. The bugle sounded "forward" and that line of cavalry started on a walk. The infantry in front ceased firing, and went to the right of us at a double-quick, and the field was clear of our men. While our cavalry was walking, they kept a pretty good line, each man glancing to the right for a guide.

As we neared the place where our infantry had been stationed, it was necessary to break up a little to pass dead and wounded without riding over them, and when falling back to keep from hurting a wounded comrade, a look at the line up and down showed that it was almost a mob, with no shape, but after geting forty rods, we passed the field where men had fallen, and the order to "close up, guide right," was given, and in an instant the line was perfect. Then came the order to trot, and we went a short distance, until the rebels could be plainly seen behind trees, logs, and in line, firing.

We halted and fired a few rounds from carbines, and then dropped the carbines, on orders. For a moment nothing was done, when officers ordered every man to draw his revolver, and when the six charges had been fired, after nearing the enemy, to drop the revolver in the holster, and draw sabres, and every man for himself, but to rally on the colours, at the sound of the bugle, and not to go too far. Talk about being sick, and going to the hospital, or driving mules! Coward as I was, and I knew it, there was something about the air that made me feel that I wouldn't be in the hospital that day for all the money in the world. All idea of being sorry for the enemy, all charity, all hope that the war might close before any more men were killed, was gone.

After looking in the upturned faces of our dead and wounded on the field, the more of the enemy that were killed the better. It is thus that war makes men brutal, while in active service. They think of things and do things that they regret immediately after the firing ceases. The next ten minutes was the nearest thing to hell that I ever experienced, and it seemed as though my face must look like that of a fiend. I felt like one. The bugle sounded "forward," and then there was an order to trot, and the revolver firing began, with the enemy so near that you could see their countenances, their eyes.

Some of them were mounted, others were on foot, some on artillery caissons, and all full of fight. It did not take long to exhaust the revolvers, and then the sabres began to come out, and the horrible word "charge," came from a thousand throats, and every soldier yelled like a Comanche Indian, the line spread out like a fan, and every soldier on his own hook. Sabres whacked, horses run, everybody yelled. Men said "I surrender," "What you jabbing at me for when I ain't fighting no moah," "Drop that gun, you Johnnie, and go to the rear." Ones of pain and anguish, and awful sounds that a man ought never to hear but once. The business was all done in ten minutes.

Many of our men were killed and wounded, and many of theirs were treated the same way. Those who could get away, got, and those we passed without happening to hit them, were prisoners, because the infantry followed and took them back to the rear. Jim and me stayed as near together as possible, and we noticed one young Confederate on a mule. His left arm was hanging limp by his side, and as Jim passed on one side of him and I on the other, he said, as he held up his right hand, "I dun got enough, and I surrender." The thing was about over, the bugle having sounded the "recall," and we turned and went back with this Confederate.

He was as handsome a boy as ever fired a gun, and while he was pale from his shattered left arm, and weak, he said, "You gentlemen are all fine riders, sir. You fought as well as Southern men, sir." That was a compliment that Jim and me acknowledged on behalf of the northern army. He couldn't have paid our regiment a higher compliment if he had studied a week.

Then he said: "I was a fool to be in this fight. I was a prisoner and was only exchanged last week. I might have remained at home on a furlough, but when our army came along yesterday, and the boys said there was going to be a fight, I took my sisters mule, the only animal on the place, and came along, and now I am a cripple."

I looked at the mule, and I said to Jim, in a whisper, "I hope to die if it isn't the angel's mule. That must be her brother."

Jim was going to ask him what his name was, when we neared the place, where our regiment was forming and the surgeon of our regiment came along, and I said, "Doc, I wish you would take this young fellow and fix up his arm nice. He is a friend of mine. Take him to our regimental hospital."

Then we went back to the regiment, the prisoners were taken away, and after marching around through the woods for an hour we rode back to our camp, and the battle was over. Two or three hours later I went over to the regimental hospital and found the black-eyed confederate with his arm dressed, and he was talking with our boys as though he belonged there. Someone asked how he happened to be there, and the old doctor said he believed he was a relative of one of our officers. Anyway he was going to stay there. I gave him a bunch of sutler cigars, and left him, and an hour later the "angel" showed up, pale as death, and wanted someone to go with her to the battle held to help find the body of her dead brother.

She said he had arrived home from the North the morning before, and had gone into the fight, and when the Confederates came back, defeated, past their plantation, her brother was not among them, and she knew he was dead. I have done a great many things in my life that have given me pleasure, but no one that I remember of that made me quite so happy as I was to escort the girl who had been so kind to me, to the hospital where her brother was.

His wound was not serious, and he sat on a box, smoking a cigar, telling the boys the news from Wisconsin. He had just come from there, where he was a prisoner, and he couldn't talk enough about the kindness of the "people of the nowth." His sister almost fainted when she found him alive, then hugged him until I was afraid she would disturb his arm, and then she sat by him and heard him tell of his visit to Wisconsin. Before night he was allowed to go home with his sister on parole, and Jim and I were detailed to go and help bury the dead of the regiment.

CHAPTER 19

I am Covered with Red Mud

After the battle alluded to in my last chapter, it took us a week or more to get brushed up, the dead buried, and everything ready to go to living again. A battle to a regiment in the field is a good deal like a funeral in a family at home. When a member of a family is sick unto death, all looks dark, and when the sick person dies it seems as though the world could never look bright again. Every time the relatives and friends look at any article belonging to a deceased friend, the agony comes back, and it is quite a while before there is any brightness anywhere, but in time the tear-stained faces become smiling, the lost friend is thought of only occasionally, and the world moves along just the same. So in the army. For a few days the thought of comrades being gone forever, was painful, and no man wanted to ride the horse whose owner had been killed, but within a week the feeling was all gone, and if a horse was a good one he didn't stay in the corral very long on account of some good fellow having been shot off his back.

The boys who couldn't remember what was trumps on the day of the battle—(and a soldier has got to be greatly interested in something else to forget what is trumps) returned to their card-playing, and no one would know, to look at them, that they had passed through a pretty serious scare, and seen their comrades fall all around. We told stories of our experience in the army and at home, and entertained each other. I couldn't tell much, except what a good shot I was with a shotgun and rifle, and I told some marvellous stories about hitting the bull's eye.

It got to be tiresome waiting around for my commission to arrive, and I did not quite enjoy being a commissioned high private. Everybody knew I had been recommended for a commission, and they all called me "Lieutenant," but all the same I was doing duty as a private.

For two or three clays I was detailed to drive mules for the quarter-master, and that was the worst service I ever did perform. It seemed as though the colonel wanted to prepare me for any service that in the nature of things I was liable to be called upon to perform. I kicked some at being detailed to drive a six-mule team, but the colonel said I might see the time when I could save the government a million dollars by being able to jump on to a wheel mule and drive a wagon loaded with ammunition, or paymaster's cash, out of danger of being captured by the enemy.

So I went to work and learned to gee-haw a six-mule team of the stubbornest mules in the world, hauling bacon, but there was no romance in taking care of six mules that would kick so you had to put the harness on them with a pitchfork, for fear of having your head kicked off. If I ever get a pension it will be for my loss of character and temper in driving those mules. I have been in some dangerous places, but I was never in so dangerous a place, in battle, as I was one day while driving those mules. One of the lead mules got his forward foot over the bridle some way, and I went to fix it, and the team started and "straddled" me.

As soon as I saw that I was between the two lead mules, and that the team had started, I knew my only-safety was in laying down and taking the chances of the three pairs of mules and wagon going straight over me. To attempt to get out would mix them all up, so I fell right down in the mud, which was about a foot deep, and just like soft mortar. As the mules passed on each side of me, every last one of them kicked at me, and I was under the impression that each wheel of the wagon kicked at me, but I escaped everything except the mud, and when I got up on my feet behind the wagon, the quartermaster, who was ahead on horseback, had stopped the team.

He called a coloured man to drive, and told me I could go back to the regiment. I tried to sneak in the back way, and not see anybody, but when I passed the chaplain's tent a lot of officers, who had been sampling his sanitary stores, come out, and one of them recognized me, and they insisted on my stopping and talking something with them. Honestly, there was not an inch of my clothing but was covered with, red mud, that every soldier remembers who has been through Alabama. They had fun with me for half an hour and then let me go. I have never been able to look at a mule since, without a desire to kill it.

I had said so much about my marksmanship with a rifle, that one day I was sent for by the colonel. He said he had heard I was a crack shot with the rifle, and I admitted that I was a pretty good shot. He asked me if I could hit a man's eye every time at ten paces. I told him I was almost sure I could. He said he had a duty that must be performed by some man that was an excellent shot, and I might report at once with forty rounds of ammunition. I don't know when I had been any more startled than I was at the colonel's questions, and his manner.

Could it be that he had some secret expedition of murder that he wanted to send me on. I had never deliberately aimed at a man's eye, and if there was anybody to be killed I would be no hand to do it in cold blood. It seemed as though I had rather give anything than to kill a man, but that was evidently the business the colonel had in his mind. Was it a lot of prisoners that were to be killed in retaliation for some of our men who had been treated badly by the enemy. I reported shortly, with my carbine and forty cartridges, and the colonel told me to go to a certain place on the bank of the river, a mile away, and report to the chaplain, who would be there to see that everything was done properly.

Then when I started off I heard the colonel say to the adjutant that there were about forty to be killed, and while it seemed cruel, it had to be done, and he hoped they would suffer as little as possible. If I could have had my way, I wouldn't have gone a step. I reflected on the pained look on the colonel's face, and wondered why I was picked out for all these sad events, but I thought if the chaplain was there everything would be all right. Arriving at the placed I found the chaplain sitting on a stump, on a big bluff overlooking the river. He sighed as I came up and said:

"Death is always a sad thing."

I told him that no one appreciated it more than I did, and I sighed also.

"But," said he, as he took a chew of navy plug tobacco, "when death is necessary, we should make it as painless as possible, I have been studying this matter over a good deal, and trying to figure out how to make the death the least painful to these poor victims, and it has occurred to me that if we place them on the edge of the precipice, and you shoot them through the brain, while at the same time I push them, they will fall down a hundred feet into the river, and if they are not killed instantly by having the brain blown out, they will certainly drown. How does that strike you?"

I thought the chaplain was about the most heartless cuss I ever heard talk about killing people, but I said that seemed to me to be the best way, but a cold chill went over me as I thought of shooting anybody through the head and the chaplain pushing him down the cliff into the water. I was just going to ask him what the men had done, when he said:

"Ah, there they come."

I looked, and a lot of coloured men were leading about forty old back-number horses and mules, afflicted with glanders and other diseases.

"Are the niggers to be killed?" I asked.

"Naw," said the chaplain. "The horses and mules."

I was never so relieved in all my life as I was when I found that my excellent marksmanship was to be expended on animals instead of human beings. But I did feel hurt, the idea of a brevet officer, a man qualified to do deeds of daring, being detailed one day to drive mules and the next-to shoot sick horses. But I decided to do whatever I had to do, well, and so preparations were made for the executions.

The glandered horses were brought out first, and then the ones with sore backs. Many of them were first-rate horses, their only fault being sores made from the saddles, and as it would take months to cure them up, and as the army was going to move soon, it had been decided to kill them rather than leave them to fall into the enemy's hands, or take them along to be cured on the march. I shot about a dozen glandered horses, that being the largest game I had ever killed, and the bodies fell down into the river. Then there was a mule that was ugly, and it occurred to me I would have some fun with the chaplain.

We were outside the lines, and quite a number of men had gathered from the plantations, on hearing the firing, to see what was up. I suggested to the chaplain that it was a shame to kill so many good horses, when they might be of use to some of the planters, but he said they were all rebels, and it was not the policy of the government to set them up in business, by giving them horses to use tilling crops. I argued that the men had come home from the confederate army—this was in 1864—either discharged for wounds or disability, or paroled prisoners, and they were anxious to go to work, but that they hadn't a dollar, and our army had skinned every horse and mule on their places, and the niggers had gone, so that a horse would be a God-send to them.

But the chaplain wouldn't hear to it. The men, who had collected, were mostly too proud to ask for a horse from a Yankee, but I could see that they did not like to see the animals killed. I thought if I could get the chaplain, who had been sent out to the execution as a sort of humane society, to see that the animals were killed easy, to go back to camp and leave me alone with the horses, I could kill them or not, as I chose.

They brought out the ugly mule next, and my idea was to shoot the mule through the tip of the ear, while the chaplain stood near with a rail to push it over the bank, and maybe the mule would flax around and kick the chaplain up a tree, or scare him so he would leave. I took deliberate aim at the mule's ear, told the chaplain to push hard with the rail so the corpse would be sure to go over the cliff, and fired. Well, I have never seen such a scene in all my life. The mule seemed to squat down, when the bullet hit the top of his ear, then he brayed so loud that it would raise your hat right off your head, then he jumped into the air and whirled around and kicked in every direction with all four feet at once, fell down and rolled over towards the chaplain, and got up, and seeming to think the chaplain was the author of the misery, started for him, and that good man dodged behind trees until he got a chance to climb up one, which he did, and sat on a limb and shook his fist at the mule and me.

He used quite strong language at me for not killing the animal dead. Finally the niggers caught the mule and the chaplain dismounted from the limb, and came to me. I told him my carbine was out of order, and I should have to take it apart and fix it, and that there was no knowing whether it would shoot where I aimed it or not, after it was fixed, and I might have trouble with the rest of the horses. It would take an hour at least to fix the gun. He said he guessed he would go back to camp, and leave me to finish up the slaughter, and that was what I wanted.

The coloured men were anxious to go back too, so I let them tie the horses to trees, and all go back except one, whom I knew. After they had all gone I went up to the dozen southern men who had been watching the proceedings, and asked one who was called colonel by the rest, if he didn't think it was wrong to kill the horses when by a little care they could be of much use in tilling crops. "Well, sah," said he with dignity. "If it is not disloyalty, sah, for a southern gentleman to criticize anything that a Yankee does, I should say, sah, that it was a d——d shame, sah, to steal our horses, and after using them up, sah, kill them in cold blood, sah. Each one of those animals sah, would be a gold mine, sah, at this time, to us who have come from the wah, sah, destitute, with nothing but our bare hands to make a crop, to keep our families from want, sah."

The other gentlemen nodded at what the colonel had said, as though that was about their sentiments. I told him that I felt about that way myself, but there was an objection. If I gave the horses away, for use on the plantations, and the animals should be used hereafter in the confederate army, it would not only be wrong, but I would be liable to be dismissed from the army.

The colonel said he should want to be dismissed from the Yankee army if he was in it, but I might feel different about it. But he said he would pledge me his word as a Southern gentleman, that if the animals could be lent to them, they should never be used for war purposes. He said he was poor, and his friends there were poor, but they would not take a horse as a gift from a stranger, but if I would lend them the horses for a year, they would use them, and return them to the proper officer a year hence, if the army was yet in existence, or they would take them in exchange for horses that had previously been stolen from them by our army. He said there was not a gentleman present but had lost from two to a dozen horses since the army had been in their vicinity. I admired the dignity and honesty of the old gentleman, and I knew mighty well that we had picked up every horse we could find, and I said:

"Colonel, here are about thirty horses I have been ordered to kill. If I do not kill them I take a certain responsibility. I feel under obligations to many Southern people for courtesies, and I feel that the nursing I received during a recent sickness, from one of your Southern ladies, about the same as saved my life. I believe the war is very near over, and that neither you nor our men will have occasion for much more active service. You have come home to your desolate plantations, and found everything gone. This is the fate of war, but it is unpleasant all the same. If you can use these animals for your work, in raising crops, you may take them in welcome, and if there is any cussing, I will stand it.

"My advice would be to take them to some isolated place on your plantation, and keep them out of sight for a time. Our army will move within a week, and perhaps never come back here. The animals are branded 'U. S.' which will always remain. If the horses are found in your possession, later, you may have to say that they were given to you by an agent of the quartermaster. If they are taken from you, grin and bear it. If you are permitted to keep them, and they do you any good, I shall be very glad. If I get hauled over the coals for giving aid and comfort to the enemy, I will lie out of it some way, or stand my punishment like a little man. The horses are yours, as far as I am concerned."

"Well, sah, you are a perfect gentleman, sah," said the colonel, as he took my hand and shook it cordially. "And I should be proud to entertain you at my place, sah. We have got little left, sah, but you are welcome to our home at any time. I am an old man, with a bullet in my leg. Two of my boys are dead, in Virginia, sah, and I have one boy who is a prisoner at the north. If he comes home alive, we will be able to make a living and have a home again. The war has been a terrible blow to us all, sah. I reckon both sides, sah, have got about enough, and both sides have made cussed, fools of themselves. When this affair is settled, sah, the north and south will be better friends than ever, sah. I wish you a long life, sah."

The other gentlemen expressed thanks, and they picked out two or three horses apiece and led them away, it seemed to me as happy a lot of gentlemen as I ever saw. I called the coloured man, and we started for camp. For a five dollar bill, and a promise to always take a deep interest in the coloured man's welfare, I got his promise that he would never tell anybody about my giving the horses away, and for nearly a year he kept his promise. I went back to headquarters and reported that the animals had been disposed of, and that evening I was invited to set into a poker game with some of the officers, and when we got up I had won over a hundred dollars. I looked upon the streak of luck as a premium for my kindness to the gentlemen who took the horses, but some of the officers seemed to have a suspicion that I concealed cards up my sleeve. It is thus that the best of us are misunderstood.

CHAPTER 20

I Cause a General Stampede

When I went away from the party of officers, where we had been playing draw-poker, with a hundred dollars in my pocket, which I had won from men who thought they were pretty good poker players, I felt as though I owned the earth. I had my hand in my pocket, hold of the roll of greenbacks, and in that way constantly realized that I was no common pauper. I had never thought that I was an expert at cards, but this triumph convinced me that there was more money to be made playing poker than in any other way. I figured up in my mind that if I could win a hundred dollars a night, and only played five nights a week, I could lay up two thousand dollars a month. To keep it up a year would make me rich, and if the war lasted a couple of years I could go home with money enough to buy out the best newspaper in Wisconsin.

It is wonderful what a train of thought a young man's first success in gambling, or speculation, brings to him. I went to bed with my hundred dollars buttoned inside my flannel shirt, and dreamed all night about holding four aces, full hands, and three of a kind. All that night, in my sleep, I never failed to "fill" when I drew to a hand. I made up my mind to break every officer in the regiment, at poker, and then turn my attention to other regiments, and win all the money the paymaster should bring to the brigade. I got up in the morning with a headache, and thought how long it would be before night, when we could play poker again, and I wondered why we couldn't play during the day, as there was nothing else going on. It got rumoured around the regiment that I had cleaned the officers out at poker the night before, and the boys seemed glad that a private had made them pay attention. I had not yet got my commission, and so any victory I might achieve was considered a victory for a private soldier.

Several of the boys congratulated me. The nearest I ever come to quarrelling with my old partner, Jim, was over this poker business. I showed him my roll, and told him how I had cleaned the officers out, and instead of feeling good over it, Jim said I was a confounded fool. I tried to argue the matter with Jim, but he couldn't be convinced, and insisted that they had made a fool of me, and had let me win on purpose, and that they would win it all back, and all I had besides. He said I had better let the chaplain take the hundred dollars to keep for me, and stay away from that poker game, and I would be a hundred ahead, but I didn't want any second-class chaplain to be a guardian over me, and I told Jim I was of age, and could take care of myself. Jim said he thought I had some sense before I was commissioned, but it had spoiled me. He said in less than a week I would be borrowing money of him.

I knew better, and went around camp with my thumbs stuck in my armholes, and felt big. It was an awful long day, but I put in the time thinking how I would draw cards, and bet judiciously, and finally night came, and I went over to the major's tent, where the officers usually congregated. I was early, and had to wait half an hour before the crowd showed up. As they came in each had something to say to me. "Here's the man who walked off with our wealth last night," said one. "Here's our victim," said another. "We will send him to his tent tonight without a dollar." They chaffed me a good deal, but I made up my mind that I could play as well as they could, and some of them were old fellows that had played poker before I was born. Well, we went to work, and the first hand I got I lost ten dollars. It was the history of all smart Aleck's, and there is no use of going into details. In less than an hour they had won the hundred dollars, and fifty that I had sewed inside my shirt to keep for a rainy day, and they had joked me every time I bet until I was exasperated to such an extent that I could have killed them.

Winning or losing money with them was a mere pastime, and they seemed to enjoy losing about as much as winning. I was too proud, or too big a fool to leave the game when I had lost all I had, and I borrowed a little of each of them, and lost it, and then I said I was tired and I guessed I would go to bed, and I went out, dizzy and sick at heart, and the officers laughed so I could hear them clear to my tent. On the way to my tent, and as I walked around for half an hour before going there, I thought over what a fool I was, how I had forgotten all the good advice ever given me by my friends.

Knowing that I was not intended by nature for a gambler, I had gone in with my eyes open, made a temporary success, got the big head, as all boys do, and gone back and laid down my bundle, and become the laughing stock of the whole crowd. I figured up that I was just an even hundred dollars out of pocket, and decided that I would never try to get it back. I would simply swear off gambling right there, forget that I knew one card from another, pay up my gambling debts when I got my first pay, and never touch a card again.

That was the wisest conclusion that I ever come to. After I had walked around until my head cleared off a little, I went in the tent sly and still, to go to bed without letting Jim hear me. I was ashamed, and didn't want to talk. I heard Jim roll over on his bunk, and he said:

"Bet ten dollars, pard, that you lost all you had."

"Jim, I won't bet with you. I have sworn off betting intirely."

"Help yourself," said Jim, as he reached over his greasy old pocketbook to me. "Take all you want, now that you have come to your senses. But you must admit that what I said about your being a fool, was true."

"Yes, and an idiot, and an ass," I said, as I handed back Jim's money. "But that settles it. I will never gamble another cent's worth as long as I live, and if I see a friend of mine gambling, I will try and break him of the habit. There is nothing in it, and I went to sleep, and didn't dream any more about winning all the money in camp."

Two days before Christmas our cavalry, consisting of a full brigade, started on a raid, or a march through the enemy's country, and as I could not act as an officer very well, before my commission arrived, and as the colonel seemed to hate to see me in the ranks when I was looked upon as an officer, he sent me to brigade headquarters on a detail to carry the brigade colours. The brigade colours consisted of a blue guidon, on a pole. The butt end of the pole, or staff, was inserted in a socket of leather fastened to my stirrup, and I held on to the staff with my right hand when on the march, guiding my horse with my left hand, When the command halted the colours were planted in the ground in front of the place which the brigade commander had selected.

On the march I rode right behind the brigade commander and his staff, with the body guard to protect the precious colours. I was glad of this position, because it took me among high officials, and if there was anything I doted, on it was high officers. The colonel had told me that I must be on my good behaviour, and salute the officers of the staff, whenever they came near me. He said the brigade commander was a strict disciplinarian, and wouldn't put up with any monkey business. The first hour of my service as colour bearer came near breaking up the brigade. I was perhaps forty feet behind the brigade commander and his staff, riding as stiff as though I was a part of the horse, and feeling as proud as though I owned the army. Suddenly the colonel and staff turned out of the road, and faced to the rear, and started to ride back to one of the regiments in the rear. I saw them coming, and felt that I must salute them.

How to do it was a puzzle to me. If I saluted with my left hand, it would be wrong, besides I would have to drop the reins, and my horse might start to run, as he was prancing and putting on as much style as I was. If I saluted with my right hand, I should have to let go the flag staff. The salute must be sudden, so I could grasp the staff very quick, before it toppled over. It took a great head to decide what to do, and I had to decide quick. Just as the brigade commander got opposite me I let go the flag staff, brought my right hand quickly to the right eye, as nice a salute as a man ever saw, and returned it to grab the flag staff. But it was too late.

As soon as my right hand let go of the staff, it fell over and the gilt dart on the end of the staff struck the general's horse in the flank, he jumped sideways against the adjutant-general's horse, and his horse fell over the brigade surgeon's horse, the general's horse run under a tree, and brushed the general off, and the whole staff was wild trying to hold their horses, and jumping to catch the general's horse, and pick the general off the ground. In the meantime my horse had got frightened at the staff and flag that was dragging on the ground, with one end in the socket in the stirrup, the pole tickling him in the ribs, and he began to dance around, and whirl, and knock members of the colour-guard off their horses, and they stampeded to the woods leaving me in the road, on a frightened horse, whirling around, unmanageable, the start striking trees and horses, until the staff was broken.

The regiment in the rear of us saw the commotion, saw the general dismounted, and the colours on the ground, and a general stampede in front, and, thinking the general and staff had been ambushed by the rebels, and many killed, the colonel ordered his men forward on a charge, and, in less time than it takes to write it, the woods were full of charging soldiers, looking for an imaginary enemy, a surgeon had opened up a lot of remedies, and all was confusion, and I was the innocent cause of it all. I had seen my mistake as soon as the flag staff knocked the general off his horse, and when I dismounted and picked up the flag, and the pieces of the staff, and found myself surrounded by excited troops, I wondered if the general would pull his revolver and shoot me himself, or order some of the soldiers to kill me.

For choice I had rather have been killed by a volley from a platoon of soldiers, but I recognized the fact that the general had a perfect right to kill me. In fact I wanted him to shoot me. I was trimming the limbs off a sapling for a makeshift flag staff, when I saw the crowd open, and the general walked towards me. His face was a trifle pale, except where the red clay from the road covered it, and I felt that the next moment or two would decide in what manner I was to meet my doom. I remembered what the colonel had told me, about the general being a strict disciplinarian, and wondered if it wouldn't help matters if I should fall on my knees and say a little prayer, or ask him to spare my life. I wondered if I would be justified in drawing my revolver and trying to get the drop on the general. But I had no time to think it over, for he come right up to me, and said:

"I beg your pardon, my young friend, for the trouble and annoyance I have caused you. I should have known better than to ride so near you, and frighten your horse, when you had only one hand to guide the animal. Are you hurt? No; well, I am very glad. Ah, the flag staff is broken! Let me help you tack the flag on the sapling. Orderly, bring me some nails. Let me whittle the bark off the sapling, so it will not hurt your hands. When we get into camp tonight, and the wagons come up, I will see that you have another staff. There, don't feel bad about it. There is no damage."

Bless his soul! I could, have hugged him for his kindness. When he came towards me, I was mad and desperate, and when he spoke kind words to me, my chin trembled, and I felt like a baby. He stopped the brigade for half an hour, to help fix up my flag, and all the time talked so kindly to me, that when the thing was fixed, I felt remorse of conscience, and said: "General, I am entirely to blame myself. I tried to perform the impossible feat of saluting you and holding the colours at the same time, which I am satisfied now cannot be done successfully. Lay it all to me."

"I knew it," said the good old general, "and I was going to tell you that you are not expected to salute anybody when you have the colours. You are a part of the flag, then. You will learn it all by and by," and he mounted his horse and rode away about his business, as cool as though nothing had happened, and left me feeling that he was the best man on earth. Further acquaintance with the old man taught me that he was one of nature's noblemen. He was an Illinois farmer, who had enlisted as a private, and had in time become colonel of his regiment, and had been placed in command of this brigade. Every evening he would take an axe and cut up fire-wood enough for headquarters, and he was not above cleaning off his horse if his servant was sick, or did not do it to suit, and frequently I have seen him greasing his own boots.

Two days out, and we were in the pine woods of Alabama, with no habitation within ten miles. After a day's march we went into camp in the woods, and it was the afternoon before Christmas. The young pines, growing among the larger ones, were just such little trees as were used at home for Christmas trees, and within an hour after getting the camp made, every man thought of Christmas at home. The boys went off into the woods and got holly, and mistletoe, and every pup tent of the whole brigade was decorated, and they hung nose bags, grain sacks, army socks and pants on the trees. Around the fires stakes had been driven to hang clothes on to dry, and as night came and the pitch pine fires blazed up to the tops of the great pines, it actually looked like Christmas, though there was not a Christmas present anywhere.

After supper the brigade band began to play patriotic airs, with occasionally an old fashioned tune, like "Old Hundred," the woods rung with music from the boys who could sing, and everybody was as happy as I ever saw a crowd of people, and when it came time to retire the band played "Home, Sweet Home," and three thousand rough soldiers went to bed with tears in their eyes, and every man dreamed of the dear ones at home, and many prayed that the home ones might be happy, and in the morning they all got up, stripped the empty Christmas stockings off the evergreen trees, put them on, and went on down the red road, and at noon the army entered Montgomery, Alabama, the first capital of the confederate states, took possession of the capital building in which were millions of dollars of confederate money and bonds.

Every soldier filled his pockets and saddle bags with bonds and bills of large denominations. It was a poor soldier that could not count up his half a million dollars, but with all the money no man could buy a Christmas dinner. A dollar in greenbacks would buy more than all of the wagon loads of confederate currency captured that day. And yet the people of Montgomery looked upon the arrival of the Yankees much as they would the arrival of a pestilence. However, it was not many days before a better understanding was arrived at, and Yankee blue and Confederate gray got mixed up, and acquaintances were made that ripened into mutual respect and in some cases love.

CHAPTER 21

I Turn Horse-Thief

Let's see, the last chapter left me with a million dollars, more or less, of confederate money in my possession, and yet I had not enough to buy a square meal. I think there was no one thing that caused, the people of the confederate states, outside of their army, to realize the hopelessness of their cause, along in '64, as much as the relative value of confederate money and greenbacks. Of course the confederate soldiers, poor fellows, realized the difference some, when they could get hold of greenbacks, but the people of the south who did not have rations furnished them, and who had to skirmish around and buy something to live upon, early learned that a greenback was worth "two in the bush," as it were.

No community in the south was more loyal to the confederacy than the people of Montgomery, Alabama. They tried to use confederate currency as long as there was any hope, and they tried hard to despise the greenbacks; but when it got so that a market basket full of their own currency was looked upon with suspicion by their own dealers in eatables, and a greenback was sought after by the dealer, and its possessor was greeted with a smile while the overloaded possessor of confederate currency was frowned upon, more in sorrow than in anger, however, a wild desire took possession of the people to get hold of the hated greenbacks; and a soldier or army follower who had a good supply of greenbacks was met more than half way in reconciliation; and little jobs were put up to get the money that made many ashamed, but they had to have greenbacks.

Many would have given their lives if confederate money could have been as good as the money of the invaders, but it was not and never could be, and it was not an hour after the enemy was in Montgomery before people who had been loyal to the south up to that hour and believed in its currency, went back on it completely, and they cherished the greenback and hugged it to their bosoms like an old friend. They had rather had gold, but good green paper would buy so much more than any currency they had known for years, that they snatched it greedily.

And many of them enjoyed the first real respect for the Union that they had had for four years, when they met the well-fed and well-clothed Union soldiers, who did not seem as bad as they had been painted, the poorest one of which had more money in his pockets than the richest citizen of supposed wealth. The people seemed surprised to meet well-dressed private soldiers who could converse on any subject, and who seemed capable of doing any kind of business. Fires broke out in many places in the city, and Union soldiers went to work with the primitive fire apparatus at hand and put out the fires. Locomotives had been thrown from the track of the railroad in an attempt to destroy them, and private soldiers were detailed to put the locomotives together and run them, which they did, to the surprise of the people.

An officer would take charge of a quantity of captured property, and he would detail the first half-dozen soldiers he met to go and make out an invoice of the property, and the boys would do it as well as the oldest southern merchant. A planter that could not speak anything but French would come to the captain, of a company to complain of something, and the captain after vainly trying to understand the man, would turn to some soldier in his company and say, "Here Frenchy, talk to this man, and see what he wants," and the soldier would address the planter in French, politely, and in a moment the difficulty would be settled, and the planter would go away bowing and smiling. Any language could be spoken by the soldiers, and any business that ever was transacted could be done by them. A soldier printer visited the office of a city paper, and in a conversation with the editor informed him that there were editors enough in his regiment to edit the New York *Herald*.

At first the better class of citizens, the old fathers in Israel, of the confederacy, stood aloof from the new soldiers in blue, expecting them to be insolent, as conquerors are sometimes supposed to be; but soon they saw that the boys were as mild a mannered and friendly and jolly a lot as they ever saw, not the least inclined to gloat over their fallen enemy, and at times acting as though they were sorry to make any trouble; and it was not long before boys in blue and citizens in gray were playing billiards together, with old gentlemen keeping count for them, old fellows, who a week before would have been insulted if anyone had told them they would ever speak to a Yankee soldier.

The second day the southern ladies, who had kept indoors, came out and promenaded the beautiful streets, and seemed to enjoy the sight of the bright uniforms, and before night acquaintances had been made, and it did not cause any remark to see Union officers and soldiers waiting with ladies, talking with animation, and laughing pleasantly. It almost seemed, as though the war was over.

It was about this time that I stole my first horse. I had ridden horses that had been "captured" from the enemy, in fair fights, and that had been accumulated in divers ways by the quartermaster, and issued to the men, but I never deliberately stole a horse. Two or three companies of my regiment had gone off on a scout, to be gone a couple of days, leaving the command at Montgomery, and one day we were encamped on an old abandoned field, taking dinner. The horses and mules were grazing near us, and there was no indication that any epidemic was about to break out.

We were about sixty miles from Montgomery, and were cooking our last meal, expecting to make a forced march and be back before morning. I had got the midday meal for Jim and myself cooked, the bacon, sweet potatoes, coffee and so forth, and spread upon a horse blanket on the ground, and we were just about to sit down to eat, when a mule that had been browsing near us, and snooping into our affairs, attracted our attention. All of a sudden the animal became rigid, and stood up as stiff as possible, then its muscles relaxed, and it became limber, and whirled around and brayed, backed up towards us, and as we rushed away to keep from being kicked, the mule fell over in a fit directly on our beautifully cooked dinner, rolled over on the bacon and potatoes and coffee, and trembled and brayed, and died right there.

I looked at Jim and Jim looked at me. "Well, condam a mule, anyway," said Jim. "That animal has been ready to die for two hours, and just to show its cussedness, it waited until we had our dinner cooked, the last morsel we had, and then it fell in a fit, and expired on our dining table." I made some remark not complimentary to the mule as a member of society and we went to the corpse and pulled it around to see if we couldn't save a mouthful or two that could be eaten. We could not, as everything was crushed into the ground. I suggested that we cut a steak out of the mule, and broil it, but Jim said he was not

185

going to be a cannibal, if he knew his own heart.

While we were looking at the remains of our meal, my horse, the rebel horse that I had rode so many months, and loved so, which was hitched near, lay down, began to groan and kick, and in two minutes he was dead. Then Jim's horse went through the same performance and died, and by that time there was a commotion all around camp, horses and mules dying suddenly, until within half an hour there were only a dozen animals alive, and forty cavalrymen, at least, were horseless. The camp looked like a battle field. Nobody knew what was the matter of the animals, until an old negro, who lived near, came out and said, "You uns ought to know better than to let you horses eat dat sneeze weed. Dat is poison. Kills animals, just like rat poison." And then he showed us a weed, with a square stem, that grew there, and which was called sneeze weed.

He said native animals would not touch it, but strange animals eat it because it was nice and green. Well, we were in a fix. The men were called together, and the major told them there was nothing to do but to take their saddles and bridles on their backs and walk to Montgomery, unless they could steal a horse. He advised us to scatter into parties of two or three, enough to protect ourselves from possible attack, go on cross roads, and to plantations, forage for something to eat, and take the first horse or mule we could find, and report to Montgomery as soon as possible. Jim and I, of course, decided to stand by each, other, and after the men who had not lost their horses, had rode away, the forty dismounted men shouldered their saddles, and started in different directions, seeking some other men's horses.

I never had realized that a cavalry saddle was so heavy, before. Mine seemed to weigh a ton. We struck a cross road, and followed it for two or three miles, when I called a council of war, with Jim. I told him that it was all foolishness to lug those heavy saddles all over the Southern Confederacy. If we succeeded in stealing horses, we could probably steal saddles, also, or if not we could get a sheepskin. I told Jim I would receipt to him for his saddle, and then I would leave them in a fence corner, and if we ever got back to the regiment I would report the saddle lost in action.

Jim said I had a great head, and he consented, and we left our saddles and moved on. Jim said that now we had only a bridle and a pair of spurs, we were more like regularly ordained horse-thieves. He said the most successful horse-thief he ever knew in Wisconsin never had anything but a halter as his stock in trade. He would go out with a halter, with a rope on the end, pick up a horse, put the rope in the horse's mouth, and ride away, and nobody could catch him. I asked Jim if he didn't feel humiliated, a loyal soldier, to class himself with horse-thieves. He said when he enlisted he made up his mind to do nothing but shoot rebels through the heart or the left lung.

It was his idea to be a sharpshooter, and aim at the button on the left breast of the enemy, but when he found that lots of the rebels didn't have any buttons on their coats and that he might shoot all day at a single rebel and not hit him, and that shooting into them in flocks didn't seem to diminish the enemy the least bit, he had made up his mind to turn his hand to anything; and if the rebellion could be put down easier by his stealing horses at thirteen dollars a month, he would do it if ordered. He said we were only putting in time, promenading around, and we should get our salary all the same. And so we wandered on, talking the thing over.

When we came to a plantation we would walk all around it, and examine the woods and swamps adjacent, because the people of the South had learned that a horse or a mule was not safe anywhere out of the most impenetrable swamp. It was dark when Jim and I decided to camp for the night, and we went into a deserted cotton gin and prepared for a sleep. It was almost dark, and Jim said he had just seen a chicken, near a cabin, fly up in a peach tree to roost, and he was going to have the chicken as soon as it was dark. I laid down on some refuse cotton, and Jim went out after the chicken. I had fallen asleep when Jim returned, and he had the chicken, and a skillet, and a couple of canteens of water.

I crawled out of my nest and built a fire, while Jim dressed the chicken, and got the water to boiling, and the chicken was put in. For three hours we boiled the chicken, but each hour made it tougher. I told Jim he might be a success as a horse-thief, but when it come to stealing tender poultry he was a lamentable failure, but he said it was the only hen on the place, and if I didn't want to eat it I could retire to my couch and he would set up with the hen. I was so hungry, and the smell of the boiling hen was so savoury, that I remained awake, and at about midnight Jim announced that he had succeeded in prying off a piece of the breast, so we speared the hen out of the water, laid it on the frame of a grindstone in the gin-house, and sat down to the festive board. "Will you have the light or the dark meat," asked Jim, with a politeness that would have done credit to a dancing-master.

I told, him I preferred the dark meat, so he took hold of one leg and I the other, and we pulled the hen apart. The hen seemed to be copper-riveted, for when I got a chunk of it down, and it chinked up a vacant place in the stomach, it did seem as though there was nothing like hen to save life. We eat sparingly that night, because we were weak, and the hen was strong, and we laid down and slept peacefully, and awoke in the morning hungry.

When the hen became cold, in the morning it *was* tough. "Will you have some of the cold chicken," said Jim, and I told him I would try a little. It was better than India rubber, and we made a breakfast and started on. It was Sunday. As we came out to the main road, we saw people dressed up, that is, with clean shirts. As ten o clock approached we could see coloured people and white, wending their way to a little church in the pine woods. We kept out of sight, and waited, several parties passed us on horseback, some in carriages, and many on foot.

Presently three soldiers of our scattered party came along carrying saddles, and we called them into the woods, where we were. I unfolded to them my scheme, which was to surround that church, hold the worshippers as prisoners inside, while we stole the horses that would be hitched to the fence. Jim kicked on it. He said he had rather walk than to interfere with people who were enjoying their religion. He said he was never very pious himself, but his parents were, and he should always hate himself if he helped to raid that church. The other fellows were for going for the horses. Pretty soon four more of our boys came along, and we called them in. They had got on to the church services, and had their eyes on the horses. That made nine of us, and as we were armed, we believed we could capture those old men and women and negroes, and get the horses.

Being a brevet officer I was placed in command of the party, and a plan was agreed upon. We were to scatter and surround the church, and ask the people outside to step inside, and then lock the door, and place a guard on three sides of the little old church where there were windows, but not to fire a gun unless attacked, and not to speak disrespectfully to any person. If there was any argument with anybody, I was to do the talking. We decided to take about fifteen horses, if there were that number there, because we would be sure to find some of our scattered boys dismounted before we got far toward Montgomery, and it was a good idea to take horses when we had a chance.

Well, it was a job I did not like, but what was a fellow to do. We were sixty miles from headquarters, on foot and out of meat. I had never been in a church row before. It seemed as though religious worshippers ought to be exempt from war, with its wide desolation. But business was business. We surrounded the church, walking up quietly from different directions, and as we closed up on the sacred edifice half a dozen men, white and coloured, were standing in front, and two men were talking over a horse trade. The minister was expounding the gospel, talking loud, and all else was still.

We invited the outsiders to go in, which they did with some reluctance, the door was fastened on the outside, guards were placed, and the preaching stopped. The minister had been informed that the Yankees had captured the place. There were only two sides of the church with windows, so two guards were sufficient, and the rest of us went to work skinning the harnesses off the horses. A window was raised and an old man stuck his head out and said, as one of the boys was mounting an old mare belonging to him, "I forbid you touching that mare." A carbine was pointed at the window, and the old man drew in his head, and the window was slammed down.

We had got sixteen pretty good horses, when a window on the other side opened, and the minister's head was put out, and he said, "In the name of the church I command you to desist." He looked so fierce that Jim, who was on guard on that side, and who had objected to the scheme on account of its being a church, cocked his carbine and pointed it at the minister and said, "gol darn you, dry up!" He dried up, the window closed and except for the heads at the windows, and faces looking very mad, all was quit.

When we had got the horses strung out, and the men were mounted, I looked in a carriage, accidentally, and saw a basket, covered over with a paper. The paper was a religious one, published at Savannah, and being a newspaper man, I looked at the leading editorial, which was headed, "The Lord will provide." I never took much stock in regular stereotyped editorials, but when I turned my eye from the editorial to the basket, I realized than an editorial in a religious newspaper, was liable to contain much truth, for the basket was filled with as fine a lunch as a man ever saw.

It seemed that the people came quite a long distance to church, and brought their dinner, remaining to the afternoon services. O, but I was hungry. I looked in several other carriages, and found baskets in each. Every man in my party was as hungry as a she wolf, and I knew they would not leave a mouthful if they once got to going on the lunches, and as it wasn't the policy of my government to take the

I FORBID YOU TOUCHING THAT MARE

bread from the mouths of Sunday-school children, I decided to divide the lunches. So I appointed Jim and an Irishman to help me, and we opened all the baskets and took half. Jim came to one basket with two loaves of bread and two bottles of wine, and he stopped.

He said, "Pard, that layout in the big basket, with the silver pitcher, is for the communion. I'm a bold buccaneer of the Spanish main, but I'll be cussed if I touch that."

The Irishman said no power on earth could get him to touch it, and he crossed himself reverently, and we left the communion lay-out, and passed the half we had taken from the baskets around among the boys, and they eat as though a special providence had provided them with appetites and means of satisfying them. After enjoying the meal the boys said we ought to return thanks for the good things the pious people had provided for us, so I went to the door of the church, opened it, and faced the congregation.

There were old and young, and some of them looked mad, and I didn't blame them. In a few well chosen remarks I addressed the minister, telling him I regretted the circumstances, but it was necessary to do what we had done. We had tried to do it as pleasantly as possible, but no doubt it seemed hard to them. I said we had got to go to Montgomery, and that if any of them who had lost their horses, would come there within a few days, I had no doubt the proper authorities would return them their horses, but that they must stand the loss of a half of their lunch, as we had divided it up as square as we knew how.

One young Confederate soldier, with an empty sleeve, who had come to church with his mother, and who could, no doubt, realize the situation better than the rest, said, "That is all right, Mr. Yankee. I would do the same thing, under the circumstances, if I was in your country, horseless and hungry." There were some murmurs of dissatisfaction, some smiled at the situation, and we mounted and rode away. Before we were out of sight the whole congregation was out of the church, under the pine trees, taking an account of stock, or lost stock, and no doubt saying hard things of the Yankees.

We travelled all day and nearly all night, picked up some of our dismounted men, and arrived in Montgomery the next day before noon. In a few days my one-armed confederate soldier, who was home from the army in Virginia, having been discharged for disability, came to Montgomery with the people who had lost their horses at the church, and I had the satisfaction of seeing many of them either receive their animals back, or vouchers from the quartermaster, by which they got pay from the government for the animals. And I entertained the one-armed confederate for two days, and we became great friends. Two years ago I met him in Georgia, grown gray, and found him connected with a Georgia railroad, and we had a great laugh over my capture of the congregation.

CHAPTER 22

I was Tempted to Have
My Horse Shot

It seemed to me that my luck was the worst of any man's in the army, and I was constantly getting into situations that caused, my conduct to be talked about. When we raided the church, mentioned last week, for horses, I saw a nice white horse with red spots on him, with a saddle, and being the commander of the squad of horse-thieves, it was no more than right for me to take my choice first, so I chose the spotted horse, and thought I had the showiest horse in the army. The animal was a sort of Arabian, and before I had rode him a mile I was in love with him. then I got to Montgomery a man told me that horse used to belong to a circus that closed up there the first year of the war, and was sold to a planter. He said the horse was considered one of the finest ever seen in the South.

I felt much elated over my capture, and refused several offers to trade. I thought no horse was too good for me, and for two or three days I did nothing but feed and groom my spotted horse, until his coat shone like satin, and he felt so kitteny that I was almost afraid to get on his back. One morning an order was issued for the regiment to turn out in a body to attend the funeral of a major of one of the regiments, who had died, and I was sent for to carry the brigade colours, a position I had been relieved from after we arrived at Montgomery. The boys all dressed up in their best, and I looked about as slick as any of them, and with my spotted horse, I felt as though I would attract about as much attention as any of the officers in the procession.

At the proper time I mounted my horse and rode over to brigade headquarters, not without some difficulty, for my horse saw the crowd on the streets, and evidently thought it was circus day, for he pranced and snorted, and walked with one fore-foot at a time, pawing as you have seen a horse in a circus, trained to walk that way. As I rode up to brigade headquarters and stopped, I must have touched my horse with my foot somewhere, for he got down on his knees, and as I got off, the horse laid down right in front of the colonel's tent, just as he would in a circus. Even then I did not realize that the confounded brute was a circus trick-horse. He had been taught to lay down, evidently, at a certain signal. And he laid there, looking up at me with his cunning eyes, waiting for me to give the signal for him to get up, but I "did not know the combination," and he wouldn't get up for kicking, so I stood there like a fool waiting to see what he would do next.

The colonel commanding the brigade, the nice old man who had helped me out of my difficulty with my other horse, on the march when he got on a tantrum, come out of his tent and said he guessed my horse was sick, and he told an orderly to go to the cook house and get a little red pepper and let the horse take a snuff of it. In the meantime my horse got up on his fore feet and sat on his haunches, like a dog, just as circus horses always do, reached up his neck and took a nice white silk handkerchief out of the breast of the colonel's coat, and held it in his mouth.

It was a circus trick, and I knew it, but the colonel said, "Poor horse, he is sick," and as the orderly come with the red pepper the colonel held it to the horse's nose. The horse got up, and I mounted, and it must have been about that time that the red pepper began its work, for my horse stood on his fore feet and kicked up, then got on his hind feet and reared up, and snorted, and come down on the colonel's tent, and crushed it to the-ground, and broke the colonel's camp cot, got tangled in the guy ropes, and tore everything loose and jumped out in the street, and began to paw and snort. I suppose there was a thousand people around by that time, soldiers and citizens, and I sat there on that horse and wished I was dead, and I guess the colonel did so too.

Finally it was time to move, and the colonel sent out the brigade colours to me, and the start started up street towards the funeral. My horse started with them, and seemed proud of the flag, and I guess he would have gone along all right, only a band down the street began to play a waltz. Do you know, that spotted horse began to waltz around just as though he was in a circus, and I couldn't keep him straight to save me. The colonel seemed mortified, as we were approaching the place where the services were to be held, and it was necessary to appear solemn.

Finally we began to get out of hearing of the band, and my horse stopped waltzing, but he kept up a-dancing, and snorting from the red pepper, until I could have killed him. When the colonel and his staff, including myself and the circus-horse, arrived at the place where the funeral was, another band was playing a very solemn sort of a funeral tune, and for a wonder my horse did not act up at all. He seemed to stand and think, as though trying to make out what kind of music it was. He had evidently never heard such music in the circus and did not know what to do.

When the body was brought out of the house, and the procession started down the street for the grave, a drum major, with a staff in his hand, came along by me, and I have always thought my horse took the drum major for the ring master of a circus, for he reared up and walked on his hind feet, and pawed the air, and made a spectacle of me that made me so ashamed that I wanted to be killed. I had the brigade colours in one hand, and had only one hand and two feet to cling on the horse by, and I must have looked like a cat climbing the roof of a whitewashed barn. The drum major got scared at my horse walking towards him in that way, and he lost his bear-skin cap off and fell over it, and rolled in the sand, and the horse, thinking that was a part of the circus turned and kicked at the drum major with both his hind feet, until the poor assistant musician got up and climbed over a fence.

The horse got quiet then, only he began to nibble his fore leg, as though trying to untie a handkerchief that the clown had tied on, as they do in the circus. The colonel rode up to me, and with a good deal of indignation, asked me what I meant by causing ourselves to become a spectacle for gods and men on so solemn an occasion. He said he was tempted to have my horse shot, and me placed in the guard-house. I told him I hoped to die if I could help it. I said the horse seemed to be possessed to do some circus business wherever he went. I confided to the colonel that the horse had been a circus-horse before the war, and the music and tinsel, and crowd that he saw, had turned his head and made him think that he was again with his beloved circus, where he had spent the best years of his life.

The colonel said I ought to have known better than to bring a circus horse to a funeral. Well, when the drum major got out of sight the horse acted better, and we went along all right, the solemn music of the march to the grave seeming to take the circus out of him. He didn't do anything out of the way on the march, except to put out his fore-feet stiff, and keep time to the music, like a trained circus horse, which attracted a good deal of attention among the citizens on the street, who seemed to know the horse.

Just as we got out at che edge of town he *did* make one raw break. There was a coloured drayman, with his dray backed up towards the procession, and when my circus horse saw the dray, before I could prevent him, he whirled around and put his fore feet upon the hind end of the dray, put one foot on the top of a stake on the dray, and stood there for a minute, like a horse statute, until I jerked him down off of there.

O, I was so mortified that my teeth fairly ached, and the perspiration stood out on me in great beads. A staff officer of the general commanding, came along to the colonel, presented the compliments of the general, and asked if he could not do something to prevent that redheaded clown on the spotted horse from doing any more circus acts until after the last sad rites had been performed. The colonel said it should be stopped, and told the start officer to present his compliments to the general and say that he was humiliated beyond endurance by the performance of the horse, but that the young man riding the horse was not to blame, as he had done all in his power to keep the circus tendencies of the horse down, but he added that he would have the horse shot if there was any more of it.

The horse kept quiet until we had got to the cemetery, and returned to town. As we got into a wide street there was an old circus ring, partly grown up with weeds, near where the division quartermaster had a large tent inside a picket fence, filled with quartermaster stores. If I had known anything, I would have kept the horse's head turned away from the circus ring, and the tent, but I thought there would be no more trouble. Just as we got opposite the ring, the band, which had heretofore played dead marches, struck up a regular ripety-rap-rap-boom-boom circus tune, and I felt the horse tremble all over. Before I could think twice, the confounded horse had tried to jump through the bass drum, had knocked the drummer down, and jumped into the circus ring.

I sawed on the bit and tried to stop him, and dug into his ribs with the spurs, but he galloped around the circus ring three or four times, and stopped still, as though expecting a clown would come up and say, "What will the little lady have now?" O, if I could have had one more hand to use, I would have drawn my revolver and put a bullet through the brain of the wretched horse, who was making me the laughing

I JERKED HIM DOWN OF'N THERE

stock of the whole army, and the citizens.

The procession moved on towards camp, the colonel seeming relieved to have me out of sight, with my spotted horse, and a crowd of citizens, boys and niggers collected around the ring, yelling and laughing. I made one desperate effort and reined the horse out of the ring, and just then he caught sight of the quartermaster's tent across the road, and evidently thinking it was the dressing-room of the circus, he started for it on a run, jumped the picket fence as though it was a circus hurdle, and rushed in the door of the tent where a dozen clerks were weighing out commissary stores, stopped suddenly, and I went over his head, into a barrel of ground, coffee. The clerks picked me out of the coffee, and laid me on a pile of corn sacks, and then the horse began to lay back his ears and chase the clerks out of the tent, and it was awful the way the animal acted.

After I had recovered from the effects of my fall into the coffee barrel, I got up and took the horse by the bridle, and led him out of the gate, and up the street to headquarters, with the brigade flag in my hand. I finally got to headquarters and left the flag, and the colonel told me he never wanted me around brigade headquarters again. He said I was a regular Jonah, that brought bad luck. I apologized the best I could, told him I would never bother him again, and led my horse back to my regiment. The chaplain of my regiment, who had not been to the funeral with us, and knew nothing about the circus, met me, and, as usual, bantered me to trade horses. I felt as though if I could saw that horse off on to the chaplain, and fix him so he could engage in the circus business, life would yet have some charms for me, so after some bantering we got down to business.

The chaplain asked me if I thought it would cause any remark if he should ride a spotted horse, and I told him I did not know why it should, if the chaplain behaved himself. He said he didn't know but the boys might think that a spotted horse was too gay for a chaplain. I told him I didn't know why a spotted horse couldn't be just as solemn as any horse. He asked me if the horse had any tricks, and if he was sound. I told him I had not had him long, but it seemed to me if the horse had any tricks I should have found it out by this time, and I knew he was sound, because I jumped a fence with him not an hour ago, and he took the fence just as though he had jumped fences all his life. I asked ten dollars to boot, and the chaplain said if I would warrant the horse not to have any tricks he would take him.

I told him I couldn't warrant the horse not to have any tricks, but that the colonel commanding the brigade wanted my horse, and he certainly would not want a horse that had tricks. What the colonel wanted was a horse noted for its strict attention to business. Then the chaplain said he would trade, and we changed saddles, and the chaplain led the spotted horse away, and I was revenged for many things the chaplain had done me.

When the chaplain led the spotted horse to his tent, and all the boys in the regiment saw that I had traded the brute off, and they thought what a picnic they would have the first time the chaplain rode the horse down town, there was a laugh all through the regiment, but nobody squealed, or told the chaplain what a prize package he had secured. I cannot account for it, how I could have coolly traded that dastardly horse off on to the chaplain, but I was young then. Now, after arriving at a ripe old age, I would not play such a trick on a chaplain.

The next day there was to be a review, and when the regiment was notified, I got sick and could not go. I felt as though I did not want to be a witness of the chaplain's attempt to exhibit a solemn demeanour, on that circus horse. I thought I should probably die right in my tracks if the horse acted with him as he did with me, so I remained in my tent with a wet towel on my head, and saw the regiment ride out to review, the chaplain on the spotted horse beside the colonel, not dreaming that it was going to be the most eventful day of his life.

CHAPTER 23

I am Court Martialed

In the last chapter I told of trading my circus-horse to the chaplain, and how the chaplain had rode away with the regiment for review, and I remained in camp, pretending to be sick. The result of that scheme on my part was not all my fancy painted it. I stood in front of my tent with a wet towel around my head, and saw the regiment return from review, the chaplain's spotted circus horse with no rider, being led by a coloured man, the horse looking as innocent as any horse I ever saw. Where was the 'chaplain? Had he been killed? I noticed half the men were laughing and it seemed to me they wouldn't laugh if the good chaplain was dead. I also noticed that the colonel and his staff wore faces clouded with anger, and that they seemed as though they would like to kill somebody.

Before the regiment had got fairly dismounted, a sergeant and three men marched to my tent, and I was arrested, and was informed that I would be tried at once, by court-martial, for conduct prejudicial to good order and military discipline. I knew the sergeant, and tried to joke with him, telling him to "go on with his old ark, as there wasn't going to be much of a shower," but he wouldn't have any funny business, and kindly informed me that I had probably got to the end of my rope, and that I would no doubt spend the remainder of my term of enlistment in the military prison. I asked him what the row was about, and he said. I would find out soon enough. One soldier got on each side of me, and one behind with sabres drawn, to stick me with if I attempted to get away, and we started for the colonel's tent.

On the way there, the chaplain came towards us, covered with red clay, and begged the sergeant to allow him to kill me right there. He was the maddest truly good man I ever saw. He fairly foamed at the mouth, and said, "O, sergeant, turn him loose, and let me chew him

200

up." I said to the sergeant:

"Now, look-a-here, don't you let that savage get at me, or he will get hurt. I don't want to have any trouble with the church, but if any regularly ordained ministerial cannibal of a sky pilot attempts to chew me, he will find a good deal more gristle than tender loin, and I will italicise his nose so he will look so crossed-eyed that he can't draw his pay."

My thus showing that I was not afraid of a non-combatant, seemed to have the desired effect, for he spit on his hands, jumped up and cracked his heels together, said he would wipe the Southern Confederacy with my remains, and he went to his tent to change his clothes, and get ready for the court-martial. The guard took me to the colonel's tent, and I walked right in where the colonel and major and several others were, and I said Hello, and smiled, and extended my hand to the colonel. None of them helloed, and none of them returned my smile, and the colonel did not shake hands with me. He said, however, that I had brought disgrace on the regiment, and broken the heart of a noble man, the chaplain.

I told him I didn't think the chaplain's heart was very badly broke, as he had just ottered to whip me in several languages, and threatened to eat me. The colonel had me sit down on a trunk and keep still, while the court-martial convened. It was not many minutes before the officers had arrived, and organized, the adjutant read the charges and specifications against me. Not to go into the military-form of charges and specifications, the substance of them was that I had with malice aforethought, procured a trick-horse from a circus, with the intention of inducing the chaplain to trade for it, with the purpose of causing the aforesaid chaplain to become a spectacle for laughter.

When the charges were read I was asked what I had to say, and I told the Judge Advocate it was a condemned lie. That made him mad, and he was going to commence whipping me where the chaplain left off, when the colonel smoothed matters over by asking me if I didn't mean to plead "not guilty." I said, "Certainly, not guilty. It is false. I did not secure the horse for the purpose of sawing it off on the chaplain. I jayhawked it, and when I found it was not the kind of a horse for a modest fellow like me, who didn't want to make any display, I thought I would trade it to some officer with gall, and the chaplain was the first man who struck me for a trade, and he got it, and from his remarks to me, and from these court-martial proceedings, I was satisfied the chaplain did not like the horse."

The officers laughed then, and I suppose they were thinking of something that happened to the chaplain on review. The colonel asked me if I wanted anybody to defend me, and I told him I had a printing office once next door to a lawyer's office, and I knew a little about law, and would defend myself. The chaplain came soon, and began to tell his story, but I insisted, that he be sworn, and then he proceeded to tell his tale. He said that he was a God-fearing man, and meant to do right, and was willing to take his chances in the lottery of war, but when a man got him to ride a circus trick-horse, and bring upon his sacred calling the ribald laughter of the wicked, he felt that civilization was a failure.

He said he traded for the spotted horse in good faith, and that he was particular to ask me if the horse had any tricks, and I said he had none, and he traded on that understanding, that he rode the afore— said horse to the review, and as soon as the aforesaid horse heard the band play, he waltzed out into the middle of the street, whirled around more than fifty times, waltzed into an infantry regiment, breaking the ranks of the soldiers just as the reviewing officer come along, causing the reviewing officer to say, "get out of the ranks, you d——d fool, and take that horse back to the circus," thus causing him, the chaplain, to be scandalized. He said he would have stood that, but the horse carried him to a battery of artillery which was in position, and began to jump over the guns, and that a gunner took a swab with which he had been cleaning a gun, and punched him, the chaplain, in the face, covering his face with burnt powder which smelled badly.

Then the horse carried him out on the field in front of the reviewing officers, got up on its hind feet and walked for half a block, making the chaplain appear as though climbing up the horse's neck, and when some of the general's staff came out to arrest him, the horse whirled around and kicked, in every direction at once, and broke the sabre of one of the staff-officers. That the horse seemed to be possessed of the devil. That he finally got the horse to go back to the regiment where he belonged, but on the way he had to pass brigade headquarters, when the horse stopped in front of the commanding officer and sat down like a dog, on his hind parts, and tried to shake hands with the colonel commanding, who was offended, and told the chaplain he was an ass, and to go away with his museum, or he would have the chaplain put in the guard house. That a coloured man near the review ground had a ginger bread stand, with a sheet tacked up to keep the sun off, and the spotted horse attempted to jump through the sheet, evidently thinking it was a paper hoop in a circus.

And in conclusion, after making the chaplain so mortified and ashamed that he wished he might die, the horse laid down in the road and rolled over the aforesaid chaplain, leaving him in the road covered with dirt, while the horse run across the street and walked up a pair of stairs, outside a store, went into the rooms occupied by some milliners and scared the women so they put their heads out of the windows and yelled fire, and said a regiment of Yankee cavalry had raided their homes. That the review was made a farce, the chaplain a laughing stock, and that it took ten men to get the horse down stairs, and half the regiment to console the milliners, and convince them that no harm was intended. He said he demanded that I be sentenced to be shot.

The colonel asked me if I had anything to say, and I asked permission to cross-examine the witness. Permission being granted, I asked the chaplain what his business was. He said he was a minister. I asked him if he didn't consider trading horses one of the noblest professions extant. He said he didn't know about that. Then I asked him if he didn't take advantage of me when I came to the regiment, as a raw recruit, and trade me a kicking mule, that made my life a burden. He said he remembered that he traded me a mule. I asked him if he didn't know the mule was balky, vicious, and spavined, that it would kick its best friend, bite anybody, that it was so ugly that he had to put the saddle on with a long pole, that he warranted the mule sound when he knew it had all the diseases that were going.

He said he objected to being asked such questions, but the judge-advocate said I had a right to bring out any previous transactions in the horse-trade line, as it would have some effect in this case. Then I asked him if he didn't know the horse he beat me out of was sound, a splendid rider, and that the mule was the worst one in the army. He admitted that he knew the animal was not a desirable animal, but he thought a recruit could get along with a kicking mule better than a chaplain. I had saved my best shot for the last, and I said, "knowing the mule was unsound, a vicious animal, and that my horse was sound and desirable, and worth more than a dozen such mules, did you consider that you was pursuing your calling as a minister when you gained my confidence, and not only sawed the mule off on to me, bereaved me of a fine horse, but took twenty dollars of my hard-earned bounty money as boot in the trade? In doing that to an innocent and fresh recruit who had confidence in you, did you not pave the way for me to get even with you on a horse trade, and haven't I got even, and do you blame me for doing it?"

The chaplain was perspiring while I was asking the questions, and all the officers were looking at him as though he had caught a tartar, but he blushed, choked, and finally answered that perhaps he did wrong in trading me that mule, and he asked to be forgiven.

Then I turned to the officers and said, "Gentlemen, I admit that I traded the spotted circus-horse to the chaplain. I did it on purpose to show him that there is a God in Israel. When I came to the regiment, right fresh from the people, I needed salting. The boys all salted me whenever they got a chance, and I took it like a little man. In turning to the chaplain for comfort, I did not expect that he would salt me worse than all of the boys combined, but when I found that he had gone through me, and taken advantage of my guileless innocence, and laughed at my woe when I found the confounded mule was not all his fancy had painted it, and that it laid awake nights to devise ways to kick my head on, I took a blooded oath that before the cruel war was over I would salt that chaplain on a horse trade, until he would own up the corn. I leave it to you, gentlemen, if I have done it or not.

"When that spotted horse fell to me, by the fortunes of war, I was not long in learning that it was the relic of a circus. I rode the horse one day last week at a funeral, and it acted in such a manner as to almost wake up the late lamented. I was made the laughing stock of the brigade, and of the town. It was government property, and I could not kill the horse, and I thought the time had arrived for me to get even with my old friend. He was mashed on my spotted horse, and bantered me for a trade. Finally we traded, and I got ten dollars to boot. The result has been all that I could desire. I have had the satisfaction of demonstrating to this truly good man that all is not gold that glitters. I have shown him that however spotted a man may be, if he rides a spotted circus horse, he will get there. I will leave it to the chaplain, now, if I was not justified in trading him that horse, after what he had done to me, and will ask him if he was not served perfectly right, and if in trading me that mule he did not do to others as he would have others do to him, and if so, if he does not think the others did it to him in great shape. I am done. I leave my life in your hands."

When I quit they were all laughing except the chaplain, and there was a quiet smile around his mouth, as he thought of his experience on the spotted horse. The colonel asked the chaplain, if he had anything to say, and he said he had just been thinking that he could go over to a New Jersey regiment and trade that spotted horse to the chaplain of that regiment, and if he could, he would be willing to drop the case. He said that chaplain played a mean trick on him once, and he wanted to get even. The court martial acquitted me, and while we were all taking a drink with the colonel, the chaplain went out, and pretty soon we saw his servant leading the spotted horse over towards the camp of the New Jersey regiment, and later the chaplain sauntered off in that direction on foot, as though there was some weighty subject on his mind. The weighty subject was the spotted circus-horse.

I do not suppose any incident ever caused so much talk as did the chaplain's circus. The boys were talking and laughing about it in every company all that afternoon, and when it was found that I had not been punished, for trading the horse to him, the boys were wild. They wanted to show their appreciation of the fun I had given them, so a lot of them got together to give me a sort of reception.

They sent for me to come over to Co. D., and when I got over there they grabbed me and carried me off on their shoulders. I felt proud to see them so joyous and friendly, until they put me in a blanket and tossed me up into the trees, and caught me in the blanket as I came down. Of all the sensations I ever experienced, that of being tossed up in a blanket was the worst. I tried to laugh, at first, but it became serious, as I went into the air twenty feet, let loose of the air and came down, expecting to be crushed maimed, killed. My breath forsook me, I was dizzy, but I struck the blanket easy, and after being sent up a dozen times they let me go, and my reception was over.

CHAPTER 24

Mingled Reminiscences

Long before this I should have related a little experience I had on my first journey south, when I was a fresh recruit. After leaving Wisconsin, in the winter, a lot of us recruits were corralled at Benton Barracks, St. Louis, and for six weeks we had a picnic. There were about fifty of us, that belonged to the cavalry, our regiments being down the Mississippi river, and the commanding officer of the barracks seemed to be waiting for a chance to send us to our regiments. I have often wondered what he waited six weeks for, when we were not doing any duty in camp, and were making him trouble enough every day and every night to turn his hair gray.

He was a Colonel Bonneville, if I remember right, a regular army officer of French extraction. Anyway, he always swore at us in French. The camp was run in a slack sort of a way, and it was easy for us to get out and go down town, or wander off into the country, and, as we had plenty of money, and were dressed better than soldiers in active service, we were welcome to all the saloons, and painted old St. Louis all the colours of the rainbow, returned to the barracks at unseasonable hours, crawled through the fence and went to our quarters howling, waking up the old general, who invariably ordered the provost-guard to arrest us, which the provost-guard invariably didn't do, for some reason or other.

The old colonel was fast aging, in trying to lead a quiet life in the vicinity of "dose d——d cavalry regruits," and he said he "would order them all shot if they didn't behave." Benton Barracks was the greatest place for the breeding of rats that I ever saw. In every house there were millions of them, and at night they were out in full force. One night our crowd of recruits, about forty in number, had been down to St. Louis on a painting expedition, and it was midnight when camp was reached. Every recruit had a revolver, and it was decided that if the rats insulted us, as they had often done before, we would shoot them. It was a beautiful moonlight night, as still as death, and we could almost hear the snoring of the excitable colonel in his house across the parade ground.

As we came near our barrack, a few thousand rats crossed our path, and I drew my revolver and fired at a large one that seemed unusually impudent, and the rest of the crowd opened fire, and there was a battle in no time. A bugler got out and blowed some call that I did not know, a drum sounded a continuous roll, men rushed out and formed in line, and before we had fired the six charges from our revolvers, the Invalid Corps came hobbling across the parade ground, the colonel behind them with his shirt on, his pants in his hand, and swearing in French, and ordering the troops to arrest the whole crowd of recruits. We went right in the barrack, and retired, as soon as the troops showed up, and were snoring, with smoking revolvers under our pillows, when the guard entered.

The colonel came in with the guard, and then put on his pants, after which he woke up some of us, and asked what was the cause of the firing. Every recruit swore that he had not fired a shot, but that he had heard some firing over the fence, on the outside, at a road-house and saloon, where bad men from St. Louis congregated and drank to excess. It seemed very hard to thus lie to so estimable a gentleman as the colonel, but as he was only half-dressed, and sleepy, and excited, it didn't seem as though the lies ought to count. But they did. The colonel apologized for waking us up, when we were enjoying our much-needed rest, and he went away with the guard.

Then we all got up and danced a can-can, in our army under-clothes, passed a series of resolutions endorsing the colonel as one of the ablest officers in the army, recommended that he be promoted to brigadier-general at the first opportunity, gave three cheers and a tiger for the Union, and went to bed. That is one thing that we recruits always come out strong in, i e., three cheers for the Union. We had enlisted to save the Union, and as there was no fighting that we could do, during our stay at St. Louis, whenever we got a chance we gave three cheers for the Union.

Sometimes it was not appreciated, however. I remember one evening our crowd went into a saloon and ordered beer all around, and after we had drank it, I proposed three cheers for the Union, which we gave in a hearty manner, and went out without paying for the beer. You would hardly credit it, but the saloonkeeper, an Irishman named Oppenheimer, became offended, and wanted us to pay cash for the beer. The boys wanted me to reason with him, and I began by asking him if he was a loyal man, and he said he was. Then I asked him if he didn't believe in supporting the Union. He said he did, but he couldn't pay the brewer for his beer by giving three cheers for the Union.

He had to put up cash. I confess that his remarks made quite an impression on me, as I had not thought of it in that light before. I proposed that we give three cheers for Oppenheimer, which was done, and I thought that would settle it, but he insisted on having cash. I told the boys, and they said he was a rebel. I told Oppenheimer, and he got out a wooden bung-starter, and said he could clean out the whole party. Finally we compromised, in this way. We had given two rounds of cheer, one for the Union and one for Oppenheimer, which were a total loss, so it was agreed that if Oppenheimer would give three cheers for the Union and three for us we would pay him for the beer, if he would agree to set 'em up for us, at his own expense.

He agreed, and then we tried to get him to onset the beer he was going to give us, for the beer we had drank, and not pay him for that we had consumed. That, to any business man, we thought, would seem fair, but he wouldn't have it. So, after he had returned our cheers to us, we paid him, and then he treated. I mention this to show the hardships of a soldier's life, and the difficulties of inculcating business methods into the minds of the saloon-keepers. Oppenheimer meant well, but he did not appreciate cheers for the Union. He got so, after that when we came in his saloon, in a gang, he would say, "Poys, of you dondt gif any jeers fun dot Union, I set 'em oop," and we would swallow our cheers for the Union, and his beer.

The next day after the battle of the rats, an order was issued for the recruits to board the steamer "City of Memphis," and go down the river to join our several regiments, in the vicinity of New Orleans. In a few hours we had drawn rations to last a week, and were on board the steamer, and had started downstream. I think every soldier that is now alive will remember that when he took his first trip on a transport, as a recruit, during the war, he laboured under the impression that he owned the boat, or at least a controlling interest in it. That was a very natural feeling. The opinions of the steamboat officials, it will be remembered, were different. I had never been on a large steamboat before, and after tying my knapsack and other baggage to a wood-pile on the lower deck, after I had vainly attempted to induce the proper official to give me checks for my baggage, I began to climb up stairs, and soon found myself on top of the Texas, beside the smoke stack, viewing the ever changing scenery of the grand old Mississippi.

I was drinking in the scenery, and the fresh air, and wondering if it could be possible that there could be war, and killing, anywhere in this broad land, when all was so peaceful and beautiful on the river, when I felt something strike me on the pantaloons most powerfully, and I looked around and a gentleman was just removing a large sized boot from my person. I was about to reprove him for kicking me, a total stranger, who had not even presented letters of introduction to me, when he said, in a voice that was deep down in his chest, "get down below." I did not feel like arguing with a man of so violent a nature, and I went down the narrow stairs, after he had said he would throw me overboard if I did not hurry.

I learned afterwards that he was the mate of the steamboat. I could see that he had mistaken me for a common soldier, which I would not admit was the case, but I went down stairs, probably looking hurt. I was hurt. I went into the cabin and sat down on one of the sofas, to think, when a coloured person told me to get off the sofa. As he seemed to know what he was talking about I got on. I saw a bar, where officers of the army and passengers were drinking, and I went up and asked for a whisky sour, thinking that would relieve the pain and cause my injured feelings to improve. The bar tender told me to go out on deck and I could get plain whisky through a window where the negro deck hands got their drinks, but I could not drink with gentlemen. That was the first day that I realized that in becoming a soldier I had descended to a level with negro deck hands and rousta-bouts, and could not be allowed to associate with gentlemen.

Soon the gong rung for supper, and I went into the cabin and sat down to the table for a square meal, the other seats being filled with army officers and passengers. I was going to give my order to a waiter, when he called an officer of the boat, who told me to get up from the table and go below, as the cabin was intended for gentlemen and not soldiers. My idea was to kick against being turned out, but I thought of the mate's boot, and I went out, went down on the lower deck with the recruits, and eat some bread and meat. I was rapidly becoming crushed.

I talked my experience over with the boys, and they all agreed with me that the way we were treated was an outrage on American soldiers, which we would not stand. We began to wonder where we were going to sleep, when I remembered seeing state-rooms on the deck above, with berths, and it seemed to me they must be intended for us, so we agreed to go up and go into the state-rooms from the doors that opened out on deck, believing that those who got in first would be allowed to occupy them.

About fifty of us got into state-rooms, while the officers and passengers were playing poker in the cabin. I was asleep, when I heard a noise out on deck, and raising up in my berth I looked over the transom and saw about twenty of the recruits being driven along by officers of the boat, kicks and cuffs, and loud talking being the order. "I'll teach you brutes to steal the beds of passengers on this boat. You dirty whelps, to presume to sleep in beds. Get down stairs and sleep on the wood-pile with the niggers," shouted the captain.

If there was going to be any fuss about it, I didn't want to stay in the state-room. I didn't want to be broke of my rest, of course, but if it was not customary for common soldiers to indulge in such luxuries, I would go out. Just then there was a knock at the door leading into the cabin, and I heard a female voice say, "Powtaw, I am afraid one of those dirty soljaws has got into my state-room," and then I heard the mate's voice say, "Wait till I get at him." Of course, under those circumstances I could not remain.

No gentleman would occupy a lady's birth, and cause her to sit up all night. To be sure there were two berths, and I could remain in the upper one, and she could turn in below, and I would turn my face to the wall and not look, but I doubted if a lady, who was a perfect stranger, and whose opinion of soldiers was so pronounced, could compromise on such a basis, so when the mate knocked at the door I took my pants and shoes and went out the door leading on deck, and went below, without being discovered. I found my companions, who had been routed out of their beds, dressing themselves as best they could by the light from the furnace, when the stokers would put in wood, and they were about as mad as I was.

The treatment we had received was not what we had a right to expect when we enlisted. We decided to set up all night, and growl and discuss the situation. Several of the recruits made remarks that were very scathing, and the officials of the boat were held up to scorn, and charged with inhumanity. We sat there till daylight, and then organized an indignation meeting, and appointed a committee to draft resolutions indicative of the sense of the meeting. I had been lightning on resolutions before I enlisted, having attended several county conventions, and I was appointed to draft the resolutions. As near as I can remember the following were the words:

"*Whereas*, The undersigned, members of the army of the union, in the course of our duty as soldiers, have been ordered to proceed to our several regiments down the Mississippi River, on board of the *City of Memphis*, and,

"*Whereas*, We have been treated by the officers of the aforesaid boat more like animals than human beings, in being deprived of luxuries to which we have been accustomed, have been driven from the public dining-table, driven from our beds at the dead hour of night, that shoulder-strapped officers might be made comfortable, and kicked down stairs, therefore, be it

"*Resolved*, That we demand of the captain of the steamer *City of Memphis*, that we be allowed the same privileges on this boat that others enjoy. 'We hold these truths to be self-evident,' that one man is just as good as another, no matter what his rank. We demand that we be allowed to eat at the table in the cabin, to sleep in the state-rooms, to drink at the bar if we so elect, and to go to any place on the boat that other passengers are allowed, and that we be treated like white men, which we, have not up to the adoption of these resolutions.

"*Resolved*, That a copy of these resolutions be presented to the captain of the boat, that a copy be sent to the secretary of war, and that the resolutions be published in the newspapers."

When I read the resolutions to the boys they were passed unanimously, after a few amendments had been voted down. One of the boys wanted a resolution passed demanding that the mate be discharged, and one moved the captain be requested to apologize. I argued that if the captain received the resolutions in the proper spirit, and acceded to our demand, that would be an apology in itself, and in that case the mate would probably resign. I was appointed one of a committee of three to wait on the captain, and read the resolutions to him, after the boys had all signed them.

I had rather someone else had been appointed, as I had been kicked once already, but the boys said it needed somebody that was equal to making a little speech, as it would be necessary to say something before reading the resolutions. They also said, it needed a man with plenty of gall, one that was not afraid to stand up be-fore the world and ask for our rights. I felt flattered at being selected, but I took the precaution to place a gunny-sack, nicely folded up, in the seat of my pants, because I didn't know what might happen. After breakfast, I took the committee and the resolutions, and went up into the cabin, and told a coloured man that he might tell the captain that a committee wished an audience with him. He was playing poker in the ladies' cabin, and I have always thought he had an idea there was a committee of passengers who wanted to present him with a gold headed cane, a thing that was often done on the boats.

Anyway he came along smiling, and when the nigger pointed me out, and the captain noticed that I had a large paper in my hand, he said, "What is it, gentlemen?" This was the first time I had been alluded to in that manner since I enlisted. I asked him to be seated, and he sat down on a lounge, and I proceeded. I forgot to make any speech, but went right at the *whereases* at once. I say the captain smiled when he came up.

Of course, reading the resolutions, as I was, I could not see his face change, but afterwards one of the committee told me about it. I could not tell that a storm was coming. I noticed that quite a number of people had collected around the captain, from curiosity, I supposed. I had just got to the last resolution where it spoke of sending a copy to the secretary of war, when there was a howl. The captain got up and grabbed me by the throat, while somebody else took me by the hind legs. As we went towards the door, I noticed other men were carrying the rest of the committee.

My idea was that they would throw us overboard, and as I could not swim, I closed my eyes and said, "Now I lay me." The stairs leading to the lower deck were covered with brass. I remember that distinctly, because I rode down the stairs on the small of my back, and we had a committee meeting at the foot of the stairs. I brought up on top of the rest of the committee. We sat there a moment, and decided, unanimously, that we had been unceremoniously chucked down stairs, resolutions and all, and we picked ourselves up and limped back to where our companions were, and so reported. The expedition was a total failure, for in a short time a notice was tacked on the foot of the stairs, stating that all enlisted men were forbidden from occupying any portion of the boat except the lower deck, and if one was found above that deck, he would be turned over to the first army post, a prisoner. So we remained on the lower deck, and took it out abusing the officers, and hoping the boat would blow up. But the scenery was just as nice from the lower deck.

CHAPTER 25

Our Party of Recruits own the Earth

Let's see, I forget whether I have ever told about getting strung up on a bayonet, near New Orleans, when I first went south as a recruit. It was before I had joined my regiment, and I was with a gang of recruits, all looking for the regiments we had enlisted in. We had come down from St. Louis on a steamboat, our regiments being scattered all over the Department of the Gulf. We were not in any particular hurry to find our regiments, as the longer we kept away from them the less duty we would have to do. I do not think, out of the whole forty recruits, there was one who was in the least hurry to find his regiment, and none of them would have known their regiments if they had seen them, unless somebody told them.

They had enlisted just as it happened, all of them hoping the war would be over before they found where they belonged. They didn't know anybody in their respective regiments, hence there were no ties binding them. But they had been together for several months, as recruits, until all had got well acquainted, and if they could have been formed into a company, for service together, they might have done pretty good fighting. The crowd was becoming smaller, as every day or two some recruit would come and bid us all good bye. He had actually stumbled on to his regiment, and when the officers of an old regiment, in examining recruits, found one assigned to his regiment, he never took his eyes off the recruit until he was landed.

I have seen some very affecting partings, when one of our gang would find where he belonged and had to leave us, perhaps never to meet again. The gang was rapidly dropping apart, and when we got to New Orleans there were only twenty or so left. We reported to the commanding officer, and he quartered us at Carrollton, near the city, in what had once been a beer-garden and dance-house. We slept on the floor of the dance-house, cooked our meals out in the garden, spread our food on the old beer tables, and imagined we were proprietors of the place, or guests of the government. We always ordered beer or expensive wines with our meals. Not that we ever got any beer or wine, because the beer garden was deserted, but we put on a great deal of style.

We found a lot of champagne bottles out in the back yard, and I do not think I ever took a meal there without having a champagne bottle sitting beside me on the table, and when any citizens were passing along the street we would take up the bottles, look at the label in a scrutinizing way, as though not exactly certain in our minds whether we were getting as good wine as we were paying for. The old empty bottles gave us a standing in Carrollton society that nothing else could have given us. Some of the boys got so they could imitate the popping of a champagne cork to perfection, by placing one finger in the mouth, prying the cheek around on one side, and letting it fly open suddenly.

We would have several of the boys with aprons on, and when anybody was passing on the street, one of us would call, "Waiter open a bottle of that extra dry." The waiter would say, "Certainly, sah," take a bottle between his knees, run his finger in his mouth and make it pop, and then pretend to pour out the champagne in glasses, imitating the "fizzing" perfectly. It was the extra dryest champagne that I ever had. But all that foolishness had the desired effect. It convinced the citizens of Carrollton that we were no ordinary soldiers. We were all nicely dressed, had no guards, and apparently no officers, had plenty of money, which we spent freely at the stores, and the impression soon got out that we were on some special service, and there was, of course, much curiosity to know our business.

I learned that we were looked upon as secret service men, and I told the boys about it, and advised them not to tell that we were recruits, but to put on an air of mystery, and we would have fun while we remained. One day an oldish gentleman who lived near, and who had a fine orange plantation, or grove, toward which we had cast longing eyes, called at the dance-house where we were quartered. We had just finished our frugal meal, and the empty bottles were being taken away. He addressed me, and said, "Good day, Colonel." I responded as best I could, and invited him to be seated. I apologized for not offering him a glass of champagne, but told him we had cracked the last bottle, and would not have any more until the next day, as I had only that morning requested my friend, the general commanding at New Orleans, to send me a fresh supply, which he would do at once, I had no doubt.

Well, you ought to have seen the boys try to keep from laughing, stuffing handkerchiefs in their mouths, etc. But not a man laughed. The old citizen said it was no matter, as he would drop in the next day, and drink with us. We talked about the war, and it is my impression he was anxious for us to believe he was a loyal man. But after a while he asked me what particular duty I was on, there at Carrollton. I hesitated a moment, and finally told him that I hoped he would excuse me for not telling him, but the fact was it would be as much as my "commission" would be worth to unfold any of my plans. I told him that time alone would reveal the object of our being there, and until such time as my government thought it best to make it public, it was my duty as an officer, to keep silent. He said certainly, that was all right, and he admired me for keeping my own counsel. (I was probably the highest private and rawest recruit in the army.)

He said there was a natural curiosity on the part of the people of Carrollton to know who we were, as we lived so high, and seemed such thorough gentlemen. I admitted that we were thorough gentlemen, and thanked him for the high opinion that the cultured people of Carrollton had of us. He wound up by pointing to his orange grove, and said he would consider it a special favour if we would consider ourselves perfectly free to go there and help ourselves at any time, and particularly that evening, as a number of young people would be at his house for a quiet dance. I told him that a few of us would certainly be present, and thanked him kindly. When he was gone I told the boys, and they wanted to give three cheers, but I got them to keep still, and we talked all the afternoon of the soft snap we had struck, and cleaned up for the party.

My intention was to pick out half a dozen of the best dressed, recruits, those that could make a pretty fair showing in society to go with me, but they all wanted to go, and there was no way to prevent it, so all but one Irishman, that we hired to stay and watch our camp, went. Well, we ate oranges fresh from the trees, joined in the dance, ate refreshments, and drank the old gentleman's wine, and had a good time, made a good impression on the ladies, and went back to camp at midnight.

On the way over to the party I told the boys the gentleman was coming to see us the next day, and we should have to get a bottle of champagne somewhere, to treat him, as I had told him we expected, some more up from the city. When we came back from the party a German recruit pulled a bottle of champagne out of his pocket, which he had stolen from the man's house in order to treat him with the next day. The gentleman came over to our quarters the next day, and we opened our bottle, and he drank to our very good health, though I thought he looked at the label on the bottle pretty close. For a week we frequented the gentleman's orange grove every day, and ate oranges to our heart's content.

Several times during the week we were invited to different houses, where we boys became quite interested in the fair girls of Louisiana. It was ten days from the time we settled in the beer garden, and we had kept our secret well. Nobody in Carrollton knew that we were raw recruits that had never seen a day of service, but the impression was still stronger than ever that we were pets of the government. We had an old map of the United States that we had borrowed at a saloon, and during the day we would hang the map up and surround it, while I pointed out imaginary places to attack.

This we would do while people were passing. Everything was working splendidly, and we decided to give a party. We hired a band to play in the dance house, ordered refreshments, and invited about forty ladies and gentlemen to attend. The day we were to give the party we sent a recruit down town to draw rations, and he told everybody what a high old time we recruits were having at Carrollton. The commanding officer heard of it, and, probably having forgotten that we were up there waiting to be sent to our regiments he sent a peremptory order for us to report at New Orleans before noon of that day. How could we report at noon, when we were going to give a party at night? It was simply impossible, and I, as a sort of breast corporal in charge, sent a man down town to tell the commanding officer that we had an engagement that night, and couldn't come before the next day. I did not know that it was improper to send regrets to a commanding officer when ordered to do anything.

The man I sent down to New Orleans came back and I asked him what the general said. The man said he read the note and said, "The hell they can't come till tomorrow. The impudence of the recruits. They will come tonight!" I did not believe we would. In my freshness I did not believe that any commander of troops would deliberately break up a ball, and humiliate brave soldiers. I thought my explanation to the commander that we had an engagement, would be sufficient, that he would see that it was impossible to hurry matters. We had been to a good deal of expense, and it was our duty, after accepting the hospitalities of those people, to pay our indebtedness in the only way we knew how, and so, as the boys had gathered around me to see what was to be done, I said, "On with the dance. Let joy be unconfined."

Our guests arrived on time, and shortly after it became dark, the Dutch band we had hired from, a beer hall down town, struck up some sort of foreign music, and "there was a sound of revelry by night." We danced half a dozen times, smiled sweetly on our guests, walked around the paths of the old garden, flirted a little perhaps, and talked big with the male guests, and convinced them anew that we were regular old battle-scarred vets, on detached duty of great importance. Near midnight we all set down to lunch, around the beer tables, and everything was going along smooth.

The old gentleman who had been first to make our acquaintance, and who had been the means of getting us into society, proposed as a toast, "Our brave and generous hosts," and the boys called upon me to respond. I got up on a bench and was making a speech that, if I had been allowed to continue, would have been handed down in history as one of the ablest of our time. It was conciliatory in tone, calculated to cement a friendship between the army and the citizens of the south, and show that while we were engaged in war, there was nothing mean about us, and that we loved our neighbors as ourselves.

I was just getting warmed up, and our guests had spatted their hands at some of my remarks, when I heard a tramp, tramp, tramp on the sidewalk outside, and before I could breathe a squad of infantry soldiers had filed into the garden, surrounded the dance-house, a dozen had formed in line before the door, and a sergeant had walked in and ordered the citizens to disperse, and said the recruits were under arrest. Well, I have been in some tight places in my life, but that was the closest place I ever struck. The old gentleman, the leader of our guests, turned to me and asked what this all meant, and I told him to be calm, and I would fix everything. I got down off the bench and approached the sergeant, to argue the thing.

I found that he was, a coloured man, and that his soldiers were also coloured troops. This was the unkindest cut of all. I could stand it to be arrested by white soldiers, but the sending of a lot of "niggers" after us white fellows was more than human nature could bear. We had most of us been Democrats before enlisting, and had never looked upon the coloured man with that respect that we learned to do, later.

217

I went up to the sergeant, as brave as I could, and said, "Look-a-here, boss, you have made a dreadful mistake. We are gentlemen, enjoying ourselves, and this interruption on your part will cost you dear. Now go away with your men, quietly, and I promise you, on the honour of a gentleman, that I will not report you, and have you punished," and I looked at him in a tone of voice that I thought would convince him that I was a friend if he should go away, but if he remained it would be at his peril.

He said he didn't want any foolishness, or some of us would get hurt, and just then one of the Irish recruits, who had tried to skin out the back way, got jabbed in the pants by a bayonet, and he began to howl and cuss the "niggers." The sergeant called up half a dozen of his sable guard, and they surrounded me and some of the boys. Our guests were becoming frightened, ladies had put on-their wraps, and there was a good deal of confusion, when I shouted, "Boys, are we going to submit to this insult on the part of a lot of nigger field hands? Never! To the rescue!" Well, they didn't "to the rescue" worth a cent.

A coloured man with a bayonet had every recruit's breast at the point of his weapon, three soldiers surrounded me, and one run his bayonet through the breast of my coat and out under my arm, and held me on my tiptoes, and I was powerless, except with my mouth. The old gentleman, our most distinguished guest, came up to me, and I said to him, in confidence, so our guests could hear, however, with a smile, "This may seem to you a singular proceeding. I cannot explain it to you now, as I am pledged to secrecy by my government, but I will say that the duty we are on here is part of a well-laid plan of our commander, and this seeming arrest is a part of the plan. This coloured sergeant is innocent. He is simply obeying orders, and is a humble instrument in carrying out our plan. I expected to be arrested before morning, but hoped it would be after our party. However, we soldiers have to go where ordered. We shall be thrown into prison for a time, but when this detective or secret service work on which we are engaged is done, we will take pleasure in calling upon you again, wearing such laurels as we may win. We bid you goodnight, and wish you much happiness."

They all shook hands with us, evidently believing what I had said, and even the sergeant seemed to take it in, for, after the crowd had gone, the sergeant said, "You will excuse me, kernel, for what I have done. I didn't know about any 'plan.' All I knew was dat the provost-marshal told me to go up to Carrollton and pull dem recruits dat was camping at de beer garden, and fotch 'em to de guard-house." I told him he did perfectly right, and then we recruits packed up our things and marched with the coloured soldiers to New Orleans, about six miles, and we slept in the guard-house. The next morning the provost-marshal called upon us, damned us a little for not insisting on being sent to our regiments, found out that my regiment was up the river two hundred miles, and seemed mad because I passed it when I come from St. Louis. I told him I was not expected to go hunting around for my regiment, like a lost calf. What I wanted was for my regiment to hunt me up. That afternoon he put me on an up-river boat with a tag on my baggage telling where I belonged, and I bid goodbye to the recruits, after having had three months of fun at the expense of Uncle Sam.

CHAPTER 26

I Begin Taking Music Lessons

The last two chapters of this stuff has related to early experiences, but now that it is probable the chaplain has got over being mad at my trading him the circus-horse, I will resume the march with the regiment. For a month or more I had been waiting for my commission to arrive, so that I could serve as an officer, but it did not arrive while we were at Montgomery, and we started away from that city towards Vicksburg, Miss., with a fair prospect of having hot work with strolling bands of the enemy. I was much depressed. It had got so they didn't seem to want me anywhere. It seemed that I was a sort of a Jonah, and wherever I was, something went wrong.

The chaplain wouldn't have me, because he had a suspicion that I was giddy, and full of the devil, and I have thought he had an idea I would sacrifice the whole army to perpetrate a practical joke, and he also maintained that I would lie, if a lie would help me out of a scrape. I never knew how such an impression could have been created. The colonel said he would try and get along without me, the adjutant didn't want any more of my mathematics in his reports and the brigade commander said he would carry the brigade colours himself rather than have me around, as I would bring headquarters into disgrace some way. So I had to serve as a private in my own company, which was very hard on a man who had tasted the sweets of official position.

O, if my commission did not come soon I was lost. After we had marched a couple of days it began to look as though we were liable to have a fight on our hands. Every little while there would be firing in advance, or on the flanks, and things looked blue for one who did not want to have any trouble with anybody. One morning when we were cooking our breakfast beside a pitch pine log, a little Irishman, who was a friend of mine, as I always lent him my tobacco, said: "There will be a fight today, and some wan of the byes will sleep cold tonight."

A cold chill came over me, and I wondered which of the "by's" would draw the ticket of death. The Irishman noticed that I was not feeling perfectly easy, and he said, "Sorrel top, wud yez take a bit of advice from the loikes of me?" I did not like to be called sorrel top, but if there was any danger I would take advice from anybody, so I told him to fire away. He told me that when we fell in, for the march of the day, to arrange to be No. 4, as in case we were dismounted, to fight on foot, number four would remain on his horse, and hold three other horses, and keep in the rear, behind the trees, while the dismounted men went into the fight. Great heavens, and that had never occurred to me before.

Of course number four would hold the horses, in case of a dismounted fight, and I had never thought what a soft thing it was. It can be surmised by the reader of profane history, that when our company formed that morning I was number four. We marched a long for a couple of hours, when there was some firing on the flanks, and a couple of companies were wheeled into line and marched off into the woods for half a mile, and the order was given to "prepare to fight on foot." It was a momentous occasion for me, and when the three men of our four dismounted and handed the bridle reins to me, I was about the happiest man in the army. I did not want the boys to think I was anxious to keep away from the front, so I said, "Say, cap, don't I go too?"

He said I could if I wanted to, as one of the other boys would hold the horses if I was spoiling to be a corpse, but I told him I guessed, seeing that I was already on the horse, I would stay, and the boys went off laughing, leaving about twenty-five of us "number fours" holding horses. Now, you may talk all you please about safe places in a fight, but sitting on a horse in plain sight, holding three other prancing, kicking, squalling horses, while the rest of the boys are behind trees, or behind logs, popping at the enemy, is no soft thing. The bullets seemed to pass right over our fellows on foot, and came right among the horses, who twisted around and got tangled up, and made things unpleasant.

I was trying to get a stallion I was holding to quit biting my legs, when I saw my little Irishman, who had steered me on to the soft snap, dodge down behind his horse's head, to escape a bullet that killed one of the horses he was holding, and I said, "This is a fine arrangement you have got me into. This is worse than being in front." He said he believed it was, as he backed his other horses away from the dying horse, but he said as long as they killed horses we had no cause to complain. There was a sergeant in charge of us "number fours," and he was as cool as any fellow I ever saw. The sergeant was a nice man, but he was no musician. He was an Irishman, also, and when any bugle-call and when any bugle-call sounded he had to ask someone what it was. There was a great deal of uncertainty about bugle-calls, I noticed, among officers as well as men.

Of course it could not be expected that every man in a cavalry regiment would be a music teacher, and the calls sounded so much alike to the uncultivated ear, that it was no wonder that everybody got the calls mixed. In camp we got so we could tell "assembly," and "surgeon's call," and "tattoo," and quite a number of others, but the calls of battle were Greek to us. The bugle sounded down in the woods, and the sergeant turned to me and asked, "Fhat the divil is that I dunno?" I was satisfied it was "To horse," but when I saw our fellows come rushing back towards the horses it looked as though the order was to fall back, and I suggested as much to the sergeant. He thought it looked reasonable, too, and he ordered us to fall back slowly toward the regiment.

We didn't go so confounded slow, and of course I was ahead with my three horses. The sergeant heard the captain yell to him to hold on, and he got the most of the "fours" to stop, and let the boys get on, but the little Irishman and myself couldn't hold our extra horses, and they dragged us along over logs and through brush, the regiment drew sabres to "shoo" the horses back, waived their hats, my horse run his fore feet into a hole, fell down, and let me off over his head, the other horses seemed to walk on me, I became insensible, and the next thing I knew I was in an ambulance, behind the regiment, which was on the march, as though nothing had happened.

I felt of myself to see if anything was broke, and finding I was all right I told the driver of the ambulance I guessed I would get out and mount my horse, but he said he guessed I wouldn't, because the colonel had told him if I died to bury me beside the road, but if I lived to bring me to headquarters for punishment. The driver said the boys whose horses I had stampeded, wanted to kill me, but the colonel had said death was too good for me. Well, nobody was hurt in the skirmish, and about noon we arrived at a camping place for the night, and the ambulance drove up, and I was placed under guard.

It seems the sergeant had laid the whole thing to me. He had admitted to the colonel that he didn't know one bugle call from another,
and he supposed I did, and when he asked me what it was, and I said
it was to retreat, he supposed I knew, and retreated. The colonel asked
me what I had to say, and I told him I didn't know any bugle call
except get your quinine, get your quinine. That when I enlisted there
was nothing said about my ability to read notes in music, and I had
never learned, and couldn't learn, as I had no more ear for music than
a mule. I told him if he would furnish a music teacher, I would study
hard to try and master the difference between "forward and back," but
that it didn't seem to me as though I ought to be held responsible for
an expression of opinion, however erroneous, when asked for it by a
superior officer.

I told him that when the bugle sounded, and I saw the boys coming back on a hop, skip and jump, it seemed to me the most natural
thing in the world that the bugle had sounded a retreat. That seemed
the only direction we could go, and as my natural inclination was to
save those horses that had been placed in my charge, of course I in-
terpreted the bugle call to mean for us to get out of there honourably,
and as the only way to get out honourably was to get out quick, we
got up and dusted. The colonel always gave me credit for being a good
debater, and he smiled and said that as no damage had been done, he
would not insist that I be shot on the spot, but he felt that an example
should be made of me.

He said I would be under arrest until bed time, down under a
tree, half a mile or so from headquarters, in plain sight, and he would
send music teachers there to teach me the bugle calls. I thanked him,
in a few well chosen remarks, and the guard marched me to the tree,
which was the guard-house. I found another soldier there, under arrest, who had rode out of the ranks to water his horse, while on the
march, against orders, and a Confederate prisoner that had been captured in the morning skirmish, a captain of a Virginia regiment. The
captain seemed real hurt at having been captured, and was inclined to
be uppish and distant. I tried two or three times to get him into conversation on some subject connected with the war, but he wouldn't
have it.

He evidently looked upon me as a horse-thief, a deserter, and a bad
man, or else a soldier who had been sent to pump information out of
him. I never was let alone quite as severely as I was by our prisoner,
at first. But I went to work and built a fire, and soon had some coffee

boiling, bacon frying, and sweet potatoes roasting, and when I spread the lay out on the ground, and said, "Colonel, this is on me. Won't you join me?" I think he was the most surprised man I ever saw, He had watched every move I made, in cooking, with a yearning such as is seldom seen, and he probably had no more idea that he was going to have a mouthful of it, than that he should fly.

His eyes might have been weak, but if he had been a man I knew well, I should have said there were a couple of tears gathering in his eyes, and I was quite sure of it when the flood broke over the eye-lid dam, and rolled down among the underbrush whiskers. He stopped the flood at once, by an effort of will, though there seemed a something in his throat when he said, "You don't mean it, do you, kernel?" I told him of course I meant it, and to slide right up and help himself, and I speared a great big sweet potato, and some bacon, and placed them on a big leaf, and poured coffee out in the only cup I had. He kicked on using the cup, but I said we would both drink out of it.

He said, "you are very kind, sir," and that was all he said during the meal. But how he *did* eat. He tried to act as though he didn't care much for dinner, and as though he was eating out of courtesy to me, but I could tell by the way the sweet potato went down in the depths of my Confederate friend, and by the joyous look when a swallow of coffee hit the right place, that he was having a picnic.

When we were through with dinner and the guard and the other prisoner were cooking theirs, he said, "My friend, I do not mind telling you now that I was much in need of food. I had not eaten since yesterday morning, as we have been riding hard to intercept you gentlemen, sir. I trust I shall live long enough to repay, you sir." I told him not to mention it, as all our boys made it a point to divide when we captured a prisoner. He said he believed his people felt the same way, but God knew they had little to divide. He said he trembled when he thought that some of our men who were prisoners in the south were faring very poorly, but it could not be helped.

"Suppose I had captured you," he said, with a smile that was forced, "I could not have given you a mouthful of bread, until we had found a southern family that 'had bread to spare.'" I told him it was pretty tough, but it would all be over before long, and then we would all have plenty to eat. I got out a pack of cards, and the confederate captain played seven-up with me, while we smoked. Presently nine buglers came down to where we were, formed in line, and began to sound cavalry calls in concert. I knew that they were the music teachers the colonel had sent to teach me the calls. The confederate looked on in astonishment, while they sounded a call, and when it was done I asked the chief bugler what it was, and he told me, and I asked him to sound something else, which he did. My idea was to convince the prisoner that this was a part of daily routine. He got nervous and couldn't remember which was trumps; and finally said we might talk all we pleased about the horrors of Andersonville, but to be blowed to death with cavalry bugles was a fate that only the most hardened criminals should suffer.

The confederate evidently had no ear for music more than I had, and he soon got enough. However the buglers kept up their noise till about supper time, when they were called on. I got another meal for the confederate, and he seemed to be actually getting fat. The colonel of my regiment came down to where we were, and said, "You fellows seem to be doing pretty well," and then he had a long talk with the rebel prisoner, invited him up to his tent to pass the night, apologized for the concert he had been giving us, explained what it was for, told me I could go to my company if I thought I could remember a bugle call in the future; the captain shook hands with me and thanked me cordially, and we separated. He was exchanged, the next day, and I never saw him for twenty-two years, when I found him at the head of a manufacturing enterprise in his loved Virginia, and he furnished me a more expensive meal than I did him years before, but it didn't taste half as good as the bacon dinner in Alabama under the guard-house tree.

CHAPTER 27

A Short Story About a Pair of Boots

When I enlisted in the cavalry I bought a pair of top boots, of the Wellington pattern, stitched with silk up and down the legs, which were of shiny morocco. They came clear above my knees, and from the pictures I had seen of cavalry soldiers, it struck me those boots would be a pass-port to any society in the army. The first few months of my service, it seemed to me, the boots gave me more tone than any one thing. I learned afterwards that all new recruits came to the regiment with such boots, and that they were the laughing stock of all the old veterans. I did not know that I was being guyed by the boys, and I loved those boots above all things I had.

To be sure, when we struck an unusually muddy country, some idiot of an officer seemed to be inspired to order us to dismount. The boys who had common army boots would dismount anywhere, in mud or water, but it seemed to me cruel for officers to order a dismount, when they knew I would have to step in the mud half way up to my knees, with those morocco boots on. Several times when ordered to dismount in the mud, I have ridden out of the road, where it was not muddy, to dismount, but the boys would laugh so loud, and the officers would swear so wickedly, that I got so I would dismount wherever they told me, suppress my emotions, as I felt my beautiful, shiny boots sink into the red clay, and when we got into camp I would spend half the night cleaning my boots. The captain said if I would spend half the time cleaning my carbine and sabre that I did cleaning my boots, I would have been a model soldier.

I think that for the first year of my service I had as elegant a pair of boots as could be found in the army. But it was the hardest work to keep track of them. The first three months it was all I could do to keep the chaplain from trading me a pair of old army shoes for my boots.

The arguments he used to convince me that morocco boots were far above my station, and that they were intended for a chaplain, were laboured. If he had used the same number of words in the right direction, he could have converted the whole army. I had to sleep with my boots under my head every night, to prevent them from being stolen and twice they were stolen from my tent, but in each case recovered at the sutler's, where they had been pawned for a bottle of brandy peaches, which I had to pay for to redeem the boots.

The boots had become almost a burden to me, in keeping them, but I enjoyed them so much that money could not have bought them. When we were in a town for a few days, and I rode around, it did not make any difference whether I had any other clothes on, of any account, the morocco boots captured the town. The natives could not see how a man who wore such boots could be anything but a high-up thoroughbred. The last time I lost my boots will always be remembered by those who were in the same command. We were on the march with a Michigan and a New Jersey regiment, through the dustiest country that ever was. The dust was eight inches deep in the road, and just like fine ashes. Every time a horse put his foot down the dust would raise above the trees, and as there were two thousand horses, with four feet apiece, and each foot in constant motion, it can be imagined that the troops were dusty. And it was so hot that the perspiration oozed out of us, but the dust covered it.

The three regiments took turns in acting as rear guard, to pick up stragglers, and on this hot and dusty day the New Jersey regiment was in the rear. It was composed of Germans entirely, with a German colonel, a man who had seen service in Europe, and he looked upon a soldier as a machine, with no soul, fit only to obey orders. That was not the kind of a soldier I was. During the day's march the boys stripped off everything they could. I know all I had on was a shirt and pants, and a handkerchief around my head. I took off my boots and coat and let the coloured cook of the company strap them on to his saddle with the camp kettles.

He usually rode right behind the company, and I thought I could get my things any time if I wanted to dress up. It was the hardest day's march that I ever experienced, lungs full of dust, and every man so covered with dust that you could not recognize your nearest neighbor. Afternoon the command halted beside a stream, and it was announced that we would go into camp for the night. The coloured cook came along soon after, and he was perfectly pale, whether from dust or fright I could not tell, but he announced to me, in a manner that showed that he appreciated the calamity which had befallen the command, that he had lost my boots. I was going to kill him, but my carbine was full of dust, and I made it a point never to kill a man with a dirty gun, so I let him explain. He said:

"I fell back to de rear, by dat plantation where de cotton gin was burning, to see if I couldn't get a canteen of buttermilk to wash de dust outen my froat, when dat Dutch Noo Jersey gang come along, and de boss he said, 'nicker, you got back ahead fere you pelong, or I gick you in de pack mit a sabre, aind't it,' and when I get on my mule to come along he grab de boots and he say, 'nicker, dot boots is better for me,' and when I was going to take dem away from him he stick me in de pants wid a sabre. Den I come away."

I could have stood up under having an arm shot off, but to lose my boots was more than I could bear. It never did take me long to decide on any important matter, and in a moment I decided to invade the camp of that New Jersey regiment, recapture my boots or annihilate every last foreigner on our soil, so I started off, barefooted, without a coat, and covered with dust, for the headquarters of the New Jersey fellows. They had been in camp but a few minutes, but every last one of them had taken a bath in the river, brushed the dust off his clothes, and looked ready for dress parade.

That was one fault of those foreigners, they were always clean, if they had half a chance. I went right to the colonel's tent, and he was surrounded with officers, and they were opening bottles of beer, and how cool it looked. There was something peculiar about those foreigners, no matter if they were doing duty in the most inaccessible place in the south, and were short of transportation, you could always find beer at their headquarters. I walked right in, and the colonel was just blowing the foam off a glass of beer. He looked at me in astonishment, and I said in a voice husky from dust down my neck:

"Colonel this is an important epoch in the history of our beloved country. Events have transpired within the past hour, which leaves it an open question whether, as a nation, we are afoot or on horseback."

"*Great hefens,*" said the colonel, stopping with his glass of beer half drank, "*you vrighten me. Vot has habbened. But vait, und dake a glass of beer, as you seem exhausted, und proke up. Captain Ouskaspiel, hand the shendleman some peer. Mine Gott, bud you look hard, strancher.*"

I do not believe that I ever drank anything that seemed to go right to the spot, the way that beer did. It seemed to start a freshet of dust down my neck, clear my throat, and brace me up. While I was drinking it I noticed that the German colonel and his officers eyed me closely, my bare feet, my flannel shirt full of dust, and my hair that looked as though I had stood on my head in the road. They waited for me to continue, and after draining the last drop in the glass, I said:

"Colonel, it was no ordinary circumstance that induced you brave foreigners, holding allegiance to European sovereigns, to fly to arms to defend this new nation from an internecine foe. While we natives, and to the manor born, left our plows in the furrow, to spring to-arms, you left your shoemaker shops, the spigots of your beer saloons, the marts of commerce in which you were engaged, and stood shoulder to shoulder. Where the bullets of the enemy whistled, there could be found the brave Dutchmen of New Jersey. It brings tears to eyes un-used to weeping, to think of the German fathers and mothers of our land, who are waiting and watching for the return of sons who will never come back, and this is, indeed, harder for them to bear, when we reflect that these boys were not obliged to fight for our country, holding allegiance, as I said before to——"

"*Waid a minute, of you blease,*" said the colonel. "*Dake von more drink, and dell me, of you please, vot de hell you vos drying to get at. Captain Hem-rech, gif der shendleman a glass of beer.*"

A second glass of beer was given me, and I drank it. There was evidently a suspicion on the part of the New Jersey officers that the importance of my visit had been over-rated by them, and they seemed anxious to have me come to the point.

"On the march today," said I, wiping the foam off my moustache on my shirt-sleeve, "one of your thieving soldiers stole my boots from our nigger cook, who was conveying them for me. A cavalry soldier without boots, is no good. I came after my boots, and I will have them or blood. Return my boots, or by the eternal, the Wisconsin cavalry regiment will come over here and everlastingly gallop over your fel-lows. The constitution of the United States and the Declaration of Independence, are on my side. In civil life a man's house is his castle. In the army a man's boots is his castle. Give me my boots, sir, or the blood of the slain will rest on your heads."

The colonel was half mad and half pleased. He tapped his fore-head with his fore-finger, and looked at his officers in a manner that showed he believed my head was wrong, but he said kindly:

"*My man, you go oud and sit under a tree, in the shade, and I vill hafe your poots found if they are in my rechiment,*" and I went out. I heard the colonel say to one of his officers, "*It vas too pad dot two good glasses of beer should be spoiled, giving them to dot grazy solcher. Ve must be more careful mit de beer.*"

Pretty soon an officer came out and asked me how the boots were taken, and I gave him all the information I had, and he sent men all around the regiment, and in an hour or so the boots were brought to me, the man who stole them was arrested, the officers apologized to me, and I went back to my regiment in triumph, with my boots under my arms. The incident got noised around among the other regiments, and for months after that, when the colonel of the New Jersey cavalry rode by another regiment, the boys would yell out, "Boots, boots," or when a company or squad of the New Jersey fellows would pass along, it was "Look out for your boots! The shoemakers are coming." For stealing that one pair of boots, by one man, a whole regiment got a reputation for stealing that hung to it a long time. Ten years afterward I was connected with a New York daily paper, and one evening I was detailed to go to a New Jersey city to report the commencement exercises of a college. In the programme of exercises I noticed that a man of the same name of that of the New Jersey colonel, was one of the college professors, and I wondered if he was the same man. During the evening he put in an appearance on the stage, and I could see that he was the colonel who had given me the beer, and caused my boots to be returned to me. After the exercises of the evening, the New York newspaper men were invited to partake of a collation in the apartments of the college officials, and the professors were introduced to the newspaper men. When my turn came to be introduced, and the old colonel stood before me, I said:

"General, you were in the army, were you not?"

"*Yezzer!*" said the old man. "*I am broud to say dot I fought for my adopted country. But vy do you ask?*"

"We have met before. I, too, was a soldier. I was at your headquarters once, on a very important mission. I was entertained, sir, in your tent, permitted, to partake of the good, things you had, and sent away happy.

"*Vell, you dond't say so,*" said the old man, as he pressed my hand warmly. "*Vere vas dis dat you were my guest, and vot vas de important message?*" and he smiled all over his face at the prospect of hearing something about old times.

"It was in Mississippi, between Montgomery, Ala., and Vicksburg. Do you remember the hottest and dustiest day that ever was, when we camped on a little stream?" said I.

"*O, yah!*" said the colonel; "*very well. It vas an awful time.*"

"I went to your headquarters with information of vital importance. One of your soldiers *had stolen my boots.*"

"*Gott in himmel!*" said the old colonel, now a college professor, as he looked at me to see if there was any resemblance between the New York reporter and the dusty, bare-footed soldier of ten years before. "*Vill I never hear de last of dem dam boots? And you are de same veller, eh. I have often thought, since dat day, vot an awful gall you had. But it is all ofer now. You vatch your poots vile you are in New Chersey, for plenty of dose cavalry-men are all around here. But do me a favour now, and don't ever again say poots to me, dot's a good fellow,*" and then we all sat down to lunch, and the old colonel told the newspaper boys from New York about how I called at his tent on the march, looking for a pair of boots that had eloped with one of his New Chersey dutchmen.

LEONAUR

ALSO FROM LEONAUR
AVAILABLE IN SOFTCOVER OR HARDCOVER WITH DUST JACKET

WELLINGTON AND THE PYRENEES CAMPAIGN VOLUME I: FROM VI- TORIA TO THE BIDASSOA *by F. C. Beatson*—The final phase of the campaign in the Iberian Peninsula.

WELLINGTON AND THE INVASION OF FRANCE VOLUME II: THE BIDAS- SOA TO THE BATTLE OF THE NIVELLE *by F. C. Beatson*—The second of Beatson's series on the fall of Revolutionary France published by Leonaur, the reader is once again taken into the centre of Wellington's strategic and tactical genius.

WELLINGTON AND THE FALL OF FRANCE VOLUME III: THE GAVES AND THE BATTLE OF ORTHEZ *by F. C. Beatson*—This final chapter of F. C. Beatson's brilliant trilogy shows the 'captain of the age' at his most inspired and makes all three books essential additions to any Peninsular War library.

NAVAL BATTLES OF THE NAPOLEONIC WARS *by W. H. Fitchett*—Cape St. Vincent, the Nile, Cadiz, Copenhagen, Trafalgar & Others

SERGEANT GUILLEMARD: THE MAN WHO SHOT NELSON? *by Robert Guillemard*—A Soldier of the Infantry of the French Army of Napoleon on Campaign Throughout Europe

WITH THE GUARDS ACROSS THE PYRENEES by *Robert Batty*—The Experiences of a British Officer of Wellington's Army During the Battles for the Fall of Napoleonic France, 1813.

A STAFF OFFICER IN THE PENINSULA *by E. W. Buckham*—An Officer of the British Staff Corps Cavalry During the Peninsula Campaign of the Napoleonic Wars

THE LEIPZIG CAMPAIGN: 1813—NAPOLEON AND THE "BATTLE OF THE NATIONS" *by F. N. Maude*—Colonel Maude's analysis of Napoleon's campaign of 1813.

BUGEAUD: A PACK WITH A BATON by *Thomas Robert Bugeaud*—The Early Campaigns of a Soldier of Napoleon's Army Who Would Become a Marshal of France.

TWO LEONAUR ORIGINALS

SERGEANT NICOL by *Daniel Nicol*—The Experiences of a Gordon Highlander During the Napoleonic Wars in Egypt, the Peninsula and France.

WATERLOO RECOLLECTIONS by *Frederick Llewellyn*—Rare First Hand Accounts, Letters, Reports and Retellings from the Campaign of 1815.

www.ingramcontent.com/pod-product-compliance
Lightning Source LLC
Chambersburg PA
CBHW032049080426
42733CB00006B/210